# DOUBLING DREAMS

# DOUBLING DREAMS

***Transforming Agriculture in Modi's New India***

*Edited by*

**G. Sreedathan & Anoop A.J.**

RUPA

BlueKraft Digital Foundation

Published by
Rupa Publications India in association with
BlueKraft Digital Foundation 2019

7/16, Ansari Road, Daryaganj
New Delhi 110002

*Sales Centres:*
Allahabad Bengaluru Chennai
Hyderabad Jaipur Kathmandu
Kolkata Mumbai



ISBN: 978-93-5333-471-0

First impression 2019

10 9 8 7 6 5 4 2 3 1



Printed at Sourabh Printers Pvt. Ltd., Noida

# CONTENTS

# ACKNOWLEDGEMENTS

There are so many people whom we wish to thank for making this book possible. We are greatly indebted to Union Minister of Agriculture & Farmers Welfare Shri Radha Mohan Singh for his direction and guidance, OSD to MoAFW Smt. Durga Nagpal IAS and many senior and junior officers in the Agriculture ministry for providing us with data and materials and facilitating our travels to various locations for meeting farmers who are beneficiaries of various schemes. We are thankful to Shri Akhilesh Mishra of Bluekraft for initiating the project and supporting throughout along with his team. We are grateful to Shri Kapish Mehra, MD of Rupa Publications and his entire editorial team for bringing out this book in a short time yet taking care to maintain highest professional standards. We are glad to have a great team of contributors who took all the efforts to complete the project in a very short time, by travelling to remote locations to interact with farmers. Not least, we would like to mention our gratitude to senior journalist Shri Pankaj Joshi for his valuable inputs and our research team, namely Shri Shailesh Singhal and Ms Garima Pandey for their timely assistance.

# FOREWORD

In India, producing more food is not an option but a necessity given the country's burgeoning population. However, in our endeavour to produce more, we should not harm the earth and environment. This is a challenge as nearly 65 per cent of our population is dependent on agriculture for their livelihood. Despite producing more, the agriculture sector continued to remain in distress as our past strategies have always focused on raising agricultural output and improving food security and not farmers' welfare. This is not to discredit the past efforts which have helped India become food self-sufficient and a food exporting nation.

The National Democratic Alliance government under Prime Minister Shri Narendra Modi sought to strike a balance between the conflicting requirements and create a situation where farmers' income from agriculture is doubled. The government had set a target of 2021–22 to achieve this goal. The government has laid out many long-term strategies to accelerate farm growth and efforts have also been taken to harness all possible sources in farmers' income within and outside the farm sector. Augmenting infrastructure, effective use of technological interventions, institutional mechanisms and buoyant policy initiatives are some of the strategies put in place to increase the incomes of farmers.

All the schemes—Soil Health Card, Neem Coated Urea, eNAM, Pradhan Mantri Fasal Bima Yojana, Minimum Support Price and Pradhan Mantri Kisan Samman Nidhi—being implemented by the government are aimed at bringing about complete transformation in agriculture. These multi-pronged strategies include enhancing productivity of crops, ensuring increase in livestock production, improvement in efficiency of input use, increase in crop intensity, diversification towards high-value crops, improved price realization by farmers, post-harvest value addition, among others.

Radha Mohan Singh

(RADHA MOHAN SINGH)

# INTRODUCTION

The country witnessed severe agrarian distress in the 1990s with farmers—in hundreds—reeling under mounting debts and committing suicides due to continued losses from farming and low agricultural incomes. This trend peaked during the period between 1995 and 2004. The steps taken to address the looming agrarian crisis such as farm loan waivers that failed to generate the desired effect, as many of them were piecemeal and ineffective, and their benefits that never reached the deserving candidates. With no redemption in sight, several farmers, particularly younger age group, left farming and took up menial jobs in urban centres, posing a serious threat to the future of agriculture in the country. Increasing the incomes of farmers and reducing the gap between their incomes and of those working in the non-farm sectors were the only solutions to end the agrarian distress. But how to achieve this was a question.

Speaking at a Kisan Rally in Bareilly, Uttar Pradesh, on 28 February 2016, Prime Minister Narendra Modi stated that his government would work to realize his dream of doubling farmers' income by 2022, when the country completes 75 years of its independence. Many sceptics dismissed it saying that the goal was difficult to achieve, given the enormity and scale of the problem.

Even those who are most critical of the government would agree that this is the first time since Independence that a government has taken a holistic view of the farm sector with an intention to transform agriculture from being merely a means of attaining food security into a powerful engine of rural prosperity and growth. When Prime Minister Narendra Modi emphasized on transforming agriculture through his government's policy of Beej to Bazaar—from Seeds to the Market—he was seeking to reveal a bouquet of comprehensive policy initiatives taken for reinvigorating and financing a whole gamut of farm-related activities covering input distribution, irrigation, farming, post-harvest storage and processing, domestic market linkages and exports. The flagship Soil Health Card scheme has been highly successful and the progress of its implementation has been meticulously followed up by the government. Making neem coating of urea compulsory, the government had curbed pilferage of the subsidized fertilizer to non-farm activities. A study conducted by the Bengaluru-based Institute for Social Economic Change for paddy found that application of neem-coated urea had propelled a higher paddy output. This move has also helped bring down the government's subsidy bill.

There has been a phenomenal rise in the government's budgetary allocation to the farm sector. The government proposes to invest ₹50,000 crore through its ambitious Pradhan Mantri Krishi Sinchai Yojana, which will help cover 28.5 lakh hectare (ha) under irrigation and 26.87 lakh ha under micro-irrigation from 2014–18. The government has set up a ₹5000-crore micro irrigation fund. It has unveiled the Pradhan Mantri Fasal Bima Yojana (PMFBY to provide insurance coverage and financial support to the farmers in the event of failure of any of the notified crops as a result of natural calamities, pests and diseases; to stabilize the income of farmers to ensure their continuance in farming; to encourage farmers to adopt innovative and modern agricultural practices and to ensure flow of credit to the agriculture sector. Besides, there have been many changes in policy with regard to fixation of minimum support price, procurement of agricultural produce, imports and exports. E-platforms and other market infrastructure have been put in place to remove exploitative middlemen so that farmers get fair prices for their produce.

As most of the schemes of the government aim at increasing farm production, the resulting surpluses may lead to drop in prices impacting income of farmers. To overcome this, the Modi government has recently announced Pradhan Mantri Kisan Samman Nidhi Yojana (PM-KISAN) in the Interim Budget 2019–20, under which ₹6,000 will be given to around 12 crore farmers with cultivable land up to 2 hectares. The scheme envisages to provide multiple benefits to the farmers, which will include improving their credit worthiness. The assistance of ₹6,000 has been fixed on the basis that the average income of farmers in the year 2015–16 was around ₹30,000. When a farmer has an assured return, financial institutions can collateralize it and provide a higher credit for his farming activities.

The idea behind all these coordinated initiatives is to double farmers' incomes by 2022–23 and end agrarian distress thereby ensuring farmers' welfare.

This book aims at analysing in detail all of those initiatives taken by Modi government to transform agriculture sector and thereby achieve its ambitious plan of doubling farmers' income.

# *BEEJ SE BAZAAR TAK*: IMPROVED FARMING CYCLE

*Anoop A.J.*

Ram Bharosay is a farmer hailing from Tiwari Mathania village of Gopalganj district of Bihar. He owns two acres of land on which he mainly grows paddy, vegetables and sugarcane. He is dependent predominantly on monsoon for irrigation as diesel pump sets are an expensive deal and not a viable option. He does not get his crops insured because of the high premium charged by the insurance companies. He sells his produce in the nearby mandi through middlemen, sometimes at prices much lower than his investment cost because of adverse market forces. He mainly uses chemical fertilizers in his fields as organic manure is not readily available, and urea is inadequately available in the market because it is diverted to non-agricultural uses. He does not have a bank account and is forced to borrow money from local moneylenders at exorbitant rates of interest. Every year in winters, he travels 20 km on a bullock cart to reach the nearest sugar mill in Harakhua to sell his sugarcane harvest, but he does not get the money on time, and sometimes, what he gets is much lower with respect to the prevalent market price because of issues with sugarcane arrears. Gopalganj is a flood-affected district, which witnesses heavy flooding every year. Ram Bharosay, just like all other small farmers in the district, suffers huge losses annually, and just like all of them, he looks for divine intervention as there is no one to extend a helping hand.

This was the case with most of the farmers in his village until 2014 when the democracy of the country voted for the Narendra Modi-led NDA government in majority. Right after coming to power, the Modi government adopted various farmer-centric policies and vowed to double the farmers' income by 2022 to give the rightful share to the 'Anndata'*, which was overlooked by the previous governments.

Today, Ram Bharosay has got his Soil Health Card (SHC) made through which he has got his soil nutrients assessed and now he grows pulses, lentils, maize and tomatoes alongside other crops. He uses neem-coated urea in his farms, which has resulted in enhancing the overall productivity and provides better pest control. His crops are insured under PMFBY for which he pays minimal premium so that it does not adversely affect his pockets. He narrates examples of fellow farmers of the village who have got their claims within a short period, for the crops damaged in the rainstorms that year. The government has installed a solar water pump near his farmland, which pumps water from the nearby Gandak river and irrigates his fields.

Today, a confident Ram Bharosay along with other villagers has made up a small cooperative through which they have taken a loan under the PM Mudra Yojana to establish a ketchup-making factory from their own tomatoes, with the aim of an additional income. He has downloaded the electronic-National Agriculture Market (e-NAM) mobile app and the Bharat Interface for Money (BHIM) app on his new android phone as per the suggestion of

---

*Anndata means one who provides food.

the officials of the newly-opened Kisan Sewa Kendra in his village. Now, he is able to sell his farm produce not only to his nearest mandi but all over India for which he gets money credited in his bank account, which was opened under the massive financial inclusion drive called Pradhan Mantri Jan Dhan Yojana (PMJDY). In 2013, Ram Bharosay's average monthly income was ₹5,000, which now has become ₹9,600.

Ram Bharosay believes it is some divine intervention that has changed his life and changed the farming scenario of his village.

The way in which these lives have changed is indeed an example of the holistic approach of *Beej Se Bazaar Tak*. Envisaged by the Modi government, it brought small to big reforms at different stages of farming, took into consideration the specific issues and local problems and provided effective solutions.

The agriculture sector in our country has taken many forms and shapes ever since independence, yet the plight of the farmers has been a continuous affair. Looking back in history, we find that the National Commission on Agriculture was formed in 1970, 23 years after India awakened to independence, to study the condition of agriculture in the country and make suggestions for its betterment. The country was in deep turmoil in 1976 as excessive population growth had resulted in an increased pressure on the economy. The commission released its final report the same year in which it suggested deployment of scientific and technological means for increasing total agricultural output. After 30 years, the National Commission for Farmers was constituted in 2004 under the chairmanship of Professor M.S. Swaminathan to address the nationwide calamity of farmers' suicides in India and to suggest methods for faster and more inclusive growth for farmers.

Many suggestions of the commission were adopted by the Modi government while formulating a holistic policy aimed at doubling the farmers' income by 2022.

As per the study by a panel formed by the Modi government on doubling farmers' income by 2022, an average agricultural household in India had a monthly income of just ₹6,426 during July 2012 to June 2013, whereas it spent ₹6,223 every month. Apart from that, around 22.5 per cent of them were below the poverty line. India's average yield for most crops is far less than the global average. The major problems today are the increasing farming costs, credit unavailability, market volatility, leakages in supply chain management, lack of water resources, food wastages in addition to farmers being unaware of the right remuneration for their produce. Income uncertainty is the biggest challenge a farmer faces today, and despite being a landholder, he has to live on the mercy of his fortunes.

In a country where two-thirds of the population relies on agriculture for livelihood, the importance of this sector cannot be overlooked. It accounts for nearly 17 per cent of the country's Gross Domestic Product (GDP) and feeds 1.3 billion people. The welfare of the gigantic Indian population rests on a strong agricultural growth policy, which is guided by an income enhancement perspective. This vision might have encouraged the Modi government to embark upon a mission of doubling the farmers' income.

*Beej Se Bazaar Tak* is a comprehensive action plan to empower farmers throughout the farming cycle with the ultimate aim of doubling the farmers' income by 2022. The goal is to make farming a lucrative profession so that the share of agriculture in the overall GDP of the nation also records a positive growth. Narendra Modi has reiterated that '*Gaon, garib aur kisan*' (Village, poor and farmer) is the focus of his development paradigm, which was evident from the subsequent union budgets passed by the government with a larger share of expenditure outlay for the farming sector.

The extremely ambitious plan to double the income of millions of farmers spread throughout the length and breadth of the country by 2022 needs to be viewed, scrutinized and evaluated on the basis of the work accomplished and targets realized.

Unlike the past, the most significant aspect of the initiatives launched by the NDA government was the clarity of objectives and measurable targets. The defined targets have prompted the implementing machinery to move in the right direction with requisite determination and firmness, and achieve the desired results. Even if 100 per cent results have not been achieved in certain cases, substantial progress has definitely been made during the last four-and-a-half years, and the process is continuing and will continue unabated. Since the NDA government has come to power in May 2014, the Ministry of Agriculture and Farmers' Welfare has launched a host of initiatives and that too in a mission mode to restructure, revive and revitalize the rural landscape.

There has been a record budgetary allocation by the Modi government for agriculture and farmer welfare. If the total budget outlay for the agriculture sector was ₹1,21,082 crore in 2009–14, it almost doubled to ₹2,11,694 crore in 2014–19. The Modi government's 'New India' budget is a farmer friendly one, which is clearly evident from the fact that there has been a record allocation of ₹14.34 lakh crore for rural development and agriculture. Moreover, the Minimum Support Price (MSP) has been hiked to 1.5 times the cost of production.

In 2017–18, agricultural production had touched a new high with production of foodgrains at 277.49 metric tonne, rice at 111.01 metric tonne, sugarcane at 352.23 metric tonne, horticulture production shooting up to 305.4 metric tonne, pulses at 23.95 metric tonne and coarse grains at 45.42 metric tonne.

Under the broader policy framework of *'Beej Se Bazaar Tak'*, the government has formulated various policies aimed at holistically restructuring the agriculture sector. The schemes and programmes have been designed taking into account everything from sowing to selling. To give initial thrust to this transformation, the government's inspiring themes and messages such as Lab-To-Land, *Har Khet Ko Paani*, Per Drop More Crop, etc., have also helped in raising awareness.

The components of the seven-point strategy being pursued by the government are as follows: special focus on irrigation with the aim of 'Per Drop More Crop'; provision of quality seeds and nutrients based on soil health of each field; large investments in warehousing and cold chains to prevent post-harvest crop losses; promotion of value addition through food processing; creation of a national farm market, removing distortions and e-platforms; introduction of a New Crop Insurance scheme to mitigate risks at an affordable cost; and promotion of ancillary activities like poultry, beekeeping and fisheries.

## PRE-SOWING: SOIL HEALTH CARD

As the motto *'Beej Se Bazaar Tak'* suggests, the government endeavours to help farmers at all levels of farming—from pre-sowing of crops to cropping season up to harvest and post-harvesting of crops. In this regard, the government introduced the Soil Health Card scheme. Under the scheme, the government issues soil cards to farmers every three years, which will suggest them, based on their soil nutrients, as to what crops to plant on a given piece of land so that maximum output is achieved with minimum input and investment. More than 12.68 crore SHCs have been printed and distributed to farmers which have resulted in 8–10 per cent decrease in the use of chemical fertilizers by the farmers and a 5–6 per cent increase in the agricultural output.

## DURING SOWING: NEEM-COATED UREA

A major breakthrough introduced by the government for the sowing period was the provision of neem-coated urea. In just one year, the government has made 100 per cent neem-coated urea available and curbed unauthorized use of urea by chemical factories. Earlier, subsidized urea was diverted to non-agricultural use, which created shortages and harmed farmers. But the launch of 100 per cent neem-coated urea has made non-agricultural use impossible which has become a great boon for farmers as urea is now available in adequate quantity to them. Neem coating for indigenous urea has been done 100 per cent which was only 35 per cent pre 2014. The use of 100 per cent neem-coated urea has led to improved soil health as well as reduced pest attacks and diseases. It has also led to the increased nitrogen use which leads to efficiency and an increase in the crop yield. The efficiency of neem-coated urea is 10–15 per cent more as compared to normal urea. Apart from this, a new fertilizer policy too has been formulated by the government under which the shutdown urea factories have been reopened. This has resulted in reduction in the prices of NPK (Nitrogen-Phosphorous-Pottasium) urea along with a significant increase in urea production. It has also led to a reduction in the MRP of Diammonium Phosphate, Muriate of Potash and other complex fertilizers. Moreover, ₹50,000 crore has been allocated by the government to revive defunct fertilizer units in Gorakhpur, Sindri, Talcher, Ramagundam and Barauni, in addition to a new urea plant being set up at Namrup with a capacity of 8.4 lakh metric tonne (LMT) per annum. A special banking arrangement of ₹10,000 crore too has been made to clear fertilizer subsidy dues.

## IRRIGATION

The government has launched the Pradhan Mantri Krishi Sinchayee Yojana (PMKSY) which is being implemented in a mission mode by three ministries under which ₹86,000 crore is being spent to undertake 99 irrigation projects to cover up an area of 28.5 lakh ha. It is an end-to-end solution to our nation's irrigation problems, with the objective of *'Har Khet Ko Paani'* (Water to every field). The PMKSY intends to be a long-term solution in dealing with the problem of drought in India. A fully dedicated micro-irrigation fund with a sum of ₹5,000 crore has been set up, which will help in the achievement of 'More Crop Per Drop' as announced in the union budget. Micro-irrigation is very crucial in ensuring judicious use of water so that maximum yield is achieved by minimum water usage. It also facilitates the farmers in installing solar water pumps for in-field irrigation. Acting on the promise of 'More Crop Per Drop', the area under micro-irrigation has doubled under the Modi government. Around 4.3 lakh ha of land was under micro-irrigation in 2013–14 which is now 8.3 lakh ha in 2016–17, in a short span of just three years.

## BEFORE HARVEST: CREDIT AVAILABILITY

Farming in India has been a labour-intensive sector unlike the developed countries, and most of the farmers here are poor. Access to finance and credit is one of the biggest challenges for Indian farmers, who, with minimal cash in hand, depend on informal credit extension by moneylenders at exorbitant rates of interest, which eventually leads to debt trap and a vicious cycle of poverty. Indeed, the same has been the major cause of farmer suicides in India. Even the Kisan credit card loans have limitations as they are only for short-term duration, particularly for purchasing seeds, fertilizers, etc. There have been hardly any viable formal long-term credit facilities to farmers to purchase advanced machineries, tractors, to invest in allied activities or establish food processing units. To overcome this situation, the Modi government has been striving hard to make available affordable credit facilities to farmers. This is evident from the farm credit target for the year 2018–19 being raised to a record high of ₹11 lakh crore.

The world's biggest financial inclusion scheme—PMJDY—was successfully conducted by the government to include the poor farmers in the formal financial system of the country, which has till date opened nearly 34 crore bank accounts. This will be instrumental in fulfilling the financial necessities of the agricultural sector and safeguarding the poor illiterate farmers from taking loans from non-institutional lenders. Another scheme, the Pradhan Mantri Mudra Yojana (PMMY), has been brought in to extend loans for activities allied to agriculture such as pisciculture, beekeeping, poultry, livestock rearing, grading, dairy, agri-clinics, food and agro-processing, etc. Mudra loans which have a repayment tenure of seven years will also be covering activities such as papad-making, pickle-making, jam/jelly-making, agricultural produce preservation at local levels, including villages as well as promotion of sweet shops, bakery industry, canteen services, cold storage facilities, etc. Under the interest subvention scheme, short-term loans up to ₹3 lakh are extended at an interest rate of 7 per cent per annum. Around 24.53 lakh joint liability groups have been provided loans of ₹26,848 crore by banks across the country.

The farm credit target under the union budget has been raised to ₹11 lakh crore for 2018–19, and ₹2,000 crore has been granted for setting up of the agri-market infrastructure fund. A corpus of ₹10,000 crore is created to develop infrastructure in the fishery, aquaculture and animal husbandry sectors, and ₹1,290 crore is allocated under the National Bamboo Mission to help set up small industries. Apart from these, tax incentives are being given to promote post-harvest agricultural activities.

## CROP INSURANCE

'Agriculture requires a safety net against nature's inclemency and capacity building to counter many manmade risks'—highlighted by the report of the Committee on Doubling Farmers' Income'(Volume X). India, being a vast country with diverse climatic conditions and weather changes, has to often bear the adversity of nature. While some part of the country faces huge floods, some other part may be severely drought hit. No matter how harsh the calamity, a farmer's right to livelihood and well-being must be ensured; the PMFBY is a remarkable step in this direction and has replaced all other existing insurance schemes to avoid multiplicity and confusion. The present government has outperformed the past governments in almost all aspects pertaining to farmer welfare with its holistic schemes and initiatives. The PMFBY, which is India's biggest crop insurance initiative covering about 4.05 crore farmers and 379.06 lakh ha of land for a sum of ₹1,31,519 crore, is a milestone in the *Beej Se Bazaar Tak* mission. The PMFBY has led to a huge increase in insured farmers with its 'maximum insurance at minimum premium' model, with 4.05 crore farmers insured in kharif 2016 as compared to only 2.09 crore farmers insured during kharif 2013. There has also been a massive increase in the sum insured for farmers with ₹1,35,519 crore in kharif 2016 relative to only ₹49,454 crore in kharif 2013.

Compensation to farmers in distress is given in case of 33 per cent or more crop damage as compared to an earlier policy of compensation at 50 per cent damage. Additionally, for foodgrains damaged due to excessive rainfall, the full minimum support price shall be paid. There has been an 82 per cent rise in the provision under the State Disaster Relief Fund during 2015–20, as compared to 2010–15 which went up to ₹61,220 crore from ₹33,580.93 crore.

The PMFBY encompasses insurance coverage and financial support to the farmers in the event of natural calamities, pests and diseases and ensures that the farmers have a stable financial health. It employs a combination of innovative technological and administrative methodologies so as to provide farmers hassle-free claim assessment. Under the PMFBY, a uniform premium of only 2 per cent is to be paid by the farmers for all kharif crops, 1.5 per cent for all rabi crops and 5 per cent premium for commercial and horticulture crops. Under this scheme, post-harvest losses are also covered. The most significant feature under the PMFBY is the mandatory use of technology, wherein smartphones, drones, remote sensing, etc., are incorporated to bring down the number of Crop Cutting Experiments.

## POST-HARVEST

The present government has shown unprecedented support to farmers with the hike in the MSP and record procurement. A major policy shift brought in by the Modi government, which has been hailed as a historic decision, was the hiking of the MSP to 1.5 times the production cost for kharif crops. The extent of buffer stock of pulses was increased from 1.5 lakh tonne to 20 lakh tonne under which about 16.24 lakh metric tonne of pulses were procured.

In order to facilitate the farmers with better returns for their investment, value addition is very important along with getting the supply chain right. In order to add value to the produce, integration and promotion of infrastructure and schemes for post-harvest, marketing and processing has been envisioned by the government.

The Pradhan Mantri Kisan Sampada Yojana (PMKSY) has been launched to modernize the supply chain infrastructure which has so far been outdated, enabling leakages. In this direction, budget allocation has been doubled to push the food processing industry. Moreover, 22,000 existing rural haats are being developed into Gramin Agricultural Markets (GrAMs), and they are being electronically linked to e-NAM to facilitate direct sale to consumers and bulk purchasers. Operation Greens has been initiated to address the price volatility of perishable commodities such as tomato, onion and potato. To help the farmers in getting the best price for their produce, 585 regulated markets have been integrated under e-NAM, where 164.53 lakh tonne of farm commodities worth ₹41,591 thousands crore have been transacted. By tapping the technology for farmer welfare, the present government has already connected 87.5 lakh farmers, 89,934 traders and 46,411 commissions live on e-NAM platform.

## e-NAM

A major barrier to the growth and prosperity of farmers has been the lack of an accessible and equitable common market. Often, middlemen would buy the produce from the farmers at takeaway prices and sell it on their own later, making huge profits. National Agriculture Market (NAM), a pan-India e-trading portal, which seeks to connect all the existing Agriculture Product Market Committees (APMCs) in the country and establish a unified national market is in place. It also ends geographical obstructions and buyer-seller information asymmetry, as it brings together buyers and sellers together on a single platform. There is a provision of single-point levy of market fees, i.e., on the first wholesale purchase from the farmer. Under e-NAM, there is also a provision for soil testing laboratories in or near the selected mandi, which the visiting farmers can access. The central government has also decided to provide the software to the states at no extra cost along with a grant of up to ₹30 lakh per mandi for related equipment and infrastructure. Moreover, the gradual integration of all major mandis into NAM will ensure common procedures for issue of licences, levy of fee and movement of produce.

## STORAGE INFRASTRUCTURE

One of the major problems plaguing the farming sector is food wastage and leakages during the time when the post-harvest foodgrains move from the farm gate to the market. Due to numerous biotic and abiotic components, their storage, till they are passed on to the consumer, is very crucial. The storage infrastructure in our country has been very poor for decades despite governments being aware of the fact that it is a crucial component in the farm process. The Modi government has brought in several policy changes to reform and restructure the farming storage infrastructure. A lot of emphasis has been given on the creation of mega food parks, which were announced by the previous governments but were not carried on with required emphasis. In this direction, PMKSY, a comprehensive flagship scheme consisting of mega food parks, integrated cold chains and value addition infrastructure, food safety and quality assurance infrastructure, has been introduced by the government. It also encompasses new projects such as infrastructure for agro-processing clusters, creation of backward and forward linkages, creation and expansion of food processing and preservation capacities. PMKSY, with a huge investment of ₹31,400 crore, is expected to generate around 5.3 lakh direct or indirect employment and benefit 20 lakh farmers by the year 2019–20.

Preventing post-harvest losses of food-grains has been the top most priority of the government. Towards this end, multiple warehouses have been established by the Food Corporation of India (FCI), Central Warehouse Corporation (CWC) and State Warehouse Corporations, especially in rural areas; the existing ones have also been improved. In addition, construction of steel silos is being done through Public Private Partnership (PPP) mode to modernize the storage infrastructure and improve the shelf-life of stored foodgrains. Apart from this, a new scheme called Operation Greens has also been initiated in the line of Operation Flood, with an outlay of ₹500 crore to promote Farmer Producers Organizations, agri-logistics, processing facilities and professional management.

## PM-AASHA

Towards safeguarding the income of farmers, the central government has taken a historic step by introducing a new umbrella scheme named Pradhan Mantri Annadata Aay Sanrakshan Abhiyan (PM-AASHA). The MSP of kharif crops has been increased by the government to 1.5 times the production cost. The government has tried to relook at its outdated procurement and the MSP system because they were found to have several lacunae. A research by

NITI Aayog and other research outfits has shown that the reach of the present MSP system of procurement is inefficient in terms of both geography and the crops covered under it. Despite crores of public money being spent on the MSP operations every year, crisis in the farm sector continues. The PM-AASHA scheme is intended to check the gaps in the MSP system and to ensure that farmers get better output for their produce. It is also intended to improve the procurement system and reduce food waste and leakages.

The PM-AASHA scheme has three arms and these will complement the existing schemes of the Department of Food and Public Distribution. The Price Support Scheme (PSS) is the first arm of PM-AASHA. Under PSS, central nodal agencies will be physically procuring pulses, oilseeds and copra, and the expenditure and losses due to procurement will be taken care of by the central government. Price Deficiency Payment Scheme (PDPS) is the second arm of PM-AASHA. The centre intends to include all oilseeds and compensate the farmers for the difference between their production costs and selling price in the market. The third arm is the Private Procurement and Stockist Scheme (PPSS). Currently, on a pilot basis, its objective is to encourage the participation of private sectors in the procurement operation. For oilseeds, the state governments will be at liberty to launch this policy in certain districts and private players in such districts may purchase the produce from the farmers at the MSP, if the price of the farm produce goes below the notified MSP.

The present government has decided to give additional government guarantee of ₹16,550 crore, and thereby the total expenditure projected for PM-AASHA scheme is ₹45,550 crore. In addition, budget provision for procurement operations has also been increased, and ₹15,053 crore is sanctioned for the implementation of PM-AASHA. In the financial years 2010–14, the total procurement as per the government data was ₹3,500 crore only, whereas during financial years 2014–18, it surged up to 10 times and reached ₹34,000 crore.

## ANCILLARY ACTIVITIES

The government came out with the seven-point strategy to achieve the target of doubling the income of the farmers by 2022 and the promotion of ancillary activities like poultry, beekeeping and fisheries has been mentioned as the seventh point. It is crucial as it multiplies the income sources of the farmers thus, decreasing dependency on a single option and opening up new avenues for income generation.

Blue Revolution is the term given to the promotion of the fishery sector and in order to exploit the best of this sector, the government is using a mix of policies and scientific approaches. The government is promoting 'cage culture', which is being vouched for as the future of fisheries. An umbrella scheme, the Integrated Development and Management of Fisheries, is a remarkable step in this direction of revolutionizing the sector.

For promoting the horticulture sector, Mission for Integrated Development of Horticulture (MIDH) has been developed, which covers fruits, vegetables, roots and tuber crops, mushrooms, spices, flowers, aromatic plants, coconut, cashews, cocoa and bamboo. To develop commercial horticulture, interventions are being made in production and post-harvest management, creation of capital investment subsidy scheme to support construction and modernization of cold storages for horticulture products, promotion of mechanization and making available quality planting material. Operation Greens with an allocation of ₹500 crore aims to stabilize the supply of Tomato, Onion and Potato (TOP) crops so as to ensure availability of these crops throughout the country, round the year.

Beekeeping has immense scope for both domestic consumption and exports. To promote scientific beekeeping, the central government under MIDH is running several training programmes because a beekeeper can not only earn by selling honey but also by scientifically extracting and selling other by-products, including beeswax, royal jelly, pollen and bee venom, which can substantially increase his or her income.

To accelerate the development of livestock, the NDA government launched the National Livestock Mission (NLM) with an aim to ensure quantitative and qualitative improvement in livestock production systems and capacity building of all stakeholders with focus on improving availability of quality feed and fodder. Besides NLM, Rashtriya Gokul Mission was launched for the development of indigenous breed with an initial outlay of ₹2,025 crore. The government has set up e-pashuhaat, a portal to help farmers obtain information regarding indigenous bovine breeds as well as help them sell and purchase animals.

## EXPORTS

The national Agriculture Export Policy (AEP), which intends to play a significant role in achieving the double income for farmers, was approved by the Modi government aiming to double the farm exports to $60 billion by 2022. It is proposed to bring structural changes in the export policy and make India a dependable exporter in the world market. The AEP aims to diversify the export basket and markets. It will mainly focus on perishables and value-added products. It will promote the export of novel, indigenous, organic, ethnic, traditional and non-traditional agri-products and provide an institutional mechanism for pursuing market access, tackling barriers and dealing with sanitary issues. This policy aims to eliminate every restriction on exports of organic agricultural merchandise, which are high in demand in the global market. The National Programme for Organic Production (NPOP) is a scheme launched by the Modi government for promoting organic farming. Its standards for production and accreditation system have been recognized by various nations as equivalent to their country standards, and thereby Indian organic products are likely to be more acceptable in global market with this move.

Many old laws have been repealed, unnecessary compliances have been eliminated and services are being facilitated with provision for online applications. The Modi government has also introduced the Merchandise Exports from the India scheme, which has replaced five different schemes for rewarding merchandise exports. India's strategic position gives it a unique advantage to export food products all over the world and make it the food capital of the world.

## SCIENTIFIC FARMING AND SMART AGRICULTURE

Technology and innovation will play a crucial role in making the aspiration of doubling the farmers' income by 2022 come true. Smart farm machinery, micro-irrigation, precision farming, digital forums and stakeholder engagement are going to create a disruptive effect in agriculture, which is being termed as Farming 3.0. The idea behind smart machinery is that it is better in terms of efficiency and it produces more output for the input. Smart machines and technological breakthroughs have the potential to extend the output, lower the costs and boost farm incomes. Agro-meteorological services provided through SMS and other modes for day-to-day farming operations have been introduced. Around 21 million farmers are currently receiving such information in vernacular languages. Precision farming incorporates the use of information technology to get real-time data regarding soil health, nutrients and available resources so that precise farming could be carried out in accordance with favourable environment and with maximum output.

## FOCUS ON NORTHEAST

Northeast India, which was mostly neglected from the developmental road map, has been given special focus by the Modi government. Northeast India has been envisioned as the organic farming powerhouse. India's third agricultural research institute is coming up in Assam, which will facilitate better education and research for increased agricultural production apart from helping the farmers in adoption of better farming technologies. The Paramparagat Krishi Vikas Yojana (PKVY), brought by the NDA government to promote organic farming, aims to bring 50,000 ha of Northeast land into organic farming.

The strategies and agendas of previous governments for development of agriculture sector in India has mainly focussed on increasing the total output and ensuring food security. However, they have totally failed on the front of farmer welfare as farmers despite owning land have remained relatively poor and sidelined. It is because of the uncertainties involved in agriculture that today's youth is migrating to urban towns in search of jobs leaving chunks of land behind in villages as they do not trust agriculture to enhance their standards of living. Agriculture in India is considered as a subsistence activity, whereas in developed countries, it is the most rewarding venture. That is so because the governments in India, till now, have suffered policy paralysis and indecisive governance when it came to restructuring and reforming the agricultural sector. Land reforms could not be done to the fullest. Despite having good monsoon seasons and vast water resources, the previous governments totally failed on the management front, thus, eventually affecting the whole sector and human capital involved therein. In some parts of India, farmers are facing severe losses due to floods and in some parts, farmers are committing suicide because of drought. Hardly any steps were taken to make farming a lucrative profession, incorporating modern farming practices on scientific lines with technological aids and suggesting soil specific cropping pattern to the farmers. Moreover, age old distorting practices and systems were not adequately dealt with resulting in losses to the farming community.

The present NDA government under the leadership of Narendra Modi has well understood the plight of the farming community and has tried to replace the policies with comprehensive and holistic bottoms-up approach rendering to the specific needs and problems of the farmers. The government has also taken into account the fact that it is relatively time-consuming to double the farmers' income just by pushing to enhance agricultural productivity.

The government introduced a series of innovative and result-oriented policies and schemes, which are remarkable efforts in the history of independent India handholding the agrarian community. The NDA-led government has been the first one to take such decisive steps, from Beej to Bazaar in such a short span, which clearly manifests the government's commitment and priority towards farmers. Certainly, the government has been ambitious in these reforms and initiatives, but the results have started to show in the lives of common farmers. Narendra Modi's vision of doubling the income of farmers by 2022 will be a key milestone in India's progress as the largest global economic power and the stride to end the vicious circle of poverty.

***Anoop A.J.*** *is a researcher and policy analyst with many years of experience in policy advocacy. He has worked as a research scholar at Vivekananda International Foundation, Delhi, and as a volunteer with Vivekananda Kendra. One of the founders of policy advocacy platform Bharat Niti, he writes regular columns in dailies. Also a political activist, Anoop is the National Secretary of the youth wing of Bharatiya Janata Party.*

# HEALTHIER SOIL: SOIL HEALTH CARD

## *G. Sreedathan*

Bhaskar Porje, a resident of Khambale village in Nashik district, is a happy man now. According to Porje, a small-scale farmer, the soil health check he carried out in his fields two years ago has changed his life for the better. In the kharif season, water-guzzling paddy is the main crop here as water is available in plenty—this region gets up to 2,000 cm of rain annually. But, after the paddy harvest, resourceful farmers who have wells or farm ponds could also grow vegetables in the rabi season. Others, however, are left with no option but to work as farm labourers. For the last couple of years, Porje has been using mulching paper method to grow tomatoes in his two-acre plot. He changed the crop pattern on the advice of agriculture officials and it worked wonders for him.

Equipped with a SHC, Porje is now aware of what his soil needs. The agriculture officials explained to him how micronutrients in adequate quantity in soil help improve harvest. He now knows how to maintain organic carbon and pH levels in the soil. Porje, like his fellow farmers, now keeps a meticulous record of soil content and applies fertilizers accordingly. 'You have to give what the soil needs and not what you have. If you give that, then Prithvi Maa will give back in plenty,' he says.

According to Porje, it never occurred to him that he should

have his soil tested. Encouraged by district agriculture officials, he, along with 1,000 other farmers, conducted the soil test. For all these years, he had been following traditional farming practices. 'After the test, I came to know that the organic carbon content in the soil was very low. It also showed me the Nitrogen, Phosphorus, Potassium (NPK) and micronutrient content in the soil. I was advised by the agriculture officials to use organic manure. This had a telling effect on the quality of the soil and its water retention capacity. The organic carbon level has also gone up,' he says. This had another telling effect—even after applying less quantity of chemical fertilizers, he got four quintal more rice. 'Now my expenses on fertilizers have come down drastically and I use only that much which is required,' he says.

*Bhaskar Porje of Khambale, Nashik (Photo courtesy: Pankaj Joshi)*

The increase in income from paddy cultivation has doubled Porje's confidence. He invested the extra income in tomato cultivation. As stated earlier, he used mulching paper technique for this. The amount of water used in farming has also gone down as water retention has increased due to mulching. Earlier, he used to only have paddy cultivation, but now he has tomatoes too. Porje believes that this change has been brought about by the SHC scheme.

The story of Harishchandra Gawane, a resident of Kanchan Gaon in the same district, is no different. He used to cultivate paddy but this season, he has also grown cucumbers using the mulching paper technique. He hopes to get good returns on them. 'This is the result of SHC,' he says with a twinkle in his eye. He used to apply fertilizers without much thought. 'I applied for a SHC three years ago. On the advice of agriculture officials, I started giving measured quantities of chemical fertilizers. Despite the cut down on chemical fertilizers, the yield was really good. The rice plants were looking robust and grains were big in size. Even the incidence of pest attack had reduced,' he says.

According to Nashik district's Soil Survey and Soil Testing Officer Chhagan Padvi, the farmers have benefitted in a big way through this scheme. 'After the soil test, the farmers were able to identify the level of micronutrients, NPK and organic carbon in the soil. The farmers can take the decision on the basis of the test results. In the last four years, since the launch of the scheme, the living standard of the farmers in the district has gone up. So far, 77,745 SHCs have been distributed in the district. We tested 91,807 soil samples in the district, and in one block of Igatpur, 19,000 farmers have benefitted from this scheme,' says the officer.

*Harishchandra Gawane of Kanchan Goan, Nashik (Photo courtesy: Pankaj Joshi)*

Nashik, called the California of India, is known for three things—Kumbh Mela, wineries and onions. Located 190 km north of Mumbai, Nashik has earned the distinction of being the wine capital of India, thanks to its climate that is favourable for growing grapes.

A majority of farmers in Niphad and Dindori taluks in the district grow grapes while paddy is the main crop in Igatpuri, Trimbakeshwar, Peth and Surgana taluks. In eastern parts of the district, farmers mainly cultivate onion, pomegranate and vegetables. Compared to other farmers, grape growers are considered to be the most updated and well-informed ones. They export tonnes of grapes and wines to the US and Europe. Apart from the government facilities, the grape growers here depend on private soil testing labs in these areas. Balasaheb Pingle, a resident of Dindori taluk, says that grape cultivation requires great and meticulous care. 'We carry out soil testing three times a year and we take the help of private soil testing facilities in these areas. We also take the advice of scientists at the National Research Centre for Grapes,' he says.

*Balasaheb Pingle of Dindori, Nashik (Photo courtesy: Pankaj Joshi)*

Pingle, a graduate, has been cultivating grapes for the last 18 years. He has adopted new and innovative farming technologies. According to him, soil test is very crucial for farming and it should be the first priority of a farmer. He vouches that soil testing has helped him increase his income. Initially, he used to cultivate grapes in 2 acres but now his family does so in 40 acres of land.

Besides grapes, he also grows vegetables and maize. He lives in a bungalow, owns a car and a tractor, and his children study in good schools. He doesn't believe that farming is a non-profitable proposition. 'If one adopts right techniques and technology, one can make farming a profitable proposition; and soil testing forms the basis of all these techniques,' he says.

## HOW IT BEGAN IN GUJARAT

In order to close the gap between theory and practice and to double farmers' income in five years, Prime Minister Narendra Modi, during his tenure as chief minister of Gujarat, introduced Krushi Mahotsav in 2005. The success of this programme encouraged the state government to organize the festival as a month-long annual event in which experts, agricultural officials, farmers and representatives of agri-businesses converged at rural areas to solve the problems faced by the farming sector. The comprehensive format of the festival had all the aspects of farming, including animal husbandry. Soil testing was also a component of this exercise. Besides, 'Krushi Raths' were fanned out to villages, and experts and officials accompanying them helped in the transfer of technology to farmers. Apart from advice, poor farmers were given input kits free of cost. The government also roped in farmers' cooperatives, non-government organizations and private agencies for dissemination of information and to enhance the reach of the scheme.

The Krushi Mahotsav had a telling impact on the income of the farmers in Garudeshwar taluk of Gujarat. Amarpal Singh Gohil, a resident of Mota Amba village who owns about 5 ha of land, got information about soil health management during the Krushi Mahotsav held in 2012. The state agriculture department officials tested his soil and gave him a SHC.

In his piece of land, he used to cultivate papaya, maize, banana, cotton, sugarcane and castor. The SHC was an eye-opener for him because his soil had all those fertilizers—urea, diammonium phosphate (DAP) and potash—in excess. He was advised not to add any chemical fertilizer except small quantities of urea in instalments and instead opt for organic manure in sufficient quantity. In a few months, the results were out for all to see. According to him, in 2012–13, the papaya production jumped from 35–40 tonne/ha (fetching about ₹1.5 lakh net profit) to 55–60 tonne/ha with income netting at ₹2.25 lakh.

On the advice of agriculture officials, Gohil tried the same experiment on banana crop. The banana production increased from 65–70 tonne/ha to 95–100 tonne/ha. His income also increased Consider using correspondingly?

At first, when agriculture officials had told Gopal Patel, a resident of Vavadi village in Nandod taluk, to apply only organic manure rich in micronutrients on his land, he was taken aback. But, he decided to give it a try. His main source of income was banana plantation. He was used to grow banana on 1 ha of land and paddy and castor on another half-a-hectare. After applying organic manure, he could feel a change in the soil quality. Returns from the banana plantation also went up to ₹4 lakh against ₹2.5 lakh a year ago.

When agriculture department officials approached Akshay Kumar, a young farmer in Bharuch village of Gujarat, to explain about the advantages of soil testing, he was not game for it. He couldn't figure out how soil testing could help reduce the cost of farming or improve yield and income. Two officials of the agriculture department came and took the samples. After a few days, they advised him on the way to proceed. Now, he thanks them for their intervention for there is a remarkable decline in the input costs. Pointing to a massive banana bunch, he tells me that there is a marked difference in the texture and size of the fruit. He also grows groundnut in his six-acre plot and the yield has increased.

In the drought-prone drylands of Yadgir in Karnataka, farming is a tough job. For the impoverished population in the Yadgir taluk, there aren't many reliable alternative sources of income save farming activities. Rainfall is low and highly variable; farming yields uncertain income. A majority of people are small and marginal farmers who toil on the dry-land fields for subsistence. Even farmers with decent land holdings have learnt to live with meagre incomes. Abdul Salim, a resident of Wankasambar village, has been following what his predecessors did on his 15-acre land. He grows tur (red gram), castor and vegetables. Although he was ready for experimentation, there was no one to guide him on new agricultural practices. He used to do farming the way his father did. He didn't know there was something called micronutrients such as zinc, gypsum and boron, which help in increasing agriculture production.

Meanwhile, agriculture officers of the Karnataka government approached Salim and suggested him to undertake a soil health check under the Bhoochetana scheme, a precursor to the SHC scheme in the state. The Bhoochetana scheme was launched on 23 May 2009 with the objective of increasing agriculture productivity in dry land/rain-fed areas of the state. The highlight of the scheme was soil health analysis using advanced technology. On the advice of officers, he carried out the soil test in 2013. After analysing the soil test findings, he was advised to replace the seeds with high yielding TSR3 tur seeds and apply micronutrients such as zinc, gypsum and organic fertilizers. He took the advice. According to Salim, there was more than 60 per cent reduction in cost on account of using micronutrients and organic fertilizers that are cheap. In the following season, he was advised to use 150 kg of Di Amonium Phosphate mixed with 20 kg of urea on his 12 acres—with 6 acres each earmarked for tur and castor.

The outcome of the experiment was highly encouraging for Salim who got twice the yield with less input costs. He got 24 quintals of tur and an equal quantity of castor against 12 quintals each in the previous years.

## WHY HEALTHY SOIL IS IMPORTANT

Healthy soil is crucial for any farming activity. The success of a farmer depends on how he manages his soil in an environmentally and economically sustainable way. As majority of India's population is dependent on agriculture for their livelihood, it is important for the government to make soil conducive for sustainable agriculture. Soil health has a direct connection with human health. India's famous agricultural scientist Dr M.S. Swaminathan says, 'Soil anaemia also breeds human anaemia. Micronutrient deficiency in soil results in micronutrient malnutrition in people, since crops that are grown on such soil tend to be deficient in the nutrients needed to fight hidden hunger.' The initiatives like Green Revolution and technological interventions have led to a quantum jump in food production and bolstered the country's food security. However, this intensive crop production has depleted the soil, jeopardizing our ability to maintain production in these areas in the future. Deteriorating soil health, due to over use of fertilizers, pesticides and insecticides, has been a cause of concern and has also led to the suboptimal utilization of farming resources. A wide gap between nutrient demand and supply, 'high nutrient turnover in soil-plant system coupled with low and imbalanced fertilizer use, emerging deficiencies of secondary and micronutrients, increase in soil acidity and nutrient immobilization in red, lateritic and clayey soils' also cause deterioration of soil fertility. Faulty management of irrigation water stimulates leaching of nutrients and development of waterlogging, salinization and alkalization.

Punjab has emerged as India's food basket post Green Revolution. But, the country had to pay a heavy price for making it self-sufficient in terms of foodgrain production. Rapidly degrading soil quality has wreaked havoc on the productivity of the land and lives of farmers. During my conversations with farmers in Malwa and Muktasar districts, they revealed their underlying fears and hopelessness. Balwinder Singh, a resident of Bhuttiwala village in Muktasar district, contradicts me when I say that his village is lush green and prosperous. 'It's deceptive. Taste the soil if you want to feel the difference. It used to taste normal but now it has become salty and sterile. Punjab had the most fertile soil in the country. Now, it's all gone. Everything is poisonous here, even the mother's milk. We sow poison and harvest poison,' said a dejected-looking Singh. He has a very sad story to tell. His son-in-law and brother died of cancer. Singh said that earlier people in those regions used to grow mustard and chickpea. 'They changed the crop patterns. To produce more, farmers use more fertilizers and pesticides. The doctors who treated my son-in-law said that excessive use of fertilizers and pesticides by farmers claimed his life,' said Singh, staring at the garlanded photograph of a middle-aged Sikh man.

Besides the excessive use of fertilizers, low addition of organic matter and non-replacement of depleted micro and secondary nutrients over the years, have also resulted in nutrient deficiencies and the decrease in soil fertility in these areas. Experts suggest that another reason for Punjab's plight is the introduction of paddy during the Green Revolution. Punjab, according to them, is not suitable for cultivating paddy. A survey was conducted by the Department of Soil and Water Conservation in SBS Nagar, SAS Nagar, Fategarh Sahib, Patiala, Sangrur, Moga and Barnala and found that the cropping pattern of wheat and paddy introduced during the Green Revolution has rendered the soil unusable.

The latest estimates show that 96.40 million ha (Mha) area of India (which is 29.32 per cent of the Total Geographic Area [TGA] of the country during 2011–13) is undergoing the process of soil degradation. It has increased from 94.53 Mha (which was 28.76 per cent of the TGA in 2003–05). The states of Rajasthan, Maharashtra, Gujarat, Jammu & Kashmir, Karnataka, Jharkhand, Odisha, Madhya Pradesh and Telangana contribute 24 percent of the degraded area in the country.

According to the Population Reference Bureau, India's population will touch 1.68 billion by mid-2030. With a burgeoning population, coupled with adverse impact of climate change and increasing stress on water and land resources, our future food security hinges on our ability to increase yields and food quality using the soil that is already under production today. Around 70 per cent of India's population is living in rural areas with agriculture as their livelihood support system. A majority of Indian farmers are small and marginal, with average land holding less than two acres a household. Moreover, their farm size is decreasing further due to population growth. Heightened nutrient mining, soil erosion, depletion of water table and accumulation of toxic elements in soil and water are posing a threat to sustainable livelihood security of the rural population. Since land resources are finite, efforts should be made to reclaim degraded land and wastelands, so that the areas going out of cultivation due to social and economic reasons are replenished by reclaiming these lands.

The government has launched Soil Health Management as one of the key interventions under the National Mission for Sustainable Agriculture (NMSA). According to the operational guidelines of NMSA, Soil Health Management aims at 'promoting location as well as crop-specific sustainable soil health management, creating and linking soil fertility maps with macro-micro nutrient management, judicious application of fertilizers and organic farming practices'. The government has put in place a five-pronged strategy to achieve this:

1. Implement SHC scheme with the following objectives: to issue SHC every three years to all farmers of the country to provide a basis to address nutrient deficiencies in fertilization practices; to strengthen the functioning of soil testing laboratories through capacity building, involvement of agriculture students and establishing effective linkages with the Indian Council of Agriculture Research/state agriculture universities; to diagnose soil fertility-related constraints with standardized procedures for sampling, analysis and design taluk/block-level fertilizer recommendations in targeted districts uniformly across states; to develop and promote soil test-based nutrient management in the districts for optimum nutrient use efficiency; to build capacities of district and state level staff and progressive farmers for promotion of nutrient management practices.
2. Ensure quality control requirements of fertilizers, bio-fertilizers and organic fertilizers under the Fertilizer (Control) Order 1985, including revision of standards and testing protocols, keeping in view the advances in research and technology and covering organic inputs under quality control regime.
3. Promote Integrated Nutrient Management (INM) through judicious use of chemical fertilizers, including secondary and micronutrients in conjunctions with organic manures and bio-fertilizers for improving soil health and its productivity.
4. Support augmentation and strengthening of soil and fertilizer testing facilities and providing soil test-based recommendations

to farmers for improving soil fertility and enhancing economic return to farmers. It will also support upgradation of skill and knowledge of soil testing laboratories (STL)/extension staff and farmers and their capacity building through training and demonstration on farm fields on balanced use of fertilizers.

5. Implement PKVY to promote organic agriculture through adoption of organic village by cluster approach and Participatory Guarantee System (PGS) certification. The scheme is an elaborated component of Soil Health Management for NMSA.

## SOIL HEALTH IN INDIA

Food and Agricultural Organization (FAO) defines soil health thus:

> Soil health has been defined as the capacity of soil to function as a living system. Healthy soils maintain a diverse community of soil organisms that help to control plant disease, insect and weed pests, form beneficial symbiotic associations with plant roots, recycle essential plant nutrients, improve soil structure with positive effects for soil water and nutrient holding capacity and ultimately improve crop production. A healthy soil also contributes to mitigating climate change by maintaining or increasing its carbon content.

So, soil is said to be healthy if it is able to optimally sustain its native/acquired productivity potential and render ecological services. Often soil health and soil quality are used interchangeably. In their book, *The Nature and Properties of Soils,* Nyle C. Brady and Ray R. Weil state, 'Although these terms are often used synonymously, they involve two distinct concepts. Soil health refers to self-regulation, stability, resilience and lack of stress symptoms in the soil as an ecosystem. Soil health describes the biological integrity of the soil community—the balance among organisms within the soil and between soil organisms and their environment.' The Soil Science Society of America defines soil health as 'the capacity of a specific kind of soil to function, within natural or managed ecosystem boundaries, to sustain plant and animal productivity, maintain or enhance water and air quality and support human health and habitation'. 'The importance of soil for food security should be obvious. From the origins of civilization in early farming communities up through today, we can see how societies have prospered, thanks to healthy soils, and declined when their lands became degraded or infertile,' said FAO Deputy Director General Maria Helena Semedo.

## SOIL HEALTH CARD SCHEME

Ancient Indian scriptures have deliberated on techniques to improve soil quality and interventions needed to conserve soil. However, in the twentieth century, in our efforts to attain self-sufficiency in food production to feed the burgeoning population, soil conservation became secondary. We had to pay a heavy price for this neglect as soil degradation in our food bowls assumed dangerous proportions. By 1980s, soil conservation started gaining policy attention. However, a more focussed approach to soil management has only been adopted after 2014–15. This has coincided with the declaration of the International Year of Soils by the United Nations. Soil health is a holistic concept, which includes chemical, physical and biological health of the soil.

The National Democratic Alliance (NDA) government led by Prime Minister Narendra Modi has taken a host of initiatives to double the farmers' incomes by 2022–23 and end agrarian distress, thereby ensuring farmers' welfare. Issuing a SHC to each farmer in the country is also a part of this larger scheme. The agriculture ministry's flagship programme, launched in February 2015 in a mission mode, has the potential to transform farming in the country.

The soil health card is a central scheme promoted by the Department of Agriculture and Co-operation under the Ministry of Agriculture and Farmers Welfare. The scheme is being implemented through the Department of Agriculture of all the state and union territory governments in 50:50 sharing pattern. The card will give each farmer the status of the nutrients on his soil and advise him on the dosage of fertilizers required. It would also inform him about the soil amendments that he should undertake to maintain soil health.

The soil is tested on twelve parameters such as NPK, secondary nutrients and micronutrients such as zinc, iron, copper, manganese, boron and physical parameters such as pH, EC and OC.

After checking the soil as per the guidelines put in place by the Union Agriculture Ministry on various parameters, a card is given, which will carry crop-wise recommendations of nutrients/fertilizers required for farms, making it possible for farmers to improve productivity by using appropriate inputs. The centre provides funds to states for setting up soil testing facilities for issuing SHC to farmers. To undertake this massive project of soil testing and issuing of cards, state governments have engaged non-government organizations, agricultural students, farmers' collectives and cooperatives.

The SHC, which will be issued every three years, displays soil health indicators and the nutrient status along with recommendations on appropriate dosage of nutrients to be applied for improving soil health and its fertility. The card provides a basis for farmers to address the nutrient deficiencies in fertilization practices. As part of the scheme, efforts are taken to augment soil testing infrastructure and the functioning of the existing soil testing laboratories through capacity building, involvement of agricultural students and effective linkage with the Indian Council of Agricultural Research and other state agricultural universities. The standardized procedures for sampling across states help the governments and agencies to analyse and design micro-level intervention strategies. Experts vouch that the scheme would help develop and promote soil test-based nutrient management in the districts for enhancing nutrient use efficiency. The scheme also envisages providing financial assistance to farmers to make corrective steps to address nutrient deficiencies and popularize balance and integrated nutrient management practices for their cropping systems. According to SHC manual, the scheme aims to enhance capacities of district and state-level staff and of progressive farmers for promotion of nutrient management practices. Another objective is to reduce the consumption of chemical fertilizers by 20 per cent overall from the present usage through effective implementation of the scheme. Raising the awareness among the farmers is another one of the main objectives of the programme. The demand for organic sources of nutrients and bio-fertilizers and vermin-compost, etc., would pick up making agriculture more sustainable and environment-friendly.

Through the usage of SHC over a period of time, a farmer can determine changes in soil health that are affected by land management. On the basis of his practical understanding and knowledge of local resources, a farmer can easily understand the information on the card and take effective steps.

According to the guidelines issued by the centre, soil samples will be drawn in a grid of 2.5 ha in irrigated area and 10 ha in rain-fed area with the help of GPS tools and revenue maps.

Ideally, soil samples are collected twice a year after the

harvesting of rabi or kharif crops, respectively, or when there is no standing crop in the field. Soil collection requires training and is done from a depth of 15–20 cm by cutting the soil in a 'V' shape. Then, the soil is collected from the four corners and the centre of the field and mixed uniformly; a part of this mixture is picked up as a sample. Soil samples from under the shade are not taken for testing. The sample chosen is bagged, coded and transferred to a soil testing laboratory for analysis.

The objectives of the SHC scheme are:

1. To improve soil quality and profitability of farmers
2. Job generation for rural youth
3. Improve timelines in the analysis of soil samples
4. Introduction of single window approach from collection to issuing of SHC, minimizing the delays and maximizing the convenience to the farmers
5. Online delivery of SHC to the farmers using SHC portal
6. Provide soil testing facilities to farmers at their doorstep

## BENEFITS OF SOIL HEALTH CARD SCHEME

The impact study conducted by the National Institute of Agricultural Extension Management (MANAGE) noted that on an average 70 per cent of the farmers have benefitted from SHC, while the remaining suggested improvement. 'In most regions, except the Northeast, farmers feel that the benefits from the SHC scheme are huge in terms of reduction in fertilizer use and cost of cultivation and increased yields,' the study noted.

The study by National Productivity Council (NPC) commissioned by the Ministry of Agriculture stated, 'The overall impact of the scheme has been positive, leading to maximization and sustainable growth at farm level by cost minimization and efficient utilization of resources.'

The MANAGE assessed the impact of SHC for three important crops paddy, cotton and soybean by comparing fertilizer use and yield before soil testing and after following the recommendations of SHC. The study has assessed change in the area under the crops, in the use of major fertilizers (Urea, Di-Ammonium Phosphate [DAP]/Single Superphosphate [SSP] and Muriate of Potash [MoP]) and in the cost of cultivation and yields. According to the study, after following the recommendations, most of the farmers diversified to less input-intensive crops. It found that overall, paddy farmers reduced the use of urea by about 13 per cent, DAP/SSP by about 12 per cent and potassium by about 4 per cent. 'This is a healthy sign of moving towards a balanced use of fertilizers. All the three crops showed a decline in costs per acre by about 8 to 10 per cent. There was substantial increase in use of manures, especially in paddy, which resulted in a decreased cost of cultivation per unit area. On the other hand, soybean farmers indicated an increase in fertilizer use, although marginally. Crop yields have increased slightly after having SHC in all three crops. Among different farm size classes, small and marginal as well as large farmers experienced decline in costs in all the selected crops, while medium farmers reported decline in the case of paddy and soybean crops.'

**The National Picture**

Under the SHC scheme, the cropped area was divided into grids of 10 ha for rain-fed land and 2.5 ha for irrigated land. Only one soil sample was taken from each grid and test results were distributed to all the farmers whose area was falling under that specific grid. Based on the grid system, total 14.1 crore ha of the net cropped area would require a total of 3.46 crore grid samples (with 52 per cent of the area under rain-fed (7.3 crore ha) with 73 lakh grid samples and with 48 per cent area under irrigated (6.8 crore ha) with 2.72 crore grid samples). The target is to cover 1.73 crore grid samples per year. This comes to on average of 25,000 grid samples per district/year and 29 grid samples per village/year. With this, all 10.39 crore farmers will be covered in two years. Every year, 5.2 crore farmers need to be covered.

Under cycle 1,2.54 crore samples were collected, 2.36 crore samples tested, 9.62 crore SHCs printed, but only 9.33 crore SHCs were distributed. It indicates that 100 per cent target was achieved in sample collection, 93 per cent of the target was achieved in soil testing, but only 80 per cent of the target was achieved in SHC printing. On 24 September 2017, 97 per cent of the SHCs printed were distributed among the farmers. However, the progress is highly skewed. Some states such as Karnataka, Tamil Nadu, Chhattisgarh, Uttar Pradesh, Maharashtra, Telangana and Andhra Pradesh were better performers compared to other states.

*Source: Impact Study of SHC scheme, National Institute of Agricultural Extension Management (MANAGE), Hyderabad*

## SOIL TESTING INFRASTRUCTURE

According to the government data, there are about 1,454 labs in India, of which only 700 are equipped with micronutrient testing facilities. To meet the shortage of facilities, agricultural departments procured about 7,000 mobile kits. However, they are found to be ineffective. Impact study which was conducted by MANAGE found that this infrastructure is grossly inadequate by any standard, given the quantum of testing to be conducted. Similarly, NPC, which was commissioned by the Ministry of Agriculture to study the impact of SHC, noted that there was not enough manpower, both technical and non-technical staff, to carry out the collection and testing of soils.

Old soil testing labs should be revamped with power backup to meet the shortage of soil testing facilities plaguing the country. The NPC also suggested providing taluk-level labs with the atomic absorption spectrophotometer for testing micronutrients.

Under the scheme, state governments can outsource soil testing to experienced and technically competent private soil testing labs depending on the urgency and quantum of soil analysis work. The private labs will get payment on per sample basis with the condition that they employ qualified and trained chemists. This public–private partnership (PPP) model will be successful in those areas where there is no government presence in soil testing.

It has also been found that in some places the farmers are unable to make the best use of the SHC recommendations as they are not briefed about the soil content by the officials who hand over the cards to them. Experts suggest that there is a need for following a standard protocol to inform the farmers about the recommendations of the SHC, when it is handed over to the farmers.

The MANAGE study also suggested that the government should be more realistic while fixing the prices for soil testing for private labs as some labs charge up to ₹1,000 per sample while others charge ₹900 per sample. It also recommended strengthening and upgrading at least one soil testing lab per district as the state-of-the-art lab. 'So, nearly 700 state-of-the-art labs are needed to act as referral labs and give broad advice to the farmers. The cost per unit will be about ₹0.4–5 crore, with a total of ₹2,800 crore. However, if this resulted in ₹1,000/ha savings in fertilizer use, even if we don't consider the yield increase, it would lead to saving of ₹14,500 crore in a year to the economy.'

The MANAGE impact study recommended standardizing with mini-kits (mini-labs) as they are not accurate enough as full-fledged labs. 'However, mini-kits are useful for remote villages and tribal communities and should also be used for measuring highly volatile elements like nitrogen, which need more frequent measurement,' it said. The NPC recommended doing away with mobile soil testing labs under the scheme because its size has not been standardized yet.

For optimum results, the NPC recommends that soil testing should be conducted for all individual farm fields in a phased manner and crop-specific recommendations about the use of fertilizers and micronutrients should be provided.

**Soil Health Card Portal**

To push the implementation of the SHC scheme, the central government and Department of Agriculture and Farmers Welfare jointly launched the SHC website. A farmer who registers at the portal (www.soilhealth.dac.gov.in), along with the details of the soil samples and test lab reports, can track the test results by soil testing labs, fertilizer and nutrients recommendations, SHC generation and Management Information System (MIS) module for monitoring progress. According to agriculture ministry officials, the main objective behind the portal is to create a single national database on soil health, which can be used, in the future, for research and giving shape to strategies. Right now, the portal is in English, but soon, the content will be available in regional languages too.

**Soil Health Card Mobile App**

The central government launched a mobile app to help field-level workers as it will automatically capture the Geographic Information System (GIS) coordinates while registering the sample details at the time of sample collection in the field and indicate the location from where the sample has been collected. It works like other Geo-tagging apps developed for the Rashtriya Krishi Vikas Yojana (RKVY). It contains farmers' details, including name, Aadhaar card number, mobile number, gender, address, etc.

**Targets and Achievements**

| *Cycle No.* | *Item* | *Target* | *Achievement* |
|---|---|---|---|
| I (2015-16 to 2016-17) | Sample Collection | 2,53,49,546 | 2,53,49,546 |
| | Sample testing | 2,53,49,546 | 2,53,49,546 |
| | Printing of SHCs | 10,73,89,421 | 10,73,89,421 |
| | Dispatch of SHCs | 10,73,89,421 | 10,73,89,421 |
| II (2017-18 to 2018-19) | Sample Collection | 2,73,99,247 | 2,65,35,491 |
| | Sample testing | 2,73,99,247 | 2,38,22,886 |
| | Printing of SHCs | 12,04,52,133 | 8,26,19,866 |
| | Dispatch of SHCs | 12,04,52,133 | 7,79,03,429 |
| Source:-https://soilhealth.dac.gov.in | | | |

## PARAMPARAGAT KRISHI VIKAS YOJANA (PKVY)

The Goa government has cleared a proposal to set up 500 organic farming clusters and has plans to enter into an agreement with an Israeli company to create a centre of excellence for organic farming. Himachal Pradesh is working towards making entire farming in the state organic. Sikkim is India's first fully organic state. Uttarakhand, Himachal Pradesh, Maharashtra and Madhya Pradesh are focussing on organic farming. The Andhra Pradesh government has launched an ambitious project by which the state will become India's first 100 per cent natural farming state. The Karnataka government rolled out its revamped Organic Farming Policy in 2017 'to bring organic farming into the mainstream and transform agriculture in Karnataka into a sustainable remunerative occupation enabling production of nutritious food by promoting eco-friendly organic farming and marketing systems'. The comprehensive policy will also focus on soil health, conservation and management of water, agri-ecosystem and augmenting market infrastructure, linkages branding, labelling and packaging of organic produce. Acknowledging the growth prospects in this area, private and public sector companies such as Mother Dairy have forayed into organic business. In an attempt to make organic food products affordable, the government through National Agricultural Cooperative Marketing Federation of India (NAFED) is planning to set up online organic market.

In the last few years, organic farming has evolved as a movement in India. Experts say that there is a huge potential for Indian organic business. According to TechSci Research, by 2020, the Indian organic business will be valued at $1.5 billion, while the domestic organic market is expected to grow at a Compound Annual Growth Rate (CAGR) of over 25 per cent during 2015–20. Increased awareness about the adverse impact of chemical fertilizers on environment and human health forced farmers to make a departure from conventional towards organic farming practices. The scope for better profit margins made many farmers plunge headlong into organic farming.

The PKVY, launched in April 2015, is an effort to promote organic farming and thereby improve soil health. It is an extended component of Soil Health Management under the centrally sponsored scheme of the NMSA.

Several schemes such as NMSA, National Project on Organic Farming, National Project on Management of Soil Health and Fertility, etc., were introduced by previous governments to promote organic farming in the country. Most of the schemes failed to deliver the desired results. Prime Minister Narendra Modi-led government then introduced a comprehensive centrally-sponsored PKVY in 2015 to promote organic farming through adoption of organic village by cluster approach and Participatory Guarantee System (PGS) of certification. Under this scheme, groups of 50 or more farmers forming a cluster having a minimum of 50 acres are encouraged to take up organic farming.

Unlike the third party certification, the PGS format of organic certification is transparent, easy and mandates the involvement of producers and consumers in the process of certification. There will be no liability on the farmers for expenditure on certification. Under the scheme, the government envisages to form 10,000 clusters of 20 ha each and bring nearly 2 lakh ha of agricultural area under organic farming by 2017–18. The pattern of funding is in the ratio of 60:40 by the central and state governments, respectively. In case of north-eastern and Himalayan states, the funding pattern is 90:10 ratio, while for union territories, the assistance is 100 per cent.

Currently, organic farming is undertaken in more than 2.3 lakh ha across the country under the PKVY scheme. Under the scheme, financial assistance is given for direct marketing to the groups and clusters for procuring common packing material, printing of packing material, brochures, leaflets, preparation of labels, holograms, transportation expenses to local markets, hiring spaces on rent for specific organic markets and branding of organic products at the rate of ₹15 lakh per cluster of 1,000 ha each. According to the scheme, clusters can develop their own post-harvest, value-addition and processing facilities, preferably under their institutions such as Farmer Producer Organizations (FPOs)/Farmer Producer Companies (FPCs) for creation, collection and aggregation of post-harvest process centre (one between every 5–10 groups) at the rate of ₹20 lakh per cluster of 1,000 ha each. A cluster with 1,000 ha is eligible for an assistance of ₹53 lakh towards market linkage/brand building with FPO/small medium enterprises (SMEs), including the cost of organic fare to be provided on submission of appropriate proposal to the Executive Committee (EC) on a case-to-case basis. A farmer within a cluster can avail the benefit to a maximum of 2 ha and the limit of assistance is ₹50,000 per hectare. Out of this, ₹31,000 is given as incentives to the farmer for organic conversion, organic inputs, production infrastructure, etc., which will be provided through direct benefits transfer during the conversion period of three years. Under this scheme, an area of around 4 lakh ha is proposed to be covered in three years.

An amount of ₹947 crore has been allotted for the scheme during 2015–2018 and ₹582.47 crore has been released till date for total 11,891 clusters.

## MISSION ORGANIC VALUE CHAIN DEVELOPMENT FOR NORTH-EASTERN REGION

To promote organic farming in the north-eastern region, the Ministry of Agriculture and Farmers Welfare has launched a scheme 'Mission Organic Value Chain Development for North Eastern Region' for implementation in the states of Arunachal Pradesh, Assam, Manipur, Meghalaya, Mizoram, Nagaland, Sikkim and Tripura during 2015–16 to 2017–18. The scheme envisages development of certified organic production in a value chain mode to link farmers with market and to support the development of entire value chain starting from inputs, seeds, certification and creation of facilities for collection, aggregation, processing, marketing and brand-building initiative. Approximately ₹400 crore has been earmarked for three years. Under the scheme, assistance is provided for cluster development, on/off farm input production, supply of seeds/planting materials, setting up of functional infrastructure, establishment of integrated processing unit, refrigerated transportation, pre-cooling/cold stores chamber, branding, labelling and packaging, hiring of space, hand holding, organic certification through third party and mobilization of farmers/processors. An area of 50,000 ha has been targeted to be covered under organic farming in the north-eastern region during the period of three years i.e., from year 2015–16 to 2017–18.

*(With inputs from Pankaj Joshi)*

***G. Sreedathan** is a Delhi-based senior journalist with more than twenty years of experience in print, electronic and digital media. He has worked with* Organiser, The Pioneer, Hindustan Times *and* Business Standard, *and written columns and articles for many Indian and foreign publications. At present, he is the chief editor of* Indus Scrolls, *a news and current affairs website. He is also associated with a policy think tank—India Foundation for Rural Development Studies—as well as several civil society organisations. He has taught as guest faculty in Indian Institute of Mass Communication.*

# NUTRITION PLAN: NEEM-COATED UREA AND FERTILIZERS

*G. Sreedathan*

**10 June 2008:** The Haveri district of Karnataka witnessed large-scale violence following a farmers' protest. Agitated farmers started pelting stones when the fertilizer stocks being distributed at the Haveri Agriculture Produce Market Committee (APMC) yard got over. Firing by the police led to the death of a farmer and injuries to several others. It took several days to control the situation as violence spread to neighbouring districts.

**21 June 2008:** The farmers of Chakur village in Marathwada's Latur district started making a beeline in front of a local fertilizer distribution facility from early morning. As the day progressed, so did the length of the queue. Farmers became restless and ruckus broke out when a rumour started doing the rounds that there was a shortage of fertilizers. The police was summoned to control the crowd and one farmer was injured in the lathi charge that followed.

**25 July 2009:** More than 3,000 farmers had lined up to purchase fertilizers and manures for their kharif crops in Kudrewadi village of Solapur district of Maharashtra. The queue was more than 3-km long. Trouble started when it transpired that the facility had run out of fertilizers and the farmers would have to go home empty handed. Police had to resort to lathi charge to control the crowd injuring three farmers.

**4 September 2012:** U. Narsimhulu, a resident of Tandur village in Ranga Reddy district in Telangana, had gone to purchase fertilizers at an authorized outlet in Tandur. Farmers from nearby villages had also gathered outside the outlet from early morning. The rumour that the truckload of fertilizer that had been brought for them had been sold within two hours triggered suspicions that the fertilizer stocks had been diverted on the way. News about fresh loads arriving at another outlet in the vicinity prompted the farmers to rush there, leading to a stampede-like situation. The police had no way but to resort to lathi charge to control the crowd. Narsimhulu was badly injured on his head in the police lathi charge and still gets excruciating headaches as a result.

Such incidents were common in place till 2015. In several places, urea and other chemical fertilizers were sold under heavy police security. Reports of shortage of chemical fertilizers led to violence. Hoarding and smuggling of fertilizers had become the order of the day.

Major reasons for shortage of urea were found to be diversion to chemical industries and smuggling to neighbouring countries. More harmfully, food adulterators had been using urea as a whitening agent in the production of synthetic milk. To address the recurring shortage of urea across the country, the government of India made it mandatory for all the indigenous producers of urea to produce 100 per cent of their total production of subsidized urea as Neem-Coated Urea (NCU) in 2015. The decision had a telling effect on the farm sector.

Popatrao Mhaske, a marginal farmer hailing from Kotamgaon village near Nashik, says that before 2015, his major worry was the availability of chemical fertilizers for his crops. Many times, he had to depend on black marketers for the supply. However, after the NCU was introduced, his worries have vanished. For the last three-four years, urea is available at a reasonable price, he says.

*Popatrao Mhaske, Nashik*

## CHEMICAL FERTILIZERS

Indian soils are deficient in nutrients and chemical fertilizers form an immediate source of nutrients. Chemical fertilizers act as a key input for agriculture. To achieve self-sufficiency in food production, chemical fertilizers play a vital role and, therefore, to ensure adequate supply of fertilizers at affordable prices to the farmers, the government's focus has been on maximizing production and regulating prices. Although the government, after initiating economic reforms, decontrolled the prices and distribution of fertilizers, it kept urea untouched. This resulted in an increased consumption of Nitrogen (N) fertilizers and reduction in the use of Phosphate (P) and Potassium (K) fertilizers. The government introduced the new pricing scheme in 2003, which triggered further distortions in the NPK consumption pattern. To rectify this and to promote a balanced use of fertilizers, a Nutrient-Based Subsidy (NBS) scheme was announced in 2010. Under this scheme, subsidy was fixed on the basis of weights of different nutrients in fertilizers annually. However, urea was not covered under the scheme. As a result, there was a steady increase in the consumption of urea since 2003–04. Domestic production of urea was not able to match the burgeoning demand, forcing the government to import urea.

India's total annual consumption of urea is about 30 million tonne of which 22 million tonne is produced indigenously while 8 million tonne is imported. The price difference of urea in the international market and subsidized urea sold to farmers made procuring subsidized urea an attractive proposition for chemical industries in India and neighbouring countries. The diversion was estimated at 30 per cent—that means about 9 million tonne were diverted to chemical industries.

## IMPORTANCE OF UREA

For the healthy growth of a crop, nutrients such as nitrogen, phosphorous pentoxide and potash are very important. Although the ideal soil nutrient ratio is 4:2:1, it is highly distorted in India, thanks to various factors, including skewed nature of subsidy. According to Economic Survey of India (2013–14), the ratio deteriorated to 8:2.7:1, and in states such as Punjab and Haryana, it was as bad as 38:6:1 and 53:11:1, respectively.

Pure urea contains 47 per cent nitrogen. It is the key component of chlorophyll, the compound essential for photosynthesis. It is also a major component of amino acids, the building blocks of proteins, without which plants can't survive. Although nitrogen is found in abundance on earth, nitrogen deficiency is one of the most common nutritional problems affecting plants. This is because plants can't directly access nitrogen from the atmosphere and earth's surface.

## EXCESSIVE USE OF UREA

Excessive and wasteful use of urea costs farmers and the government ₹8,540 crore. According to Dr B.S. Dwivedi of Indian Agricultural Research Institute, New Delhi, urea is indiscriminately used by farmers in India irrespective of scientific prescriptions. It has adverse impact on soil, crop quality and ecosystem. As witnessed in Punjab and some other states, excessive usage of urea has led to deterioration of soil fertility. Farmers are forced to use more fertilizers to produce optimum yields. Nitrogen from urea applied is lost through volatilization, denitrification and leaching. Excessive use of urea results in climate change and groundwater pollution. It also leads to crop succulence, making the plants prone to disease and vulnerable to pest attack.

A report by *Down to Earth* magazine based on a 10-year study called The Indian Nitrogen Assessment by the Indian Nitrogen Group states, 'In the past five decades, every Indian farmer has, on an average, used up over 6,000 kg of urea. Only 33 per cent of this urea is consumed by rice and wheat crops. The remaining 67 per cent remains in the soil, water and environment, harming all irreparably.'

The report further pointed out, 'Nitrate ($NO_3$) concentration in dug-well and shallow bore well water in Punjab, Haryana and western Uttar Pradesh has been found to be above the limits prescribed by the World Health Organization (WHO). Haryana fares the worst with 99.5 mg per litre of $NO_3$ against the WHO norm of 50 mg per litre.'

## WHY NEEM OIL IS COATED ON UREA

Urea is coated with a layer of neem oil to enhance the soil fertility and curb pilferage of subsidized urea to chemical industry and other illegal uses such as making of harmful synthetic milk. Under the Investment Policy for Urea, the government has not only made it mandatory for all the indigenous producers of urea to produce 100 per cent of their total production of subsidized urea as NCU, but they had also directed that the imported urea be also coated with neem oil from May 2015. Through this, the government wanted to encourage efficient use of fertilizers and reduce subsidies. Compared to plain urea, neem coating results in gradual release of urea into the soil, helping the plants to gain more nutrients, which results in higher yields.

Answering a question in the Rajya Sabha on the efficacy of NCU on crops, the Minister of State for Ministry of Road Transport and Highways, Shipping and Chemicals and Fertilizers Mansukh L. Mandaviya, said that a study conducted by the Department of Agriculture, Cooperation and Farmers Welfare (DAC&FW) has found that the use of NCU results in the improvement in soil health; reduction in costs with respect to plant protecting chemicals; reduction in pest and disease attack; an increase in the yields of paddy, sugarcane, maize, soybean and tur/red gram to an extent of 5.79 per cent, 17.5 per cent, 7.14 per cent, 7.4 per cent and 16.88 per cent, respectively; and negligible diversion of highly subsidized urea towards non-agricultural purposes.

According to the minister, the availability of urea ever since the introduction of the policy is more than the requirement and sales. As diversion became minimal, some state governments have even reduced their requirement from what was initially projected. There is no report of shortages received from any of the state governments. It is, therefore, perceived that neem coating of urea has helped in curbing the diversion, the minister told the Rajya Sabha.

## IMPACT OF NCU ON PADDY AND OTHER CROPS

The Indian Agricultural Research Institute, New Delhi, conducted a research on NCU, which showed that rice grain yield has gone up by 6.3 per cent to 11.9 per cent over normal urea. Much before this, researchers have studied the benefits of neem-coated urea briquettes in paddy cultivation, especially on the Indrayani variety of rice developed by Agricultural Research Station at Igatpuri in Maharashtra. According to Vaibhav Pawar, agriculture officer, the state agriculture department adopted certain villages in the Pune region for implementing the new technique. It was found that paddy output increased from 2–3 quintals per acre to 10–15 quintals per acre after using neem-coated urea briquettes. About 15 farmers who adopted this technique reported an increase in income. The popularity of the technique led to production of neem-coated urea briquettes locally by women self-help groups resulting in employment generation. For the last 15 years, this technique has been yielding higher income to farmers engaged in paddy cultivation.

A study conducted by the Institute for Social Economic Change (ISEC), Bengaluru, found that application of NCU propelled a higher paddy output and net income in the 2015 kharif season as compared to 2014, when plain urea was used. The paddy output increased from 28 quintals an acre in 2014 to 36 quintals in 2015 kharif, while the paddy by-product increased from 62 quintals to 67 quintals. The study said that the net return for one acre increased from ₹13,492 to ₹21,474 on an average. The findings of the study reported in *The Hindu* said that about 85 per cent of paddy farmers enjoyed an increase of 12 per cent in the yield when they used neem-coated urea.

Apart from the increase in yield, NCU is found to be cost-effective as it reduces the consumption of urea by 10–15 per cent. It is also found to be environment-friendly and has helped reduce the environmental hazards. The use of NCU is also found to be effective in improving the uptake of N, P and K to a considerable extent. Compared to normal urea, the neem-coated variety is found to be agronomically superior.

Studies have shown that use-efficiency of normal prilled urea for paddy is 30 per cent while for wheat it is 50 per cent. This means 50–70 per cent urea is lost/leached down resulting in nitrate pollution in underground water. However, neem coating reduces this loss significantly by about 10–15 per cent, thereby minimizing pollution of groundwater.

National Fertilizers Limited (NFL) was the first company in India that was granted the permission to produce and market NCU in 2004. Before undertaking the production on an industrial scale, it carried out several field studies. Its website claims that at one of the locations in Uttar Pradesh, farmers have observed that the menace of neel gai has reduced significantly in the paddy crop; at Panipat, there has been no incidence of leaf folders and stem borers in the paddy crop; while at Sangrur and Gurdaspur in Punjab, farmers have observed that the incidence of white ants has reduced with the use of NCU in the wheat crop.

The ISEC study also endorses the claim of NFL. According to the ISEC study, the costs incurred on pest and disease control and on weed management have declined by 18 per cent and 20 per cent, respectively, and this was revealed by 60 per cent of paddy growers and 21 per cent of tur farmers. About 59 per cent of the paddy farmers noticed an improvement in the soil health, quality of grain and market acceptability of grains because of the application of neem-coated urea. (*The Hindu* report)

Balasaheb Mhaske, a young farmer from Kotamgaon, says that earlier farmers had to ensure a supply of water in the fields soon after the application of urea to prevent wastage of urea due to evaporation. However, neem-coated urea has solved their problem as the coating reduces evaporation rate of urea in soil, and therefore, water need not be supplied immediately.

*Balasaheb Mhaske of Kotamgaon, Nashik*

*Shivram Maske of Kotamgaon, Nashik*

Vilas Maule, a progressive farmer from Mohadi village around 25 km east of Nashik, says that he has been using neem-coated urea for cultivating wheat, coriander and grapes. Neem coating on the urea prevents accumulation of soil bacteria near plants reducing the dependence of farmers on pesticides, resulting in cost saving.

Neem-coated urea has been found to be useful in water deficient areas of Marathwada also. A farmer from Devgaon Rangari, around 50 km from Aurangabad, says that neem-coated urea has resulted in cost-saving for farmers engaged in cotton cultivation, due to prevention of loss of urea as a result of evaporation. Even the cost of fertilizers has reduced to half, which results in considerable saving for low-income farmers of this drought-prone area. In monsoon deficient years, the farmers have turned to sericulture recently. Neem-coated urea has proven useful to farmers engaged in sericulture as well.

*Vilas Maule of Mohadi village, Nashik*

*Deepak Joshi of Devgaon, Aurangabad*

## MAJOR FINDINGS OF ISEC STUDY

As regards the benefits of NCU, relative to Normal Urea (NU), a majority of the farmers have observed an improvement in the yield levels with respect to all crops and their by-products; however, differing responses are observed in respect to the cost of pest and disease control and weed management; and there is no change in the cost of NCU as well as of other fertilizers in the context of the application of NCU in place of NU.

- Nearly 52 per cent of tur farmers and 61 per cent of paddy farmers have found an improvement in the soil health characteristics such as soil texture, soil-moisture retention, water infiltration and soil softness, and a reduction in soil compaction post-NCU application.
- An improvement in soil quality post the application of NCU has been clearly reflected in the incremental increase in yield levels of main product and by-product with regard to reference crops as noticed by 98 per cent of sugarcane farmers, 63 per cent of jute farmers, 40 per cent of paddy and tur farmers each, 18 per cent of maize farmers and 4 per cent of soybean farmers. The increase in yield is to an extent of 38 per cent (1.46 quintal/acre) in soybean, 34 per cent (0.90 quintal/acre) in tur, 8 per cent each (1.62 and 1.87 quintal/acre) in paddy and maize, 5 per cent (26 quintal/acre) in sugarcane and 3 per cent (0.26 quintal/acre) in jute crops. However, in the case of by-products, an increase in yield has been observed with respect to paddy (3 per cent=0.82 quintal/acre), tur (23 per cent=0.45 quintal/acre) and soybean (11 per cent=0.80 quintal/acre), while there is no change observed with respect to jute, maize and sugarcane reference crops.

- A highest incremental yield is noticed in paddy in the case of Madhya Pradesh (17 per cent=2 quintal/acre), while the lowest in the case of Punjab (1 per cent=0.28 quintal/acre). With respect to tur, both the highest main product (56 per cent=1.8 quintals/acre) and by-product (71 per cent=1 quintal/acre) yields are observed for Maharashtra.
- An increase in the cost to an extent of 4 per cent in paddy and 1 per cent in maize has been reported. Conversely, while a reduction in cost is noticed in the case of soybean (6 per cent) and jute (2 per cent). Further, a reduction in the cost of pest and disease control and weed management has been noticed with respect to paddy, jute, maize and soybean post the adoption of NCU, whereas, these costs show an increase in tur and sugarcane.
- A partial budget based result indicates the highest incremental income in the case of tur (₹14,940/acre), followed by sugarcane (₹5,313/acre), soybean (₹2,817/acre), paddy (₹2,430/acre), jute (₹615/acre) and maize (₹363/acre) crops. Accordingly, the benefit-cost ratio works out to 10.21, 10.11, 4.28, 3.46 and 1.21 for the respective crops in the order of magnitude post the adoption of NCU.
- A significant impact to be noted is that the diversion of NU to other than crop production purposes is negligible among the farmers, and in fact, it has completely stopped post the introduction of NCU.

## NEEM COATING HELPS BRING DOWN SUBSIDY BILL ON UREA

Experts suggest that excessive and wasteful use of urea will adversely affect crops and will lead to loss of money for farmers and the government. According to an estimate, excessive use costs the farmers and the government ₹8,540 crore. As the government intends to cut down on fertilizer subsidy, it is trying to reduce the consumption of urea. Besides neem coating, the government has asked the manufacturers to come out with 45 kg bags in place of 50 kg. Most farmers use fertilizers by an estimate in terms of bags and not the actual volume. Providing urea in 45 kg bags will straight away bring down the consumption of urea by almost 10 per cent. This will roughly result in savings of ₹1,608 crore at the retail spend by the farmer (assuming the 45 kg bags are priced proportionately to current prices). Consequently, this additional purchasing power can be spent on other nutrients. Additionally, neem coating has acted as a check on urea from being diverted to non-agricultural uses across the border.

## ENSURING QUALITY NEEM OIL FOR UREA COATING

Department of Fertilizers (DoF) has instructed urea units to ensure the quality of neem oil and to procure it from genuine neem oil manufacturers only. DAC&FW, in an order, has prescribed specification of neem oil to be used for coating. DoF has directed all the urea manufacturers/importers to strictly adhere to the specifications provided by the DAC&FW for the neem oil which would be used for the purpose of producing neem-coated urea. DoF has requested DAC&FW to advise the Central Laboratories to lift samples of neem oil used for neem-coated urea from the premises of urea manufacturing units to test its quality as per the specification provided.

## FERTILIZER QUALITY CONTROL SYSTEM

In order to check the quality of the fertilizers sold in the country, there are 74 Fertilizer Quality Control Laboratories, including four Central Government Laboratories. The government enacted the Fertilizer Control Order (FCO) 1985 to regulate trade, price, quality and distribution of fertilizers in the country and to ensure adequate availability of fertilizers of standard quality to farmers. Apart from chemical fertilizers, bio-fertilizers and organic fertilizers have also been brought under the purview of FCO. As many state laboratories are facing financial problems since they are not able to maintain and upgrade the instruments and equipment needed to carryout testing, the centre has proposed a scheme to upgrade and strengthen the existing Fertilizer Quality Control Laboratories. Under this scheme, an assistance of ₹30 lakh will be provided to those state laboratories which are operating well.

Besides, there is a need to set up new Fertilizer Quality Control Laboratories, as, according to an estimate, the minimum requirement of fertilizer samples to be checked for ensuring quality is 6.5 lakh samples. The present annual analyzing capacity of 1.30 lakh samples is inadequate. Therefore, 20 new Fertilizer Quality Control Laboratories are proposed to be set up in states with central assistance of ₹75 lakh per laboratory.

***G. Sreedathan** is a Delhi-based senior journalist with more than twenty years of experience in print, electronic and digital media. He has worked with* Organiser, The Pioneer, Hindustan Times *and* Business Standard, *and written columns and articles for many Indian and foreign publications. At present, he is the chief editor of* Indus Scrolls, *a news and current affairs website. He is also associated with a policy think tank—India Foundation for Rural Development Studies—as well as several civil society organisations. He has taught as guest faculty in Indian Institute of Mass Communication.*

# MORE CROP PER DROP: MICRO-IRRIGATION FOR MITIGATING WATER STRESS

*Nivedita Khandekar*

From a community that prayed 'शंनोमित्र:शवरूण' (May Mitra, the sun, be propitious with us; may Varuna, the rain god, be propitious with us) since time immemorial to a people who proudly proclaimed its land as 'सुजलामसुफलाम' (with ample water, ample production), India has come a long way. From a successful farming community that wisely utilized natural resources, primarily water, since Vedic times to an oversized mass of people with scarce water resources, India's journey in efficient water management for farming has been tumultuous. At the turn of the millennium, the same land with bountiful monsoon has started its journey from being water-stressed to being water-scarce.

Even after 70 years of independence, much of our farming continues to be rain-fed. At a time, when erratic rainfall and rising temperatures due to changing climate, is making the situation further worrisome, it has become imperative to plan for efficient use of existing water resources. Among the technological interventions are drip irrigation system and sprinklers that are slowly yet steadily changing the face of water management in agriculture belts. Not within the reach of ordinary farmers yet, even with the government subsidy, these interventions—termed as micro-irrigation—are making a huge difference in the lives of the farmers who have adopted it. Well begun is half done, as the saying goes but, in this case, what has well begun has still a long way to go. Nevertheless, this will bring in a paradigm change if implemented well. This is an important component in the long-term plan to make agriculture sustainable by drought-proofing.

All his younger years, Deepchand Chokse, a farmer from Poama village, struggled to make ends meet with subsistence farming on his small land holding in Chhindwara district of Madhya Pradesh. He would grow maize and wheat. Fortunately for him, things started changing when he opted for installing drip irrigation system a few years ago.

Starting with just 2 acres, the earlier rain-fed crop, with almost no crop in the rabi season, turned into water-rich kharif and rabi cycles. Soon, he began growing potatoes, ginger, papaya and vegetables such as cauliflower. By 2017, his entire land of 6 acre was under drip irrigation system.

Since 2013, potatoes have given him the most rewarding monetary returns as they are much in demand from a multinational company (MNC) producing and selling chips. The MNC is very particular about the size and appearance of the yield and pays an additional ₹1 per kilo to those farmers who use drip irrigation to grow potatoes. Chokse is not alone, neither from his village nor from the district.

The Chhindwara district alone has a contract with the MNC for exclusively growing potatoes on almost 350 ha of land using the drip irrigation system. Most of the blocks in the district have red morum (laterite soil), which, agriculture officials say, makes any type of agriculture difficult. He practised flood irrigation as he had a big well. But, the problem can be overcome using drip irrigation, and nowadays mulching as well. With these two interventions, farmers have experienced that the yield has increased to almost 2.5–3 times.

*Deepchand Chokse (right), a farmer from Poama village in Chhindwara district of Madhya Pradesh with his son Mithilesh (Photograph by: Nivedita Khandekar)*

While showing me around, Chokse's son Mithilesh also told me what goes around in their farmland. For a lawyer who is now pursuing Master's in Arts, Mithilesh is in tune with agricultural matters. 'Drip irrigation helps us regulate flow of water to the potatoes, which helps improve the quality of the potatoes. Flood irrigation, on the other hand, will inevitably have an adverse impact on the potatoes,' Mithilesh told me. 'Thanks to the drip, there is ample aeration since the soil is loose, and oxygen directly reaches the roots,' he added.

Before adopting drip irrigation, a typical year for Chokses used to be a tightrope walk. The family spent approximately ₹70,000, mainly on fertilizers and about 400 kg of ginger seeds. For roughly 28 quintals of ginger, they would get ₹1 lakh, leaving them with a net profit of ₹30,000. Using the drip and mulching systems, just 200 kg of seeds were needed. Also, the income increased to ₹1.5 lakh leaving the family with a net profit of ₹1 lakh.

'But, the most important difference has been the amount of water required. Now, we need very less water than others. As a matter of fact, water-use efficiency has gone up to 95 per cent,' the senior Chokse said.

'Water-use efficiency' is an important determinant for the quality of produce. It is also affected by external factors such as the increasingly erratic rainfall which is leading to water stress in many parts across India.

It was the same story in every village I visited in the district. Apart from less water, another advantage that the farmers counted was the reduction in weeds. Drip irrigation has meant that the soil has only that much moisture as is needed. So, there are no excess weeds to share soil nutrients.

In Parasia block of the Chhindwara district is the Kondali Kala village where farmers have tube wells. Ashok Suryawanshi has 3.45 acre of land where he grows wheat, maize and potatoes. Excitedly, he told me, 'Apart from making an extra ₹25,000 per acre, I also save on labour costs plus there are no weeds. All this has made my job a lot easier. Practising this kind of agriculture has meant an increase of 60–70 per cent in production.'

*Ashok Suryawanshi (middle) and other farmers from Kondali Kala village of Parasia block of Chhindwara district of Madhya Pradesh*
*(Photograph by: Nivedita Khandekar)*

'Most importantly, I use less water overall,' he insisted. This is exactly what the Pradhan Mantri Krishi Sinchayee Yojana (PMKSY) with its slogan 'More Crop Per Drop' envisages.

Water remains the backbone of agriculture. Assured irrigation can cause wonders even in low-rainfall area. How much water is given, at what time it is given and on how many days it is given to the farm—all of these factors have an impact on the overall yield. Good seeds and fertilizers will fail to achieve anything if there is no water.

India holds only about 4 per cent of fresh water resources; at the same time, it is home to approximately 17 per cent global population. Further, this water availability and access is uneven in different areas or different states. India's water availability is 1,544 $m^3$ per person. As per United Nations (UN) Water,* when annual water supplies drop below 1,700 $m^3$ per person it is considered water stress. When annual water supplies drop below 1,000 $m^3$ per person, the population faces water scarcity and below 500 $m^3$ per person is termed as absolute scarcity. As per these international norms, India is already water-stressed and moving towards being a water-scarce country.

A December 2015 paper by NITI Aayog clearly points out, 'At present, irrigation consumes about 84 per cent of total available water. Industrial and domestic sectors consume about 12 per cent and 4 per cent of total available water, respectively. With irrigation predicted to remain the dominant user of water, "More Crop Per Drop" becomes all the more imperative. The efficiency of water use must improve to expand the area under irrigation while also conserving water.'

The same report points to government data that shows 'the share of canal in net irrigated areas has declined from 39.8 per cent in 1950–51 to 23.6 per cent in 2012–13. Alongside, the share of groundwater sources has increased from 28.7 per cent to a whopping 62.4 per cent during the same period' and warns, 'while proving to be a valuable source of irrigation expansion, injudicious utilization of groundwater through the explosion of tube wells has raised several sustainability issues'.

But, it is not just the groundwater that is posing a problem, the erratic, uncertain rainfall is also causing farmers to look beyond the obvious. With every passing year, as forests are felled and as rivers run dry, the farmers face the maximum brunt. Sensing

*http://www.unwater.org/water-facts/scarcity/#

troubled times ahead, some farmers feel it necessary to adopt newer technology to beat the water shortage problem.

N.S. Tomar, deputy director (horticulture) for Chhindwara district, threw some light on the situation on the ground. 'There is no denying that rains are uncertain every year, yet we do not have planned agriculture. We have each type of agro-climatic zone for which planning is of utmost necessity. But right now, what happens? In the flood irrigation method, our farmers are using as much as 90 per cent extra water.' In such cases, drip irrigation is most advisable for water conservation.

Shanti Mohane and her husband Buddhaman Mohane from Bisapur Kalan village of Mohkhed block of Chhindwara district have done exactly that. Between themselves, the husband and wife have 14 ha land. Both progressive farmers, they have been growing capsicum, green peas, brinjal, tomatoes and green chillies apart from wheat. A veritable combination of drip and mulching combined with the couple's zest while tending to their crops and vegetables has ensured that theirs is the best farm around.

When we reached their farm, we were greeted by heaps of brinjals, being loaded onto a truck to be sold in bigger cities. A beaming smile welcomed us. Negotiating the narrow bunds dividing two large plots, we reached the inner side of the sprawling vegetable farm. Long rows of drip lines and mulching plastic could be seen everywhere.

'After experimenting for 10 years, I have finally perfected the art of growing capsicum in this weather, ahead of season,' said Buddhaman, who was awarded the Sarvochha Krushak Puraskar (state level) for the year 2016–17. He is now a master trainer at the agriculture/horticulture department, conducting training sessions for farmers from across the state.

*Shanti Mohane and her husband Buddhaman Mohane from Bisapur Kalan village of Mohkhed block of Chhindwara district of Madhya Pradesh (Photograph by: Nivedita Khandekar)*

Speaking for his village, he said, 'We had seen these technological innovations of sprinkler, mulching and drip irrigation in other parts of the district since 2010. But, when we felt that water availability was increasingly less, we decided to go for it ourselves.'

Shifting to vegetables proved in good stead for the couple, who went on to build a pucca house for themselves, bought a two-wheeler and could give professional education to their son.

Buddhaman summed up the change in one line, 'Earlier my produce went in bamboo baskets and only to Chhindwara or Nagpur. Now, neatly packed in plastic crates, my veggies go all the way to Allahabad in Uttar Pradesh and to many other bigger cities.'

The Mohanes are the perfect showcase couple for the PMKSY.

Circa 2018, when rainfall is uncertain and irrigation still shares the maximum load for utilization of water, it becomes necessary to take a look at land under irrigation and water use. The research paper, 'A Socio Economic Study of Irrigation Projects in Maharashtra State with Special Reference to Marathwada Region'* by Prakash Vankar Salve of Dr Babasaheb Ambedkar Marathwada University, gives a neat compilation of the present status of agriculture and irrigation.

The author quotes the relevant data available from Ministry of Agriculture at national level for the period 2000–10 for the year-wise land use and irrigation statistics in India.

**Land Use and Irrigation Statistics—All India**

('000 ha)

| *Year* | *Geographical Area* | *Forest Area* | *Net Sown Area (NSA)* | *Total Cultivable Area (TCA)* | *Gross Sown Area (GSA)* | *Gross Irrigated Area (GIA)* | *Net Irrigated Area (NIA)* |
|---|---|---|---|---|---|---|---|
| 1 | 2 | 3 | 4 | 5 | 6 | 7 | 8 |
| 2000–01 | 328726 | 69843 | 141336 | 183455 | 185340 | 76187 | 55205 |
| 2001–02 | 328726 | 69720 | 140700 | 183551 | 188286 | 78420 | 56920 |
| 2002–03 | 328726 | 69821 | 132051 | 183449 | 174108 | 73094 | 53884 |
| 2003–04 | 328726 | 69968 | 140708 | 183132 | 189669 | 78038 | 57046 |
| 2004–05 | 328726 | 69960 | 140642 | 182946 | 191119 | 81076 | 59218 |
| 2005–06 | 328726 | 69994 | 141162 | 182685 | 192756 | 84280 | 60831 |
| 2006–07 | 328726 | 70002 | 139848 | 182508 | 192408 | 86756 | 62744 |
| 2007–08 | 328726 | 70020 | 141377 | 182691 | 195138 | 67980 | 63291 |
| 2008–09 | 328726 | 70034 | 141929 | 182514 | 195357 | 88867 | 63740 |
| 2009–10 | 328726 | 70042 | 140022 | 182466 | 192197 | 86423 | 83256 |

*Source: Ministry of Agriculture, Directorate of Economics & Statistics; Office of the Registrar General of India (2014)*

*http://hdl.handle.net/10603/81241

As the table indicates, only about 45 per cent of cropped area in the country was irrigated during the period 2006–07 to 2009–10. It is also very clear that almost 55 per cent of the sown area—gross or net—doesn't have any irrigation facility.

Another set of statistics shows source-wise net irrigated area in India. Needless to add, the table makes it amply clear that the major source of irrigation is groundwater. 'Wells (considering all types of wells viz. dug well, shallow tube well, deep tube well, etc.) provided about 62 per cent irrigation followed by canals with 26 per cent at an all-India level. Tanks and other sources have minor share in the net irrigated area in India. Also, there is an increase in the net irrigated area by wells (5,224 Thousand Hectares), other sources (2,971 Thousand Hectares.) and canals (685 Thousand Hectares.), but there is a drop in the net irrigated area by tanks during this decade,' the research pointed out.

**Source-wise Net Irrigated Area in India**

('000 ha)

| *Year* | *Canal* | *Tank* | *Wells* | *Other Sources* | *Total (All Sources)* |
|---|---|---|---|---|---|
| 1 | 2 | 3 | 4 | 5 | 6 |
| 2000–01 | 16012 | 2466 | 33818 | 2909 | 55205 |
| 2001–02 | 15200 | 2186 | 35183 | 4350 | 56920 |
| 2002–03 | 14071 | 1803 | 34348 | 3662 | 53884 |
| 2003–04 | 14455 | 1916 | 36383 | 4292 | 57046 |
| 2004–05 | 14763 | 1734 | 35189 | 4531 | 56218 |
| 2005–06 | 16716 | 2083 | 36070 | 5962 | 60831 |
| 2006–07 | 17026 | 2078 | 37641 | 5998 | 62744 |
| 2007–08 | 16812 | 1978 | 38400 | 6103 | 63291 |
| 2008–09 | 16945 | 1985 | 38795 | 6015 | 63740 |
| 2009–10 | 16697 | 1638 | 39042 | 5880 | 63256 |
| Total | 158697 (26.62) | 19867 (3.33) | 364869 (31.20) | 52702 (8.84) | 596135 (100) |

*Source: Ministry of Agriculture, Directorate of Economics & Statistics; Office of the Registrar General of India (2013)*

The net irrigated area during Agriculture Census 2010–11 was 64.57 Mha, out of which 48 per cent was accounted for by small and marginal holdings; 44 per cent by semi-medium and medium holdings and 8 per cent by large holdings.

Out of five sources of irrigation for which the data was collected in the Agriculture Census, viz., canals, tanks, wells, tubewells and other sources, tube wells emerged as the most popular source of irrigation in 2010–11 (29.16 Mha of irrigated land) followed by canals (16.91 Mha), wells (11.92 Mha) and tanks (2.25 Mha). Other sources accounted for 4.33 million hectares.

The two tables above and the Agriculture Census data are pointers to the fact that centralized capital-intensive dams and major or minor irrigation projects have not helped achieve as much potential as desired. And, given the water stress, there is hardly any scope for newer projects on any rivers big or small. Hence, it is here that the decentralized micro-irrigation, working under the PMKSY, can help tide over the complicated water situation.

Another aspect is that the source for irrigation notwithstanding, the most common method almost across the country is flood irrigation. This leads to massive loss of water and also has an adverse impact on the crop quality. Technological interventions under the PMKSY such as drip irrigation system or the sprinkler system not just minimize water loss but also drastically improve crop yield. Experts told me that both drip and sprinkler systems are very useful where water is in lesser amounts, but its popularity is proving well even in areas with better rainfall.

This brings me to the PMKSY itself. I dig into the government records to find further details. With the dream of providing water to even the remotest farmer, irrespective of his land holding size, the Cabinet Committee on Economic Affairs chaired by Prime Minister Narendra Modi accorded approval for the PMKSY* in its meeting held on 1 July 2015.

The dedicated website for the scheme states that the government of India is committed to accord high priority to water conservation and its management. 'To this effect, PMKSY has been formulated with the vision of extending the coverage of irrigation (Har Khet Ko Pani) and improving the water-use efficiency (More Crop Per Drop in a focussed manner with end-to-end solution on source creation, distribution, management, field application and extension activities.'

The PMKSY has been formulated by amalgamating ongoing schemes, viz., Accelerated Irrigation Benefit Programme (AIBP) of the Ministry of Water Resources, River Development and Ganga Rejuvenation (MoWRRDGR), Integrated Watershed Management Programme (IWMP) of Department of Land Resources (DoLR) and the On-Farm Water Management (OFWM) of Department of Agriculture and Cooperation (DAC).

The PMKSY has been approved for implementation across the country with an outlay of ₹50,000 crore in five years.

The Press Information Bureau** release about the same carries details about a lot of components as it was in response to a question in the Rajya Sabha in May 2016.

The PMKSY has been in operation since 1 July 2015 with the objective of enhancing irrigation coverage and improving the delivery system at farm level. The scheme envisages decentralized state-level planning and execution, allowing the states to draw their irrigation development plans based on the district/block plans with a horizon of five to seven years.

---

*https ://pmksy.gov.in/Default.aspx

**(http://pib.nic.in/newsite/PrintRelease.aspx?relid=145004)

The scheme has four components which are as follows:

1. AIBP: To focus on faster completion of ongoing major and medium irrigation projects, including national ones
2. HKKP: Creation of new water sources through minor irrigation (both surface and groundwater); repair, restoration and renovation of traditional water bodies; command area development; strengthening and creation of distribution network from sources to the farm, etc.
3. Per Drop More Crop (PDMC): Precision irrigation systems, efficient water conveyance and application, micro level storage structures, topping-up of input cost beyond Mahatma Gandhi National Rural Employment Guarantee Act's (MGNREGA) permissible limits, secondary storage, water-lifting devices, extension activities, coordination and management, etc.
4. Watershed Development (WD): Ridge area treatment, drainage line treatment, soil and moisture conservation, rainwater harvesting and other watershed interventions

It has also mentioned the initial state-wise details of funds allocated under various components of PMKSY during that fiscal.

**State-wise Allocation (Tentative) under Various Components of PMKSY for 2016–17**

(Rupees in crore)

| *Sr. No.* | *State* | *Department of Agriculture Cooperationand Farmers' Welfare* | *Department of Land Resources* | *Ministry of Water Resources, River Development and Ganga Rejuvenation* | |
|---|---|---|---|---|---|
| | | Per drop more crop | Watershed Development | Accelerated Irrigation Benefit Programme | Har Khet ko Pani |

| *Sr. No.* | *State* | *Department of Agriculture Cooperationand Farmers' Welfare* | *Department of Land Resources* | *Ministry of Water Resources, River Development and Ganga Rejuvenation* | |
|---|---|---|---|---|---|
| 1 | Andhra Pradesh | 263.00 | 83.09 | | |
| 2 | Bihar | 61.00 | 19.19 | | |
| 3 | Chhattisgarh | 48.00 | 34.96 | | |
| 4 | Goa | 1.50 | 0.00 | | |
| 5 | Gujarat | 260.00 | 115.04 | | |
| 6 | Haryana | 45.00 | 12.82 | | |
| 7 | Himachal Pradesh | 18.25 | 35.40 | | |
| 8 | Jharkhand | 51.00 | 29.48 | | |
| 9 | Jammu & Kashmir | 16.00 | 25.59 | | |
| 10 | Karnataka | 190.00 | 152.17 | | |
| 11 | Kerala | 30.00 | 11.37 | | |
| 12 | Madhya Pradesh | 202.00 | 89.27 | | |
| 13 | Maharashtra | 347.00 | 186.95 | | |
| 14 | Odisha | 47.00 | 63.38 | | |
| 15 | Punjab | 14.00 | 9.49 | | |
| 16 | Rajasthan | 215.00 | 199.35 | | |
| 17 | Tamil Nadu | 142.00 | 62.31 | | |
| 18 | Telangana | 139.00 | 55.02 | | |
| 19 | Uttarakhand | 23.00 | 11.23 | | |
| 20 | Uttar Pradesh | 69.00 | 97.31 | | |
| 21 | West Bengal | 38.50 | 28.33 | | |
| 22 | Arunachal Pradesh | 4.75 | 23.12 | | |
| 23 | Assam | 44.50 | 37.62 | | |
| 24 | Manipur | 9.75 | 18.81 | | |
| 25 | Meghalaya | 6.75 | 11.56 | | |
| 26 | Mizoram | 10.50 | 16.06 | | |
| 27 | Nagaland | 9.50 | 28.20 | | |
| 28 | Sikkim | 9.50 | 2.16 | | |
| 29 | Tripura | 10.50 | 12.47 | | |
| 30 | Andaman and Nicobar Islands | 1.00 | 0.00 | | |
| 31 | Puducherry | 1.00 | 0.00 | | |
| | Grand Total | 2340.00 | 1471.75 | 1000.00 | 500.00 |

*State-wise release of Central Assistance depends upon the proposals received from the states

The scheme is to be implemented by Ministries of Agriculture, Water Resources and Rural Development. The Ministry of Rural Development is to mainly undertake rainwater conservation, construction of farm ponds, water harvesting structures, small check dams and contour bunding, etc. The role of MoWRRDGR is to undertake various measures for creation of assured irrigation source, construction of diversion canals, field channels, water diversion/lift irrigation and development of water distribution systems.

The best part is that the Ministry of Agriculture will be promoting efficient water conveyance and precision water application devices like drips, sprinklers, pivots, rain-guns in the farm (Jal Sinchan). It will also construct micro-irrigation structures to supplement source creation activities and undertake extension activities for promotion of scientific moisture conservation and agronomic measures.

The state has to draw up their own irrigation development plan based on the District Irrigation Plan (DIP) and the State Irrigation Plan (SIP). It will be operative as a convergence platform for all water sector activities, including drinking water and sanitation, MGNREGA, application of science and technology, etc., through comprehensive plans.

Although this is a central scheme, all states have an important role to play in its implementation because, as mentioned above, DIPs and SIPs form a vital component of the scheme.

## WEST BENGAL

For instance, with its fair bit of share in this scheme, West Bengal got a one-time grant of ₹90 lakh from the centre for preparing DIPs in 2015–16. Based on those plans, it now has 42 projects in 16 districts.

However, the most interesting development is that in February 2018, the PMKSY was implemented for small tea growers in Bengal with the West Bengal State Watershed Development Agency as the nodal agency. Given that 30 per cent of the tea growers are small here, effective implementation of the scheme can fetch high income for them.

The 'PMKSY, if implemented properly, will not only help in achieving India's climate agenda of 2030 but will also provide various other social, economic and environmental co-benefits namely, Sustainable Development Goals (SDG1) (reducing poverty), SDG2 (increasing agricultural productivity), SDG 6 (judicious use of water), SDG8 (economic growth) and SDG12 (sustainable production),' said Shreya Some, senior research fellow and PhD scholar at Department of Economics, Jadavpur University.

However, Shreya Some had a word of caution too, 'Injudicious implementation can lead to various adversities such as more energy use and income disparity among farmers because farmers who have electricity access can use significantly more energy per hectare compared to owners of diesel pumps. So, there are possibilities of having negative effects on SDG7 (energy use) and SDG10 (income inequalities) as well.'

Climate change indeed is an immense challenge looming large over India. The chapter on 'Climate, Climate Change and Agriculture' of the Economic Survey 2018* ominously points out the worst possible scenarios for Indian agriculture. 'A key finding—and one with significant implications as climate change looms—is that the impact of temperature and rainfall is felt only in the extreme; that is, when temperature is much higher, rainfall is significantly

*(http://mofapp.nic.in:8080/economicsurvey/pdf/082–101_Chapter_06_ENGLISH_Vol_01_2017–18.pdf)

lower, and the number of 'dry days' is greater than normal. A second key finding is that these impacts are significantly more adverse in unirrigated areas (and hence rain-fed crops) compared to irrigated areas (and hence cereals). Applying these estimates to projected long-term weather patterns implies that climate change could reduce annual agricultural incomes in the range of 15 per cent to 18 per cent on average, and up to 20 per cent to 25 per cent for un-irrigated areas. Minimizing susceptibility to climate change requires drastically extending irrigation via efficient drip and sprinkler technologies (realizing 'More Crop Per Drop') and replacing untargeted subsidies in power and fertilizer by direct income support.'

## ASSAM

Both the scenarios mentioned above are very much evident in Assam as well. In recent years, many districts in Assam have seen an increasing trend of heavy rainfall and flood situation in monsoon months and an almost dry season during winters. Other problems include arsenic occurrence that has crippled water availability for both drinking and irrigation. For instance, Sonitpur district, sandwiched between Arunachal Pradesh foothills and the Brahmaputra north bank, receives an average rainfall of 1,355 to 2,350 mm spread over 122–134 days.

Government records* show how, out of the total geographical area of 2.72 lakh ha, only 41.03 per cent area is cultivable and 27.23 per cent is under forest. At present, out of the total cultivable area, 89.61 per cent is under cultivation and remaining portion is cultivable wasteland. The area under pasture is meagre and

*http://sonitpur.gov.in/departments/detail/agriculture-department-general-statistics

marginally productive due to the prevailing system of open grazing that has been continuing since long without any replenishment of soil nutrients.

Generally, the district experiences two to three waves of floods between May and September. At present, 2,117 ha, that is, 1.9 per cent of cultivable area is chronically flood-affected. Also, only 24 per cent of cultivable area is irrigated and the main sources of irrigation are shallow tube wells (STWs) and low lift pumps (LLPs), which contribute 11 per cent to the total irrigated area. Farmers in two development blocks of the district Borchala and Bihaguri have been deprived of their main source of irrigation facility that is, STW, due to non-clearance on arsenic content of groundwater by the concerned authority.

**Basic Statistics of Sonitpur district (Agriculture)**

| *Sl. No.* | *Detailed Statistics as on April 2018* | |
|---|---|---|
| 1. | Geographical Area | 2,71,729 ha |
| 2. | Cultivable area | 1,12,281 ha |
| 3. | Net cropped area | 1,08,281 ha |
| 4. | Gross cropped area | 1,79,476 ha |
| 5. | Area sown more than once | 71,194 ha |
| 6. | Mono cropped area | 37,086 ha |
| 7. | Forest area | 74,018 ha |
| 8. | Area under horticultural crop | 27,364 ha |
| 9. | Cultivable wasteland | 303 ha |
| 10. | Chronically flood-prone area | 2,117 ha |
| 11. | Char area | 10,373 ha |
| 12. | Irrigated area under STW/LLP | 19,940 ha |
| 13. | Cropping intensity | 165.75 per cent |

*(Source: http://sonitpur.gov.in/departments/detail/basic-statistics-of-sonitpur-district-agriculture)*

'We have heavy monsoons which inevitably lead to floods every year. But, thanks to climate change, rabi season is experiencing a dry spell increasingly. That time, we need to use drip irrigation or sprinkler irrigation,' said Dr Pramod Deka of Krishi Vikas Kendra, Sonitpur.

However, drip or sprinkler, whichever the farmers are using, is economically viable only for high-value crops, he says and adds, the most common in this district are banana, strawberry and king chilli.

The farmers have been using these micro-irrigation sprinklers since 2012. During last three years, when the refurbished PMKSY was launched, there has been about 12–15 per cent increase in irrigated area while the number of farmers—mostly with medium and large land holdings—has reached about 25 per cent.

Micro-irrigation has been approved with an indicative outlay of ₹50 crore over a period of five years from 2015–16 to 2019–20 in this district. Under the PMKSY's Har Khet Ko Pani, 350 STWs have been provided to four command areas in Sonitpur district for accessing groundwater irrigation for the year 2018–19 as recommended by the Central Ground Water Board.

## MAHARASHTRA

If Assam has a problem of regular floods, there are large areas in Maharashtra that face regular drought. The traditional farming in Marathwada—the drought hotbed—has all but vanished because of continuous drought situation. Fed up with pitiable conditions, the farmers have started looking for ways to make agriculture sustainable. There is an exponential difference between the traditional crops grown in Marathwada and water requirement.

Government agencies and NGOs have been discussing and

experimenting with ways and means to bring about a revolution in farming with available water resources. There are a few farmers who have managed to grow better crops and increase the yield by judiciously planning the water resources even when facing drought.

Parali tehsil in Beed district of Marathwada is a favourable landscape to carry out water conservation works. This tehsil has a ghat (named Balaghat) which offers a lot of scope for contour planning for water conservation from the top of the ghat till foothills. And fortunately, a lot of work has been done over the last few years.

But, a moot question remains—even when all such conservation work yields good results and the groundwater is being recharged, what can be the judicious way to use it? If the future water problem needs to be tackled, then it is imperative to plan water usage for non-monsoon months.

After the severe droughts in 2015 and 2016, Marathwada is staring at yet another drought this year as monsoon rains in 2018 were inadequate. In some areas, the waterbodies have so less water that people are worried if livestock can survive with that much water. Few villages in Parali tehsil get water from Jayakwadi project at Majalgaon while some others get water from Van and other small and medium irrigation projects.

Of the approximately 66,000 ha geographical area of Parali tehsil, only about 35–40 per cent area is fertile. Sugarcane, cotton, soybean and lentils are the main crops in this tehsil, with sugarcane and cotton being the most grown crops. Therefore, the water requirement is on the higher side but awareness about water usage is low. As a result, the number of farmers who use drip or sprinkler systems is abysmally low.

However, those who have started using micro-irrigation have prospered as their income has shown exponential growth. For instance, Manoj Kumar Shambhuling Swami, a farmer from Moha village said his income tripled after he started using drip irrigation for growing cotton. 'I availed the government scheme for drip irrigation three years ago. Using drip has meant that I get more output using less water. With the same input cost, my income has tripled,' an excited Swami said.

The news spread so fast that the very next year, 13 more farmers in his neighbourhood opted for drip irrigation for their respective fields.

*Manojkumar Shambhuling Swami of Moha village of Parali tehsil of district Beed in Maharashtra (Photo courtesy: Dhananjay Ramakrushna Arbune)*

Pravin Sudamrao Deshmukh, another farmer from Moha, said that keeping in mind the precarious water condition, he replaced his regular sugarcane and cotton crops with banana. Fully aware that even banana needs a lot of water, Deshmukh chose to set up drip irrigation system for it. 'And look at it! With the same amount of water as last year, my area under irrigation has increased this year. I could conserve more water and irrigate my field better. My bananas are the talk of the town now and herds of farmers from neighbourhood are dropping in to take a look at my banana plot,' Deshmukh said.

*Farmer Pravin Sudamrao Deshmukh in front of his banana plantation in Moha village of Parali tehsil of Beed district in Maharashtra (Photo courtesy: Dhananjay Ramakrushna Arbune)*

In Parali tehsil:

| | |
|---|---|
| 356 | Number of farmers who availed benefits under the PMKSY in the year 2016–17 |
| ₹85,32,451 | Total subsidy amount |
| 612.44 ha | Irrigated area under PMKSY |
| 348 | Number of farm ponds in Parali tehsil |
| 77,109 ha | Total area of Parali |
| 1,375 ha | Forest area |
| 850.8 mm | Average yearly rainfall |
| 702 mm | Rainfall in 2017 |
| 3 | Number of medium-sized irrigation projects |
| 9,168 lakh $m^3$ | Combined storage capacity of the three medium irrigation projects |
| 10 | Minor irrigation projects |
| 13.70 lakh $m^3$ | Combined storage capacity of the three minor irrigation projects |

Along with PMKSY, Maharashtra has also seen Farm Ponds to Those Who Ask scheme. As many as 348 farm ponds have been built till date and about 200 ha has been brought under irrigation using these ponds. Moha village has 70 farm ponds, Parchundi has 16, Bhilegaon 22, Malnathpur 25, Rewali 2, Pimpalgaon Gadhe 7, Mamadapur 4, Pohner 6, Kaudgaon Huda 11, Nagpimpari 18, Hiwara (Go) 3, Jalgavhan 4, Sirsala 4, Nandagaul 20, Daunapur 1 and Loni has 12 of them.

*Inputs from Marathwada Courtesy: Dhananjay Ramakrishna Arbune*

## UTTARAKHAND

Just like the hardcore commercial crop growing farmers in Marathwada have shifted to drip irrigation, the farmers in the north hill states such as Uttarakhand have received the PMKSY very well.

The hilly state has two types of agricultural practices—rain-fed and irrigated. The first type is the one that is found across the state, contributing to major areas. On the other hand, irrigation is available only in plains and valleys. The net irrigated area in Uttarakhand is 3.38 lakh ha (2009–10) while the net irrigated area to net sown area is 45 per cent. 'What we are focussing on are alternative sources of irrigation such as rainwater harvesting, check dam construction over small streams, increasing use of technologies such as drip irrigation and sprinklers,' said an official from the state's agriculture department.

The PMKSY has watershed development programmes, minor irrigation for creation of water sources and per crop more drop component. 'Increasingly, with every passing year, hills are witnessing dry winters. There is a huge demand and scope for water conservation measures for rabi crops and horticulture under the PMKSY components and we are focussing on those. For instance, plastic-lined ponds; combination of poly-houses and drip irrigation, etc., are becoming increasingly popular,' he said.

## PUNJAB

While the farmers in the hill state of Uttarakhand have lapped up PMKSY, the farmers from the neighbouring state of Punjab are not yet that receptive to the idea. Dr R.S. Ghuman from Centre for Research in Rural Development (CRRID) agrees, 'The applicability of sprinkler or dip in Punjab is very less as this is the land of wheat or paddy.'

However, policy about electricity usage (fuel) or water could be used as an incentive. The government should think about giving priority to subsidy, but no such initiative can be seen. An experiment is being done in northern side, the sub-mountainous area of Kandi, where the response for horticulture is good but not as good as is in the rest of the state.

'Pressurized irrigation works very well when it comes to water-guzzling crops. We have tried it for vegetables earlier and now we are trying to use the drip with sugarcane. Subsurface water is also more important,' said Ghuman.

In terms of delta (total depth of water required to raise a crop over a unit area of land is usually called delta), using drip irrigation for paddy last year showed how it is possible. Now, the need is to spread awareness about discouraging flood irrigation and going in for drip.

In the wheat and paddy focussing Punjab, drip is more popular in horticulture. 'There are more takers of drip for horticulture; the idea is to share and hence we are actively discouraging paddy plantation,' said Harjinder Singh of Punjab Agriculture Department. Protected irrigation using polyhouses is also catching up fast.

Gurbinder Singh, map officer with the Soil and Conservation Department of Punjab, who is also the nodal officer for minor irrigation, explains the hows and whys of the drip business in his state. The fact is that no one has accepted drip for the paddy crop; the drip is used more for vegetables. 'The subsidy offered is huge, almost 80 per cent for general category and 90 per cent for small/marginal/SC/ST farmers, etc.; the problem is that there needs to be an assured market of processing facilities,' said Gurbinder Singh.

As on date, Punjab has 34,000 ha area under drip irrigation. Last year, with no budget to spend, the increase was just 600 ha. This is just 0.4 per cent of the total irrigated area and just 1 per cent of the potential area that can be covered under micro-irrigation. 'The bone of contention is the free power supply. With free power, farmers are inclined to pump out more and more groundwater and use it unbridled. There is no thought about saving any water,' Singh said.

Despite all such hurdles, his department has prepared a comprehensive plan—the District Irrigation Plan (DIP) for this year. The target for this year is 2,400 ha as per the sanctioned budget and as per the DIP, the target for next year is set at 20,000 ha assuming that there would be no budgetary problems.

## KERALA

Then, there is this coastal state such as Kerala. The small state has almost all agro-climatic types ranging from the Western Ghats to dense forests to even the coastal backwaters.

Kollam district is the perfect showcase for the PMKSY. The District Irrigation Plan* under the PMKSY tells us that though the district holds only 1.17 per cent of the total geographical area of the country, it accommodates 3 per cent of the country's population. Kollam districts comprises 6.4 per cent of the state's total geographical area and it has a net cultivated area of 1,23,060 ha. Even though mean annual rainfall of the district is 2,700 mm, its temporal distribution is highly uneven resulting in a long dry spell of about 5–6 months.

The command area of the district is 53,960 ha, which is only 37 per cent of the net cultivated area. Even though Kollam has an annual rainfall of 2,400 mm, which is received mostly during

*(https://pmksy.gov.in/mis/Uploads/2017/20170504123828000–1.pdf)

south-west and north-east monsoon, the water received is lost due to heavy run-off because of the poor condition of irrigation and drainage channels. In most of the villages, drainage is also a major problem, which results in crop damage during rainy season and moisture stress during summer. This condition adversely affects the total food grain production in the district.

An official from Kerala said that the three most important points of action in its strategy to implement the PMKSY are the 'promotion of scientific moisture, conservation and run-off control measures to improve groundwater recharge so as to create opportunities for farmer to access recharged water through shallow tube/dug wells and promoting efficient water conveyance and field application devices within the farms, viz., underground piping system, drip and sprinklers, pivots, rain-guns and other application devices, etc. Also, community irrigation through registered users groups/farmer producers organizations/NGOs should be encouraged'.

The major sources of irrigation in the district are government canals, private wells, tanks and lift irrigation schemes with a predominant share contributed by government canals. As rightly pointed out in the DIP, 'There is a larger role for PMKSY to play in the agricultural development of Kollam. Long-term storage of water is not a pragmatic solution for such a thickly populated area. The possible solutions are in-situ water conservation, increasing the efficiency of the existing irrigation projects through proper maintenance of main channels and distribution system and adoption of micro-irrigation methods.'

## UNSPENT FUNDS

Under the PMKSY, more than 20 lakh ha of land has been brought under micro-irrigation till 2017–18. Under the aegis of National Bank for Agriculture and Rural Development and PMKSY, a Micro-Irrigation Fund (MIF) worth ₹5,000 crore was set up in May 2018. Some states did not come up with their share of the subsidy, while in some other states, the approval for spending did not come on time. As a result, several targets were unmet in many states. But finally, after the initial hiccups, the operationalization of MIF* was finally cleared in August 2018.

So, it all boils down to what more can be done to ensure success of this scheme?

To start with, despite whatever success has been achieved so far, decentralized micro-irrigation is the way forward to drought proof agriculture. But, it needs to spread evenly across all climatic zones of all the states.

First thing, if we look at the performance of the states, it can be easily seen that Andhra Pradesh, Karnataka, Gujarat, Maharashtra and Tamil Nadu have contributed more than 75 per cent of additional coverage in 2017–18 area. Rightly so, Andhra Pradesh, Gujarat, Karnataka, Madhya Pradesh, Maharashtra, Rajasthan, Tamil Nadu and Telangana are being labelled as progressive states. Next is the list of under-performing states and those are Punjab, Jharkhand, Bihar, Chhattisgarh and Goa. But, what needs more attention are the states where micro-irrigation is yet to pick up, that is, the entire eastern, north-eastern spectrum of states namely, Arunachal Pradesh, Manipur, Meghalaya, Nagaland and West Bengal (Assam is excluded as it has done some progress). The

*https://pmksy.gov.in/MicroIrrigation/Archive/OperationalisationofPMKSY_MIF.pdf

government machinery across all the states needs to gear up its act and ensure that the scheme is implemented well.

In some cases, even when the centre had sent its share of the subsidy under the micro-irrigation fund, several states were unable to come up with whatever little contribution was required for the smooth functioning of the scheme. Follow-up meetings, incentives to the staff and officials and, then again, actual legwork in the field are 'must-do' category works that states' machinery needs to implement.

## POWER SUPPLY

Malati Sahoo is a small land holding farmer from Bisapur Kala village in Chhindwara district of Madhya Pradesh. Along with her 3 acre land, her family has 4.35 acre in her husband Shriram Sahoo's name and 3.5 acre each in her two sons', Kamlesh and Anup, names.

The family lives on the fringe of Bisapur Kala village as the village, nestled in the foothills of the Satpura ranges, faces acute drinking water shortage in non-monsoon months. 'At least, from here, the river is relatively closer,' Anup chips in. Earlier, when they were entirely dependent on rain-fed agriculture, the family barely earned enough to feed all the mouths in their home. But, as the children grew up, they decided to do something.

By 2010, they had already started witnessing water shortage. With no well in their own farmland, it was increasingly becoming difficult to earn enough to make ends meet. Water table, like in several areas across peninsular India, has been going down with scores of blocks declared dark zones. The family had heard and seen about micro-irrigation schemes in their neighbourhood since 2010, but finally in 2014, when they felt the acute pressure of non-availability of water, they opted for sprinklers first.

But, it was easier said than done. Water source, the Kulbhera river near their village, was a little less than 2 km away. They first built a check dam at the curve nearer to their farmland. Then, they constructed a horizontal storage like well almost 6,000-feet long near the river bed. Transformers were put in place, pipeline was laid till their farmland and a tank to store the water was built.

Even after all this, they could use it only when the power supply was available. So, they also brought pumps to run that and connected it directly to the sprinkler. The family grows wheat and gram using the sprinkler system and deploys drip irrigation for green peas, tomatoes, green chillies, potatoes, ginger and water melons in summers.

Now, the Sahoo family is better-off compared to about a decade ago. But, an important point to remember is that all of the above plays well only with power supply, a diesel pump or a generator.

*Farmers Malati Sahoo and her husband Shriram Sahoo from village Bisapur Kala in Chhindwara district of Madhya Pradesh (Photograph by Nivedita Khandekar)*

Micro-irrigation, be it the drip or sprinkler system, requires uninterrupted power supply, to maintain pressure and level. Hence, for successful implementation of micro-irrigation, the government needs to look at the availability of power supply in remote/rural areas. Although the power situation in the urban areas has improved a lot in the last decades, but, the rural areas continue to be treated in a partial way as compared to the city centres. As a result, it is only in the night, when the big cities go to sleep, that the farmers get power.

What do the farmers do then? Exactly what the Sahoos did. Therefore, the government needs to calculate and consider this major aspect while the preparing the panning out of micro-irrigation schemes.

## RESEARCH AND DEVELOPMENT TO BRING DOWN THE COST

As seen across many states, micro-irrigation—both drip and sprinkler—has come up as the top choice for horticulture products. But, estimates suggest that the cost per acre comes to around ₹60,000 for vegetables and ₹35,000 for fruits. Even with the handsome subsidy, this is way above the reach of really small and marginal land holding farmers, who actually need a helping hand to come out of the poverty line rut. More research needs to be carried out by both the government and the private sector Research and Development (R&D) labs to ensure that the drip or sprinkler systems are cost-effective for the smallest land holding farmer as well. If that is done, this scheme can go a long way to improve the condition of the marginalized communities along with the overall irrigation scenario of our country.

## SHIFT TO HIGH-VALUE CROPS (HVCs)

Diversification to high-value crops can potentially increase the farmers' income, which is the aim of any government scheme, the same is the case with micro-irrigation. It is well-established that agriculture consumes the largest share of freshwater available in India. For decades, since the water shortage problem started raising its head, activists have demanded a ban on water-guzzling crops in drought-prone areas. But, the situation on the ground is different.

However, with HVCs, the picture can turn around. Instead of water-intensive sugarcane, paddy and banana, the farmers should be encouraged to adopt lesser water-intensive crops such as oilseeds, vegetables, pulses and even the latest hot favourite herbal produce.

## INCREASE FUND ALLOCATION

Many experts have spoken about how the PMKSY can be a further effective scheme provided the allocation for micro-irrigation component is at least doubled, if not for all, at least for rain-fed areas.

First, the fund allocation from the centre should be smooth, then, the state component needs to be released on time and finally, when the farmers actually avail the scheme, the direct transfer to the beneficiary should be on time. The prime minister has promised that he would double the income of farmers by 2022. So, it is imperative for the government to give priority to micro-irrigation and minor-irrigation works.

Dr J.P. Mishra, adviser, agriculture, with the NITI Aayog, in his presentation 'Revitalizing Rain-fed Agriculture in India', has elaborated how rain-fed agriculture, especially for small and marginal farmers, needs a paradigm shift.

Following are the highlights:

- Move from commodity-centric to an area-focussed approach
- Investment in rain-fed agriculture at ₹50,000 per ha
- Knowledge-based agriculture
- Improved inputs, diversification and R&D
- Farmer-centric agriculture
- Farmer Producers' Organisations (FPOs), agri-marketing and warehouse receipts
- Credit, finance and insurance, capacity-building
- Industry-agriculture-farmer linkages
- Market infrastructure, export opportunities and agribusiness
- Government as the facilitator
- Mission mode approach to enhance land and labour productivity
- Governance
- Convergence matrix of programmatic interventions

## WAY FORWARD—TRADITION AND TECHNOLOGY

### Traditions

Across India, rainwater harvesting has been done by various traditional methods, the most common being 'catching the rain where it falls', be it in ponds, in johads or in percolation tanks. It was used both for domestic chores and for rabi crops.

Situation becomes tricky for hills. Be it Uttarakhand, Arunachal Pradesh or Nagaland, the problem is grim. Inspite of its high rainfall, there is acute shortage of drinking water during the dry season, that is, from November to April, in the region. Due to lack of irrigation facilities, a second crop is not possible in uplands; as a result, cropping intensity is very low (120 per cent) in Nagaland.

As per the case study for Jalkund*, a hybrid of traditional and modern water harvesting structure, one can find efficient management of water in the region in traditional farming systems. The examples are 'Zabosystem' of Nagaland and Bamboo drip irrigation of Meghalaya and rice and fish farming in Apatani valley of Arunachal Pradesh.

This simple micro rainwater harvesting structure—Jalkund—has been developed and popularized by the Indian Council for Agriculture Research (ICAR) Complex, Umiam, to solve the problem of water scarcity to a great extent. It involves development and popularization of Jalkund (5 X 4 X 1.5 m with a lining of 250 gsm silpaulin and 30,000 litres capacity) in hilltops/highlands for its efficient utilization during lean period for diversified farm activities. About 145 jalkunds were demonstrated in farmers' fields. Farmers cultivated high-value crops such as strawberry, broccoli, chillies and reared pigs, poultry, etc., with harvested water.

Strawberry crop, grown under straw and black polythene 50μ (50 microns) using harvested rainwater stored in Jalkund (30,000 litres) and irrigated using drip system under gravity flow, was evaluated for enhancing crop productivity, quality and water use efficiency. And, this has been tested successfully on all three counts. Another indigenous system is the bamboo drip irrigation system. The application of water on hill slopes for irrigation of plantation crops poses a serious problem of soil erosion. The tribal farmers in Muktapur village in Jaintia hills district of Meghalaya have developed the indigenous technique of bamboo drip irrigation.

---

*http://www.kiran.nic.in/pdf/NRM/water_mgnt/Jalkhund_Watermangt.pdf

Betel vines planted with areca nut as the supporting tree are irrigated with this system, in which water trickles or drips at the base of the crop.

Similarly, the Zabo system is an indigenous farming system of Nagaland. The word 'Zabo' means impounding of water. It is a combination method where three components of forest, agriculture and animal husbandry are combined for effective soil and water conservation. In the hilly areas, the hilltops have forests that retain water and disallows surface runoff of rainfall. Then, at the middle level of that hill, there are tanks that harvest water. And lastly, there are cattle yards and paddy fields at the base, which help in irrigation during crop period and are used as storage at other times.

## TECHNOLOGY: SOLAR-POWERED COMMUNITY MICRO-IRRIGATION PROJECT (SCMIP)

Punjab's Kandi belt comprising 10 per cent of the total area of the state is predominately rain-fed. According to Punjab government website, even the name 'Kandi' is an Urdu word meaning 'water scarce'. The area suffers from acute shortage of drinking water besides poor socio-economic conditions of farmers. Hoshiarpur district falls in this Kandi belt and is characterized by the highest number of seasonal choes (rivulets) criss-crossing its lands, but due to undulating topography and steep slopes, most of it gets wasted as run-off.

Soil erosion is another major concern in this area. During monsoon period, most of the fertile soil gets eroded, thereby leaving farmers with double whammy that is, the unavailability of assured irrigation source coupled with soil degradation. These problems are just the tip of the iceberg. Since the area is largely forested, agriculture is also threatened by wild animals. The farmers cannot even grow fruits or vegetables for their household needs because of the threat of wild animals.

Being a sub-mountainous and remote area, the electricity supply is highly unreliable, mainly because of the logistics involved. The productivity is among the lowest as the farmers are only able to cultivate a single crop in the year and that too is at the mercy of rainfall only. The government of Punjab, taking stock of this situation, had constructed the Kandi canal, which was also called the lifeline of Kandi area. But, the irony was that the area to the right of the canal, being at a lower elevation, was irrigated through gravitational flow, whereas the area to the left of the canal, being at a higher elevation, could be irrigated utilizing lift irrigation only.

The villagers of the project area approached the agriculture department in the year 2014 to find a solution to their hardships and implement a lift irrigation scheme. Acting on the complaint, the department held deliberations with various stakeholders and conceived a grid-operated traditional lift irrigation project. However, upon explanation of recurring costs of grid-connected project, the villagers expressed their inability to pay the recurring costs, until they had an assured source of income. The department, considering the concerns of the community, got to the drawing board once again and thus came the 'Integrated Solar-Powered Community Micro-Irrigation Project'.

The government of Punjab approved the project with a total cost of ₹40.94 crore with funding from the RKVY and the National Bank for Agriculture and Rural Development (NABARD). The work on the project started in April 2015 and was divided into three phases. The project was completed and commissioned on 7 August 2017. It shall be operated and maintained by the department by hand-holding the local community for the initial seven years; thus providing gestation period for farmers to develop their fiscal and technical capacity.

## PPP IN MICRO-IRRIGATION

In its draft proposal about 'Public Private Partnership (PPP) in Integrated Micro-Irrigation'*, NITI Aayog has raised concerns about the prevalent practices and suggested means and ways to deal with the problems.

For instance, highlighting what it termed as industry concerns, the document mentions that micro-irrigation, in its current avatar, focusses too much on the overarching concept. 'The current funds allocated for micro-irrigation this fiscal year are lower than the previous year's. Therefore, the funds are not keeping up with the increasing demand.'

It also suggests doing away with the 'area ceiling limit' and says, 'while only 15 per cent of the farmers in India are large- and medium-scale farmers, they account for control over 55 per cent of the total available land. Experts feel that increasing the cap to 10 ha from the current ceiling of 5 ha would be extremely beneficial to the sector. This scheme, however, does not lift that cap. Only 10 per cent of the total potential area (estimated to be 69 million ha in India) has been brought under micro-irrigationas on date. Hence, the area ceiling cap of 5 ha may be increased to 10 ha'.

And finally, warning about the 'lack of framework for scalability', the document says, 'Under the extant schemes, there is limited incentive for the farmers and the private sector to

*http://niti.gov.in/writereaddata/files/document_publication/Draft%20 Concept%20Paper%20on%20PPP%20in%20Microirrigation_Oct%202017.pdf

enter/get involved in "Participatory Integrated Micro-Irrigation Management" at a scalable level.'

The NITI Aayog document lists out some of the benefits of the PPP approach in scaling-up capacity in micro-irrigation as follows:

1. Availability of private capital and technology partnership
2. Access to functional and technical efficiency of private entities improvising the lifecycle cost
3. Risk of project completion and delivery of agreed outputs to be transferred to the private entity
4. Public funds would be expended only upon delivery of agreed outcomes
5. Achieving economies of scale

Since the PPP model has not really succeeded in any of the sectors in India (or for that matter in any developing country), it needs to be treated with caution. There are already several large land-holding farmers who are availing every kind of technology as they have access to it. The idea termed as the 'economies of scale' needs a relook; rather than being a private player in such a vital scheme, the government should promote farmers' cooperatives.

There have been enough successful farmers' collectives and cooperatives across India. What needs to be done is to apply those small, decentralized models and customize them for respective areas. Hivare Bazar, near Ahmednagar in Maharashtra, is one good example for plains. The ice stupas built by Sonam Wangchuk in Ladakh is another example of coming up with customized, localized solutions.

The government cannot and should not let private companies sneak into micro-irrigation and risk threatening the smooth ride it has experienced so far.

## JOURNEY SO FAR

Of course, the journey so far has not been bad at all. The PMKSY gave the much-needed impetus to the concept of decentralized micro-irrigation.

A quick look at the statistics, graphs and numbers can give a clear picture of the landmarks achieved. And, it gives a glimpse of what more needs to be done.

Here are the charts and figures showcasing various outputs related to PMKSY* as on 23 November 2018.

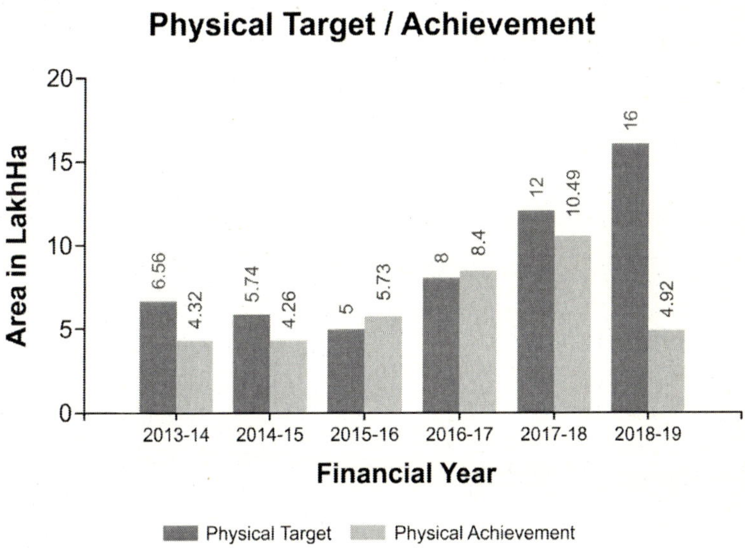


*(https://pmksy.gov.in/mis/frmDashboard.aspx)

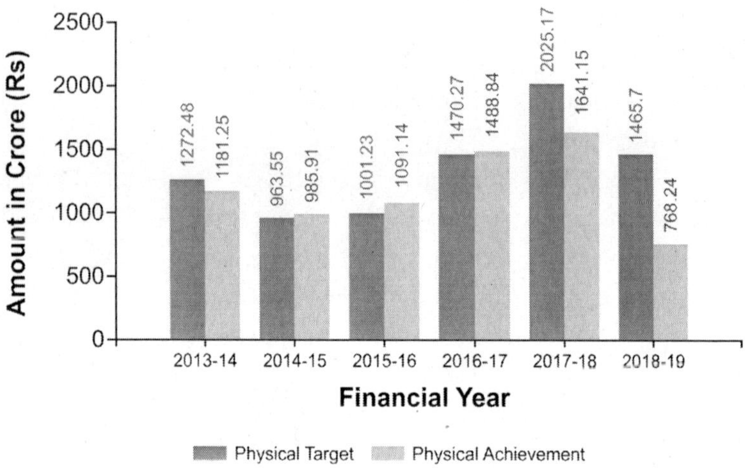
2500
2000
1500
1000
500
0
Amount in Crore (Rs)
1272.48
1181.25
963.55
985.91
1001.23
1091.14
1470.27
1488.84
2025.17
1641.15
1465.7
768.24
2013-14
2014-15
2015-16
2016-17
2017-18
2018-19
Financial Year
Physical Target
Physical Achievement

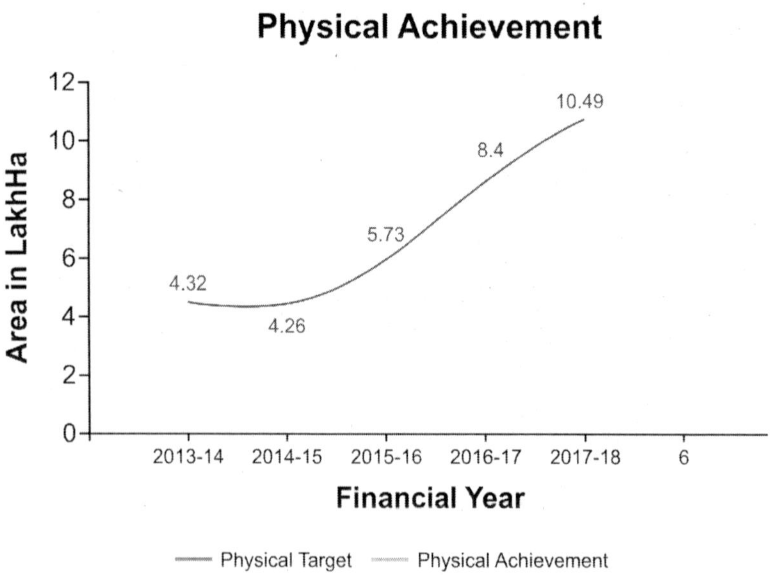
Physical Achievement
12
10
8
6
4
2
0
Area in LakhHa
4.32
4.26
5.73
8.4
10.49
2013-14
2014-15
2015-16
2016-17
2017-18
6
Financial Year
Physical Target
Physical Achievement

## Total Coverage Drip & Sprinkler from 2005-06 to 2017-18

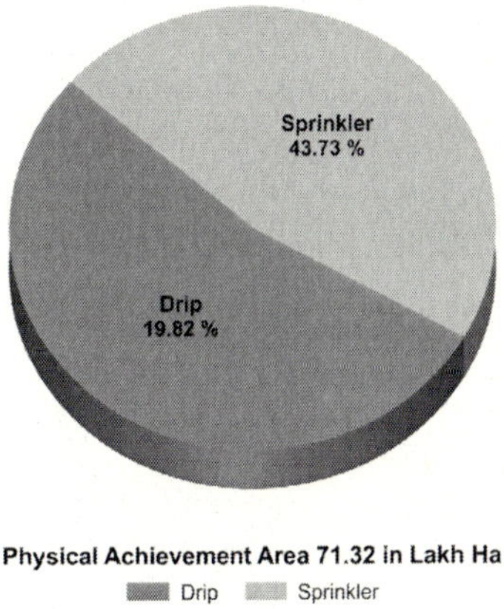


## Coverage under Drip & Sprinkler in 2015-16

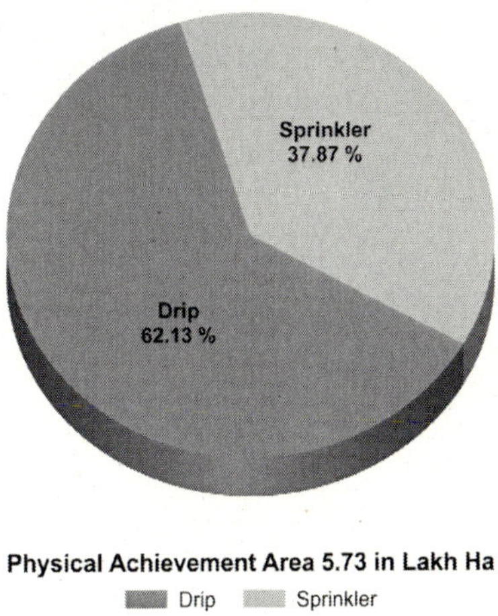

## Coverage under Drip & Sprinkler in 2016-17

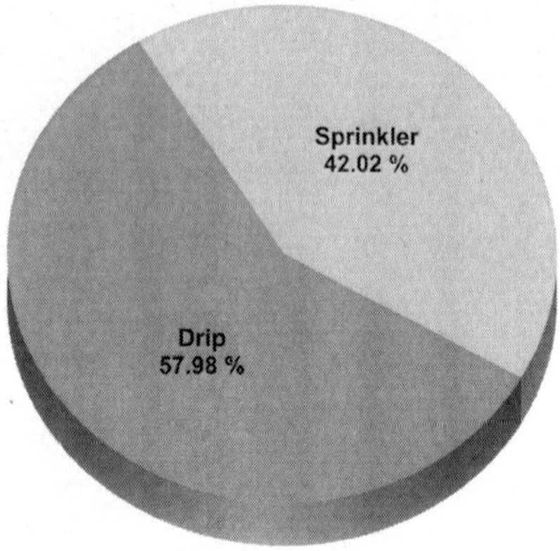


**Physical Achievement Area 8.40 in Lakh Ha**



## Coverage under Drip & Sprinkler in 2017-18

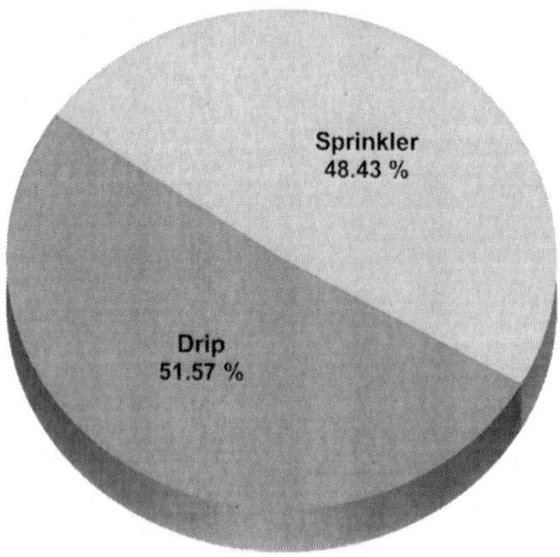


**Physical Achievement Area 10.49 in Lakh Ha**

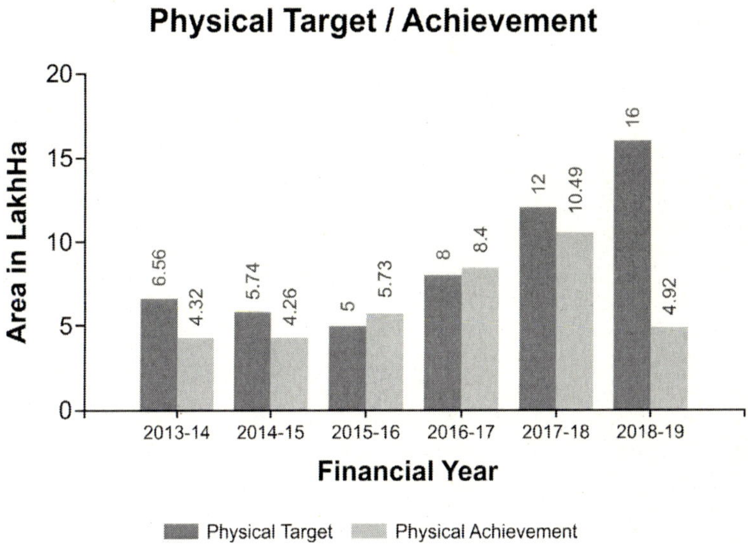
Physical Target / Achievement
Area in LakhHa
20
15
10
5
0
6.56
4.32
5.74
4.26
5
5.73
8
8.4
12
10.49
16
4.92
2013-14
2014-15
2015-16
2016-17
2017-18
2018-19
Financial Year
Physical Target
Physical Achievement

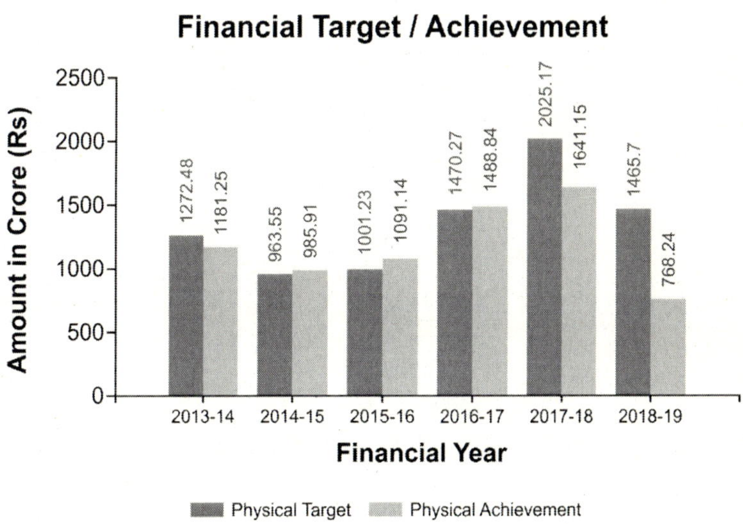
Financial Target / Achievement
Amount in Crore (Rs)
2500
2000
1500
1000
500
0
1272.48
1181.25
963.55
985.91
1001.23
1091.14
1470.27
1488.84
2025.17
1641.15
1465.7
768.24
2013-14
2014-15
2015-16
2016-17
2017-18
2018-19
Financial Year
Physical Target
Physical Achievement

# Coverage under Drip & Sprinkler in 2017-18

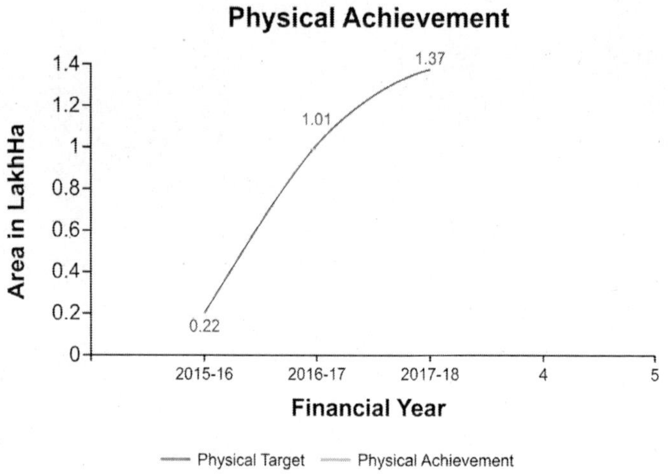


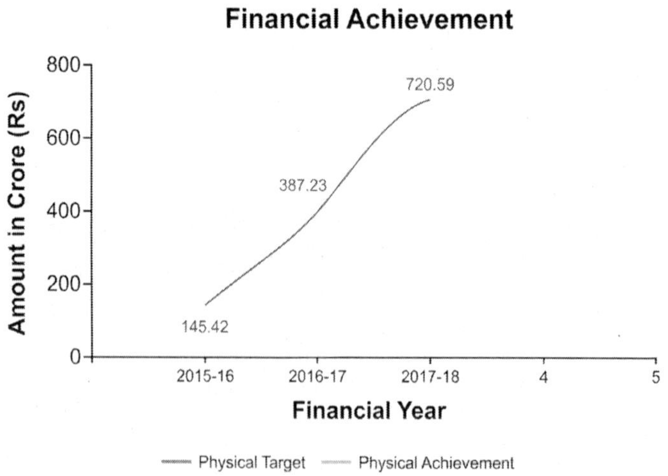

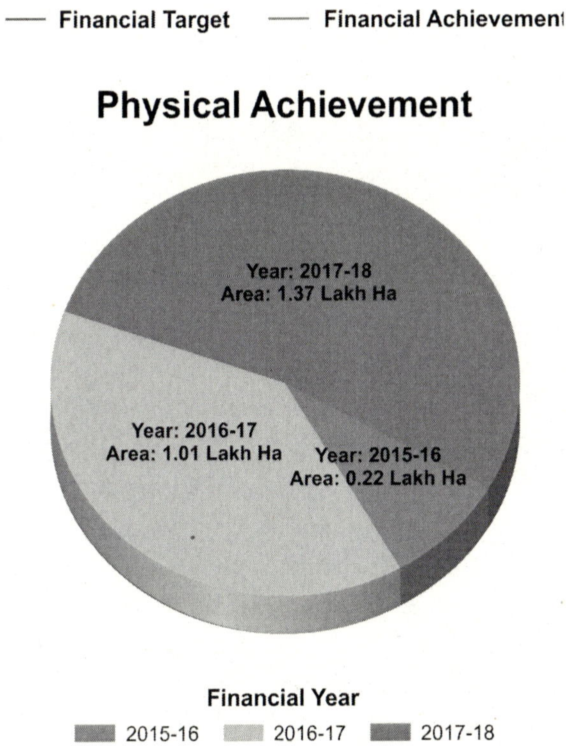


If we see the larger picture, 'More Crop Per Drop' is immensely important to attain sustainable agriculture. The PMKSY is a step towards improving agricultural water productivity in India and making the farmers happy.

***Nivedita Khandekar*** *is an independent journalist based in Delhi. She writes on environmental and developmental issues.*

# PROTECTING AGAINST VAGARIES OF NATURE: PM FASAL BIMA YOJANA

*Lekshmi Parameswaran*

Akhilesh Meena, a young man from Vidisha, Madhya Pradesh, is setting an example for his peers by taking a path less trodden by youth in today's time. He left a lucrative job in the corporate sector and decided to take up farming as a full-time profession. This change in perception among the youth is new to an India, where the agrarian crisis has been a reality for the last many years. It is estimated that in the past 21 years, more than 3,20,000 farmers have taken their lives due to the increasing debt burden. For a country where 70 per cent of its rural households are still primarily dependent on agriculture, the unfortunate reality has been that the governments in power have neglected that very section which forms the backbone of the country's economy.

In a scenario that was threatening to consume an entire sector, the first glimmer of hope came on 13 February 2016 when Prime Minister Narendra Modi announced the launch of the Pradhan Mantri Fasal Bima Yojana (PMFBY), an unprecedented step that would go on to secure the future of Indian agriculture. For the first time, the farmers were given the safety net of a crop insurance scheme that was not just wide-ranging in its scope but also held promises of erasing the unpredictability in the Indian agriculture.

The results of this are visible with youth like Meena finally viewing agriculture as a profitable and honourable profession—one which would benefit both farmers and landowners. There are no more fears of a catastrophe taking away the livelihoods of millions of people. With assured returns, the scheme has instilled confidence in Indian farmers who have been the most oppressed of all classes till date.

## HISTORY OF AGRICULTURAL INSURANCE

There is no doubt that India has had a history of agricultural insurances. The question then is: why is Fasal Bima touted as a significant step for Indian agriculture? To understand this, it is necessary to take a relook at the history of agricultural insurances in the country.

The greatest bane of Indian agriculture has been that it is always weather dependent. Floods, droughts, cyclone or pest attacks have robbed farmers of their harvest and have pushed them to utter impoverishment. Even with the advent of modern technologies and the introduction of weather forecast systems, the situation has remained unchanged. Since 1985, widespread efforts have been made to mitigate the risks through crop insurance schemes. But, the idea that farmers can pass the weather-related risks to a third party never panned out the way it was envisioned, and the inherent flaws of the schemes oppressed the farmers even further.

In 1985, the Government of India launched the Comprehensive Crop Insurance Scheme (CCIS) and it remained in operation till kharif 1999. The coverage of this scheme was limited in scope with it being extended only to loanee farmers for food and oilseed crops and the risk commitment of ₹10,000 per farmer per season. This was replaced with National Agriculture Insurance Scheme (NAIS) with effect from rabi 1999–2000. Though this scheme was wider in scope with coverage extended to both loanee and non-loanee farmers and all food, oilseed and horticulture/commercial crops with the risk commitment of upto 150 per cent of threshold yield, it could not provide the desirable results.

When the scheme was launched, it held promise for the farmers. The premium structure was rationalized and conceptualized to implement the scheme on actuarial premium rate over a period and a corpus fund had to be created to meet the catastrophic losses. It was decided that the surplus premium collected from the farmers will be deposited in the corpus fund. The problem arose when the corpus fund itself could not be created.

Apart from the operational difficulties, what went against the scheme was its failure in ensuring financial viability. The administrative premium rate ranged from 1.5 per cent to 3.5 per cent, which was charged from the farmers and the government had to bear all claims liabilities over and above the premium cost collected. Though the scheme has filled some of the lacuna as compared to CCIS, the lack of financial planning was evident throughout. The administrative costs like bank service charges, adjusting and other expenses, publicity, etc., had to be borne by the government and all the liabilities were to be shared on a 50:50 basis by the central and state governments. No mechanism had been put in place to ensure that the states were not delaying the release of share towards its committed financial liabilities and the government found it increasingly difficult to meet the rising administrative costs.

Lack of infrastructural support and proper monitoring also led to the woes of NAIS. The fields did not have the infrastructure to conduct the requisite number of Crop Cutting Experiments (CCEs)—the process used to analyse the overall yield of the village.

The most important factor that went against NAIS was that the premium amount never equalled the risk level and even in genuine cases where money had to be disbursed, the farmers seldom got any benefits—either the money never came or only too little was released.

## THE CONSTITUTION OF DR P.K. MISHRA COMMITTEE

In 2014, when the Bharatiya Janata Party (BJP) came to power, it was evident that Indian agriculture was in tatters and there was an urgent need to remedy the historical wrongs. To get a better perspective on the policy initiatives required, a high-power committee was constituted under the chairmanship of Dr P.K. Mishra with the mandate of reviewing the crop insurance schemes. The committee found an array of issues that needed immediate intervention.

Among the findings of the committee, the most prominent ones were: the area insured for a particular crop was more than the area sown; the data collected from the CCEs as well as the weather data were not reliable; many banks did not comply with the provisions of compulsory insurance for loanee farmers; the premium rates were unaffordable for marginal farmers; the dispute in settlement of claims; the lack of technical skills and capacity building of the personnel associated with crop insurance schemes and a general lack of awareness among farmers regarding the various features of the schemes.

With the problems clearly spelt out, the committee made a number of recommendations, which would help plug loopholes and address the issues that the farmers were facing for so long. Transparency was at the core of the roadmap laid out. To achieve this goal, technology was seen as the single biggest tool that would eliminate corruption in the system and put in place a policy that would solely work towards ensuring farmers' interests. The first suggestion put forth by the committee was the launch of a web portal for uploading of farmers' data. The web portal would enable financial institutions to link each farmer's existing loan account to the unique land account, facilitating detection of multiple loans taken on the same land. The committee recommended the use of mobile phone technology to capture and transmit photographs of standing crops once or twice during the season for the purpose of verification of the crops sown on a particular land. It said that the state governments should ensure the use of GPRS-enabled and camera-fitted mobile phones or handheld devices while conducting CCEs so as to transmit data on a real-time basis.

Among the recommendations, that truly took into account the varying topography of the country and the accompanying problems, was that the critical-weather elements, which trigger crop-yield losses in different crop-growth periods, should be developed for different agro-climatic regions to be used by governments and industry as benchmarks. It called for the strengthening of capacity-building measures in line with the needs of the stakeholders such as the central government, state governments, crop insurance companies and farmers. It also pointed out the need to create awareness and insurance literacy among the farmers, which should be initiated with the insurance companies and banks in collaboration with the concerned state governments.

## THE LAUNCH OF PMFBY

Taking all recommendations of the Dr P.K. Mishra committee into consideration, the government formulated the Pradhan Mantri Fasal Bima Yojana (PMFBY) and implemented it from kharif 2016 season. It was an ambitious scheme with 28 states and union territories participating in it. It was launched when Indian agriculture was reeling under one of its most difficult periods with twin droughts brought about by the El-Nino phenomenon and untimely rabi season rains and hailstorms. It was also a time when only 23 per cent of the cropped area in India had access to insurance. The immediate goal of the PMFBY was to increase the coverage to 50 per cent of the total crop area of 194.40 Mha from the existing level of about 25–27 per cent crop area. The expenditure was expected to be around ₹9,500 crore.

There were certain features that made the PMFBY stand out among the earlier crop insurance schemes and promise the Indian farmers a future that was free from all worries. To begin with, it had lower premium compared to the previous insurance schemes. The maximum insurance charges payable by the farmers was just 2 per cent of the sum insured or the actuarial rate whichever was less for the kharif season, 1.5 per cent for the rabi season and 5 per cent for annual commercial or horticulture crops. For the first time, there was no cap on the premium and reduction of the sum insured which meant that it insured the income of the farmers and not crops as was widely practised till then. The use of technology like GPS, smartphones, remote sensing and drones to access actual crop damage meant that there would be prompt and easy settlement of claims. Most significant was the clause that 25 per cent of the likely claim will be settled directly on farmers' accounts immediately after a disaster. The scheme also included provisions to cover localized crop losses such as hailstones and also provided coverage for post-harvest losses.

It was decided that the difference between the premium paid by the farmers and the premium fixed by the insurance companies will be subsidized and there will be no cap on the maximum subsidy paid by the government. The subsidy will be borne equally by the central and the respective state governments. Till then, farmers were paying an amount as high as 15 per cent of the sum insured as premium under the then existing schemes that were all consumed by PMFBY.

To streamline the process, it mandated that there will be only one insurance company for the entire state. The overall control for implementation rested with the Ministry of Agriculture and Farmers' Welfare. The choice of which insurance company was left to the states from a ministry designated/empanelled Agriculture Insurance Company of India (AIC) and some private insurance companies.

The stated objectives of the PMFBY are the following:

1. To provide insurance coverage and financial support to the farmers in the event of failure of any of the notified crop as a result of natural calamities, pests and diseases
2. To stabilize the income of farmers to ensure their continuance in farming
3. To encourage farmers to adopt innovative and modern agricultural practices
4. To ensure flow of credit to the agriculture sector

The Faal Bima Yojana will operate on the principle of 'Area Approach' in the selected Defined Areas called Insurance Unit. The state government will have to notify crops and Defined Areas covered during a particular season. For major crops, area approach was chosen as the basis of implementation with the unit of insurance being the village/village panchayat; for higher crops, a higher level, depending upon the requirement, was chosen. All the farmers growing notified crops in a notified area during the season, who have insurable interest in the crop, were termed eligible to participate in the scheme. Compulsory coverage was extended to all loanee farmers. For the proper management of the scheme, the existing State Level Coordination Committee on Crop Insurance (SLCCCI), a sub-committee to SLCCCI and District Level Monitoring Committee (DLMC) already overseeing the implementation and monitoring of the ongoing crop insurance schemes were designated.

In case of the loanee farmers under the compulsory component, the sum insured would be equal to the scale of finance for that crop as fixed by the District Level Technical Committee (DLTC), which may extend up to the value of the threshold yield of the insured crop at the option of insured farmer. Where value of the threshold yield is lower than the scale of finance, higher amount shall be the sum insured.

By multiplying the notional threshold yield with the Minimum Support Price (MSP) of the current year, one arrives at the value of sum insured. Wherever current year's MSP is not available, the MSP of previous year were to be adopted.

The crops for which the MSP is not declared, the farm gate price established by the marketing department/board was to be adopted.

The risks to be covered were:

1. Yield Losses (standing crops on a notified area basis): Comprehensive risk insurance is provided to cover yield losses due to non-preventable risks such as:
    i. Natural fire and lightning
    ii. Storm, hailstorm, cyclone, typhoon, tempest, hurricane, tornado, etc.
    iii. Flood, inundation and landslide
    iv. Drought, dry spells
    v. Pests/diseases, etc.

2. Prevented Sowing (on a notified area basis): In cases where the majority of insured farmers of a notified area, who have the intent to sow/plant and incur expenditure for the purpose, are prevented from sowing/planting the insured crop due to adverse weather conditions, shall be eligible for indemnity claims up to a maximum of 25 per cent of the sum insured.
3. Post-harvest Losses (individual farm basis): Coverage is available up to a maximum period of 14 days from harvesting for those crops that are kept in 'cut and spread' condition to dry in the field after harvesting, against specific perils of cyclone/cyclonic rains or unseasonal rains throughout the country.
4. Localized Calamities (individual farm basis): Loss/damage resulting from occurrence of identified localized risks i.e., hailstorm, landslide and inundation affecting isolated farms in the notified area.

## WHAT MAKES PMFBY STAND OUT

Chhattisgarh is a state that has seen two consecutive drought years during the period 2016 and 2017. With 96 tehsils declared as drought hit, the state, which is predominantly dependent on paddy cultivation, banned the growth of summer paddy and also took the adverse step of cutting off the electricity to some villages where water levels had hit the below-average mark. For famers who grew paddy in the kharif season, the drought meant huge losses, which made them stare at an extremely bleak future.

In Rajnandgaon of Chhattisgarh, a farmer, Nivedanlal Sahu, recounts how he did not have to sell his farm this year after the drought destroyed his entire year's harvest. 'If this drought had happened four years ago, I would have been forced to the streets with no land or occupation. Today, because I enrolled myself in the

Bima Yojana, a sum of ₹4,32,00 was credited to my bank account that came well in time for me to plan for the next season,' he said.

*Nivedanlal Sahu (Photo by Lekshmi Parameswaran)*

Another farmer, Dev Kumar Sinha, who had a sum of ₹7,15,000 credited to his account after he suffered heavy losses termed the PMFBY as a means that has made the farmers self-reliant. He pointed out that even though the farmers were made to sign-up for insurances in the past years too, this is the first time that the farmers have truly benefitted by a scheme of this nature. It gave them hope that the vicious debt cycles that they found themselves entrapped in after every natural calamity can finally come to an end.

In kharif year 2017, Rajnandgaon had an enrolment of 1,78,878 farmers in the PMFBY with 1,34,548 being loanee farmers and

44,330 being non-loanee farmers. The total area insured was 2.68 lakh ha. Once the adverse effects of the drought were known, an immediate relief of ₹61 crore was disbursed.

*Farmers from Rajnandgaon, who have got more than 3 lakh rupees in claims (Photo by Lekshmi Parameswaran)*

One particular set of figures from Rajnandgaon would aptly explain the impact that the PMFBY had in providing financial security to the farmers. According to the official statistics, in the kharif season of 2012, the amount disbursed to farmers, as part of the insurance claim, was ₹0.69 crore and in the kharif season of 2017, this figure jumped to ₹465.33 crore. This speaks volumes of the sheer scale and reach of the policy.

In another district of Mahasamund, Jagdish Singh, a farmer who owns 14 acres of land, where he cultivates seedless lemons, lets out a sigh of relief when he talks about the PMFBY. Even though he has introduced modern technology like the drip-irrigation system in his farms, the drought year meant that he still had to cope with some unforeseen losses. His enrolment in the crop insurance scheme ensured that an amount of ₹22,000 was credited to his account when he was least expecting it. As a person who has been in the farming sector for the past 35 years, he was quick to say that this was the first time he felt confident about his chosen path and he feels that he will be in a position to secure his family's future.

*Jagdish Singh, Mahasamund (Photo by Lekshmi Parameswaran)*

V. P. Choubey, Deputy Director of Agriculture, Mahasamund, who has been striving to make farmers aware of the benefits of the scheme said that claims of over ₹1 crore had already been settled immediately after the drought. He added that PMFBY figures among the schemes that have genuinely ensured the welfare of farmers.

When the nation as a whole is considered, it won't be far-fetched to state that PMFBY has been a game changer for Indian agriculture. It is the first crop insurance scheme launched by the government, which had a flat rate for premium irrespective of the crops and removed capping on premium rates that paved the way for adequate claims being paid to the farmers. In all the earlier schemes, farmers had to pay a premium as high as 3.5 per cent. The use of technology in estimating the losses have eliminated corruption and the role of middlemen. Earlier, the farmers were just silent spectators and did not have a say while the CCEs were done. Today, with awareness campaigns being done at every block, the farmers are aware of the scientific way in which the CCEs are done and can voice their concerns to the higher authorities if they feel that the method used does not meet the standards specified.

At the district level, monitoring is done by a team comprising of nodal officers, bankers and officers from the insurance company with the collector as the chairperson. This means that arbitrary decisions while estimating the losses can no longer be taken and the uploading of real-time data on the PMFBY site means that questions can be raised by any citizen of the country regarding how the figures were arrived at. The details of individual farmers are given in the portal which is a stark change from the fragmented data that was available in the earlier schemes. Such a step has facilitated the farmers to have a say in their lives which was long denied to them. It is ironical that the hands that feed the mouths of millions of Indians were the most neglected even after independence.

The two-year claim settlement delay, which had become the norm during the tenure of previous administrations has completely been done away with. The focus is now on expediting the process so that the farmers are reimbursed in a timely manner and are encouraged to sow for the next harvest season. An example of how this has worked in a phenomenal way can be found during the devastating Kerala floods of 2017. Taking into account the scale of the calamity, the prime minister had personally instructed 25 per cent of the expected claims to be directly settled into the farmers' accounts without waiting for a team to assess the damages. The benefits of the scheme could not be reaped by the state as only 2.5 per cent of the farmers were insured primarily because the state government was not proactive in implementing the scheme. The floods made the farmers realize the benefits of a weather-based insurance scheme and 55,000 farmers enrolled in the year 2018–19.

The fact that the PMFBY covers all losses from pre- to post-harvesting has ushered in an era where farmers are no longer pushed to the brink. Also, using the area approach where the village/village panchayat is taken as the unit of insurance means that the farmers are no longer at the mercy of statistics that do not give the true picture. Earlier, if a state had a good threshold yield and a calamity was to strike just one village, the farmers of that village could not claim the benefits of the insurance scheme as the overall statistics for the state never revealed any distress.

Also, the government has made it a point to keep the PMFBY as a dynamic scheme. All the difficulties that arose at the stage of implementation were being factored and solutions were constantly being evolved. For example, when the government realized that there was a delay in the settlement of claims in certain areas, it incorporated the provision of penalties for states and insurance companies for the delay. In a new set of guidelines issued, the government stated that the farmers will be paid 12 per cent interest by insurance companies for the delay in settlement claims beyond two months of prescribed cut-off dates. The state governments were also mandated to pay 12 per cent interest for the delay in the release of the state share of subsidy beyond three months of prescribed cut-off date/submission of requisition by insurance companies.

Another example of the government looking at the needs of the farmers with sensitivity is the inclusion of cloudburst and natural fire in localized calamities in addition to hailstorm, landslide and inundation. It also included, on a pilot basis, an add-on coverage for crop loss due to attacks by wild animals. These provisions were added after hailstorms resulted in huge losses for the farmers in Haryana in rabi 2017 and attacks of boars and elephants had damaged huge stretches of land in Chhattisgarh. The definition of perils by the government is a continuous process with the aim that the burden of natural calamities should never be passed on to the farmers.

*Farmers of Bagbahara, Chhattisgarh (Photo by Lekshmi Parameswaran)*

## ADDRESSING THE CONTROVERSY

Today, the media in India has alleged that the PMFBY is nothing but a scam that has only resulted in the private insurance companies being benefitted. There cannot be a more blatant accusation that is solely based on concocted analysis of figures. It is also an example of why for any analyst it is important to get the facts right before reaching conclusions. Unfortunately, for the media in India, the conclusions were drawn even before the ground realities could be analysed.

It is pertinent here to know the details of how the scheme works. There are a total of 18 insurance companies involved—five from the government sector and 13 from the private sector. There is a transparent bidding process where the tender is allotted to those who quote the lowest premium. And, when it comes to claim settlement, the primary data is provided by the state government which is uploaded on the PMFBY site. From here, the central government takes over, which calculates the final claim payable to a farmer according to the formula:

$$\frac{(\text{Threshold Yield—Average Yield})}{\text{Threshold Yield}} \times \text{Sum Insured (for every hectare)}$$

The insurance companies or any outside agency have no role to play in this. The real-time data is uploaded on the PMFBY site and farmers can keep a track of the entire process. Top officials at the agricultural ministry do video conferencing on a weekly basis with the implementing officials of every state to see to it that all the grievances are addressed immediately.

The question then arises is how was the overall data construed to play along a particular narrative? The answer lies in the details. In totality, 2016–17 and 2017–18 have been agriculturally good years for the country, which implies that the claim ratio was low. Also, it needs to be understood that this is not a welfare scheme where a particular sum of money is assured, it is an insurance scheme that pays for the losses incurred by the farmers in the face of adverse weather events. Even here, the benefits can be accrued only according to the area insured. When a farmer has paid premium for only half a hectare, the agencies can pay only for the losses incurred in that half hectare. Wherever there have been extreme natural events and the area insured was bigger, the farmers have always reaped benefits from the scheme. In the Vidisha district of Madhya Pradesh, which was reeling under agrarian distress, more than 300 farmers got amounts exceeding ₹3 lakh in claim settlements and for the first time the farmers felt that their crisis could be abated.

After understanding that the problem was also with the farmers not having adequate insurance literacy, the government has now started awareness camps at the panchayat level and also does door-to-door campaigning to make the farmers realize that their responsibility does not end with signing up for the scheme. It is up to them to take into account their needs and insure their entire farms. In the quest to save a few pennies while paying the premium then, the farmers often put at stake a lot more than what they realize.

## CHALLENGES AHEAD

All this is not to say that PMFBY is without challenges or it is a flawless scheme. Like any scheme that was launched with an ambitious vision, it also has a set of issues that will have to be addressed if the true benefits are to be reaped.

The coverage of the PMFBY is still limited to food crops, oilseeds and selected annual horticulture and commercial crops. In a country with unpredictable weather patterns, it is necessary to further reduce the unit insurance to take into account individual fields. The penetration of insurance schemes is still low in the country with only 30 per cent of farm households signing up for it annually. The situation is more dismal in the case of non-loanee farmers with most of the state administrations still struggling to convince those farmers of the benefits of the insurance scheme.

The adoption of technology remains a challenge with many states struggling to find trained hands to carry out CCEs and estimate the losses in a scientific manner when a calamity strikes. There is also a need for the farmers to come together and voice their grievances at community forums so that the state governments have an idea of their needs and can evolve the scheme accordingly. It is also true that a formula will have to be worked out that would better reflect the aspirations of the farmers. But, these are just minor glitches in a scheme that is as extensive as the PMFBY and will eventually be addressed by the government and the implementing agencies.

## THE WAY FORWARD

It needs to be understood that PMFBY is a scheme that is a result of years and years of policy apathy from the governments in power. Even when the governments were mourning about agrarian distress, there was no infusion of fresh ideas. The lethargy in policy making has resulted in huge costs being paid by the farmers of the nation. No value can be attached to the numerous lives that were lost for want of some assurance from those in power. It is this aspect that the PMFBY has addressed. It has succeeded in conveying to the farmers that they will get an assured income for their harvest and will no longer have to go to moneylenders to mitigate their losses.

It has stopped the exploitation that the farmers of our nation were subjected to since pre-independence era.

Perhaps, the greatest achievement of the PMFBY, as told by many farmers who benefitted from the scheme, is that they have become self-reliant. They are no longer at the mercy of state administrations to dole out schemes in times of calamities. They can now, with their heads held high, demand rights that have historically been taken away from them. It is often said that agriculture is the backbone of Indian economy, now in all true respects that backbone had been strengthened. Indian agriculture can finally look into a future unaffected by natural calamities, where there is greenery all around.

***Lekshmi Parameswaran*** *is a researcher with a decade's experience in the field of policy studies and international relations. She is an alumnus of Jawaharlal Nehru University.*

# FARM-GATE TO MARKET: POST-HARVEST TECHNOLOGIES AND STORAGE INFRASTRUCTURE

*Sandip Das*

*From construction of state-of-the-art silos and cold storage facilities along with promotion of modern pre- and post-harvest techniques to creation of warehouses and food parks, the Modi government has given a huge thrust on boosting infrastructure for the food processing sector, which has helped farmers in better price realization through value addition.*

Mahendra Kharat, a farmer from the Ambad taluka of Aurangabad district of Maharashtra is currently engaged in taking care of 200 'Kesar' mango plants, which have reached flowering stages. Before harvesting the juicy Kesar mangoes, which command a premium price in the US, Japan and many European countries, Kharat strictly followed the norms (for use of agricultural inputs like fungicide, fertilizer and insecticides) given by the government agencies so that his plants would give quality fruits. Kharat recalls that last year, the exporter paid him a price of ₹150 per kg for Kesar mangoes against ₹90 per kg fetched five years back.

Since the last couple of years, due to sustained effort by the central government agencies such as Agricultural and Processed Food Export Development Authority (APEDA), National Plant Protection Organization (NPPO), India has managed to create an export market for Kesar, Alphonso and other varieties of mangoes. Incentivizing the creation of pack houses, thrust on the promotion of pre- and post-harvesting techniques for ensuring better fruit amongst farmers and setting up facilities of hot water treatment and irradiation (for mangoes bound for South Korea, Japan, the US and other European countries) have helped boost mango exports as well as farmers' income. Besides mangoes, India has emerged as one of the biggest exporters of rice during the last couple of years and has also emerged as a key exporter of several other agricultural commodities such as fresh and processed fruits and vegetables, processed meat and other value-added agricultural commodities mainly because of the government's focus on creating pre- and post-harvest infrastructure for facilitating exports as well as ensuring availability of safe and the quality produce in the domestic market.

The food processing and agriculture-based industries play a vital role in boosting farmers' income, thus ensuring growth in rural income. Since coming to power in 2014, Prime Minister Narendra Modi-led government has put emphasis on helping farmers not only through increasing the Minimum Support Price (MSP) for most of the notified agricultural commodities but also through support in creating infrastructure for promoting food processing and value addition.

Today, farmers in several states are not worried about fluctuations in the prices of agricultural commodities as they have been provided with the option of getting warehouse receipts after depositing their produce in registered cold storages. These receipts are being used in agricultural marketing for buying and selling, thus protecting the farmers against volatility in the prices.

Through several measures, the government has made food processing sector as thrust areas for infrastructure such as silos, cold chains and warehouse constructions. Most of the infrastructure creation in food processing sector is done through collaboration with private sector for effective time bound implementation.

Indian agriculture has witnessed several achievements in the last decades. From a country perennially witnessing food shortage till 1960s and early 1970s, India has emerged as one of the biggest producers of several commodities such as rice, wheat, pulses, oilseeds, sugarcane, cotton, milk, inland fish, fruits and vegetables in the world. India's achievement has been noteworthy especially in the last decade or so. The production of foodgrains in the country is estimated at a record 284.83 million tonnes for 2017–18. For 2018–19, the target for foodgrain production has been fixed at 290.25 million tones. The increase in agricultural and allied commodities output is possible mainly because of the factors such as expansion in irrigation, improvement in crop varieties, mechanization, application of technologies and investment made in creating infrastructure.

Following the harvest of a commodity, it undergoes series of post-harvest operations such as handling stages, storage, processing and packaging before it reaches the consumer. Each of these operations results in losses of the commodity. The losses are caused by moisture, temperature and biological agents such as insects, rodents, birds and storage fungi. Thus, the post-harvest losses are the critical component of the entire agricultural value chain—from the farm gate to the market. The lesser the losses, the better is the availability of the commodity. The knowledge of the extent of these losses and their reasons will help in making strategies for reducing the losses.

A study was conducted by the Indian Council of Agricultural Research-Central Institute of Post Harvest Engineering and Technology (ICAR-CIPHET), Ludhiana, which was funded by the Ministry of Food Processing Industries (MoFPI) in 2012–15 to assess the extent of harvest and post-harvest losses in 45 crops and livestock produce. The study has estimated that the annual value of harvest and post-harvest losses of major agricultural produces at national level was of the order of ₹92,651 crore, which were calculated using the production data of 2012–13 at 2014 wholesale prices.

**Table 1**

| *Crops* | *Cumulative Wastage (%)* |
|---|---|
| Cereals | 4.65–5.99 |
| Pulses | 6.36–8.41 |
| Oil Seeds | 3.08–9.96 |
| Fruits and Vegetables | 4.58–15.88 |
| Milk | 0.92 |
| Fisheries (Inland) | 5.23 |
| Fisheries (Marine) | 10.52 |
| Meat | 2.71 |
| Poultry | 6.74 |

Only 2 per cent of the country's agriculture produce is processed due to lack of processing facilities, infrastructure and technology. Only 7 per cent of the total Indian perishable produce is processed, which is extremely low compared to countries such as the US (65 per cent), Philippines (78 per cent) and China (23 per cent). Realizing the need for improving the capacity of the food processing industry, the government has taken several initiatives to stimulus the growth of the sector. The food processing sector has emerged as an important segment of the Indian economy in terms of its contribution to GDP, employment and investment. During 2015–16, the sector constituted as much as 9.1 and 8.6 per cent of Gross Value Added (GVA) in manufacturing and agriculture sector, respectively.

PM Narendra Modi's government has set a goal of doubling the farm incomes by 2022 and is working with multi-modal focus towards achieving the same. From seeds and soil to access to markets, the focus has been on reforms across the agricultural cycle. There is also a renewed focus on allied activities, to aid the incomes of the farmers.

One of the significant initiatives of the government has been the Mega Food Parks scheme. The aim is to establish mega food clusters in India. The scheme is based on the cluster approach for developing food processing industries. The aim is to provide modern infrastructure facilities for food processing along the value chain from the farm to the market.

It has been the focus of the government to promote food processing industry in the country for reducing wastage of agricultural produce and minimizing post-harvest losses. The MoFPI has taken up implementation of various central sector programmes such as the scheme for the development of infrastructure for food processing having components of mega food parks, integrated cold chains, value addition and preservation infrastructure and modernization of abattoirs and the scheme for quality assurance, codex standards, research and development and other promotional activities.

## MEGA FOOD PARKS

The MoFPI has been implementing mega food park and cold chain schemes for setting up of food processing infrastructure since 2008. However, the setting up of food parks acquired momentum post 2014. The focus of MoFPI is on boosting the food processing industry so that agriculture sector grows exponentially and becomes a major contributor in doubling the farmers' income by 2022 (as announced by the government). This sector aims to contribute to the 'Make in India' initiative of the government. The mega food park scheme is being implemented for promoting value addition in the agriculture sector and for reducing food wastage at each stage of the supply chain with particular focus on perishables.

Through the creation of mega food parks, modern infrastructure facilities are made available for food processing along the value chain from farm to market with strong forward and backward linkages through a cluster-based approach. Common facilities and enabling infrastructure are created at the central processing centre and the facilities for primary processing and storage are created near the farm in the form of primary processing centres and collection centres. The scheme envisages a one-time capital grant of 50 per cent of the project cost (excluding land cost) subject to a maximum of ₹50 crore in general areas and 75 per cent of the project cost (excluding land cost) subject to a ceiling of ₹50 crore in difficult and hilly areas of northeast region including Sikkim, Jammu and Kashmir (J&K), Himachal Pradesh and Uttarakhand.

The functioning of mega food parks is closely monitored by the MoFPI through a well-established mechanism as per the scheme guidelines. This includes detailed scrutiny of the progress reports received from the Special Purpose Vehicle (SPV) formed for implementation, verification of the claims by the Project Management

Consultant (PMC) and Programme Management Agency (PMA), assessment of the progress through site visits by PMA and officers of the ministry, periodic review meetings in the ministry, etc.

Each food park is expected to have around 30–35 food processing units, an aggregate investment of ₹250 crore, expected annual turnover of about ₹450–500 crore and generation of direct and indirect employment for around 30,000 people. As on 31 December 2018, the government has sanctioned setting up of 42 mega food parks. Currently, 14 food parks are in operation across the country.

**Table 2: Status of Implementation of 42 Mega Food Park Projects as on 30.09.29.019**

| *Sr. No.* | *Project Name* | *State* | *Status* |
|---|---|---|---|
| 1 | Srini Food Park Pvt. Ltd., Chittoor | Andhra Pradesh | Completed |
| 2 | Godavari Mega Aqua Park Pvt. Ltd., West Godavari | Andhra Pradesh | Under Implementation |
| 3 | Andhra Pradesh Industrial Infrastructure Corporation (APIIC), Krishna | Andhra Pradesh | Under Implementation |
| 4 | Rongoge Mega Food Park Pvt. Ltd, Papum Pare | Arunachal Pradesh | SPV is in the process of meeting the conditions for "Final Approval" |
| 5 | North East Mega Food Park Ltd., Nalbari | Assam | Operational |

| | | | |
|---|---|---|---|
| 6 | Pristine Mega Food Park Pvt. Ltd., Khagaria | Bihar | Under Implementation |
| 7 | Indus Best Mega Food Park Pvt. Ltd., Raipur | Chhattisgarh | Under Implementation |
| 8 | Gujarat Agro Infrastructure Mega Food Park Pvt. Ltd., Surat | Gujarat | Under Implementation |
| 9 | Fanidhar Mega Food Park Pvt. Limited, Mehsana | Gujarat | Under Implementation |
| 10 | Haryana State Industrial & Infra Dev. Corp Limited (HSIIDC), Sonipat | Haryana | Under Implementation |
| 11 | Haryana State Coop. Supply and Marketing Federation Ltd (HAFED), Rohtak | Haryana | SPV is in the process of meeting the conditions for release of 1st installment. |
| 12 | Cremica Food Park Pvt. Ltd., Una | Himachal Pradesh | Under Implementation |
| 13 | RFK Greens Food Park Pvt. Ltd., Pulwama | Jammu and Kashmir | Under Implementation |
| 14 | Jharkhand Mega Food Park Pvt. Ltd., Ranchi | Jharkhand | Operational |
| 15 | Integrated Food Park Pvt. Ltd., Tumkur | Karnataka | Completed |

| | | | |
|---|---|---|---|
| 16 | Favorich Infra Pvt Ltd., Mandya | Karnataka | Under Implementation |
| 17 | Kerala State Industrial Dev Corpt Ltd (KSIDC), Alappuzha | Kerala | Under Implementation |
| 18 | Kerala Industrial Infra. Development Corpt. (KINFRA), Palakkad | Kerala | Under Implementation |
| 19 | Indus Mega Food Park Pvt. Ltd., Khargoan | Madhya Pradesh | Completed |
| 20 | Avantee Mega Food Park Pvt. Ltd., Dewas | Madhya Pradesh | Under Implementation |
| 21 | Paithan Mega Food Park Ltd., Aurangabad | Maharashtra | Ready for operational |
| 22 | Satara Mega Food Park Pvt. Ltd., Satara | Maharashtra | Operational |
| 23 | Wardha Mega Food Park Pvt. Ltd, Wardha | Maharashtra | Under Implementation |
| 24 | Zoram Mega Food Park Pvt. Ltd., Aizawl | Mizoram | Ready for operational |
| 25 | Doys Agri Resources Pvt Ltd, Dimapur | Nagaland | Under Implementation |
| 26 | Odisha Industrial Infrastructure Development Corporation (IDCO), Khurda | Odisha | Under Implementation |

| | | | |
|---|---|---|---|
| 27 | MITS Mega Food Park Ltd., Rayagada | Odisha | Operational |
| 28 | International Mega Food Park Ltd. , Fazilka | Punjab | Operational(Agenda for closure is being processed) |
| 29 | Punjab Agro Industries Corporation Ltd., (PAIC) Ludhiana | Punjab | Under Implementation |
| 30 | The Sukjhit Starch & Chemical Limited, Kapurthala | Punjab | Under Implementation |
| 31 | Greentech Mega Food Park Pvt. Ltd., Ajmer | Rajasthan | Operational |
| 32 | Smart Agro Industries Corporation Pvt. Ltd., Nizamabad | Telangana | Under Implementation |
| 33 | Telangana State Industrial Infrastructure Corporation Ltd., Khammam | Telangana | Under Implementation |
| 34 | Raaga Mayuri Agrovet Pvt. Ltd., GadwalJogula mba | Telangana | Under Implementation |
| 35 | Basavashakti Mega Food Park Pvt. Ltd, Sangareddy | Telangana | SPV is in the process of meeting the conditions for release of 1st installment |
| 36 | Sikaria Mega Food Park Pvt. Ltd., West Tripura | Tripura | Ready for operational |

| | | | |
|---|---|---|---|
| 37 | Patanjali Food & Herbal Park Pvt. Ltd., Haridwar | Uttrakhand | Completed |
| 38 | Himalayan Food Park Pvt Ltd, Udham Singh Nagar | Uttrakhand | Operational |
| 39 | VindhyachalAt tivo Food Park Pvt. Ltd,Mirzapu | Uttar Pradesh | SPV is in the process of meeting the conditions for "Final Approval" |
| 40 | Overseas Infrast Alliance (India) Pvt. Ltd, Mathura | Uttar Pradesh | SPV is in the process of meeting the conditions for "Final Approval" |
| 41 | Patanjali Food & Herbal Park Noida Pvt Ltd GautamBudh Nagar | Uttar Pradesh | SPV is in the process of meeting the conditions for release of 1st installment. |
| 42 | Jangipur Bengal Mega Food Park Ltd., Murshidabad | West Bengal | Operational |

In the coming years, mega food parks would generate huge employment opportunities at the local level and boost the food processing industry in the country. The NDA government, in its manifestos, had talked about incentivizing the setting up of food processing industry for providing better income for the farmers as well as for creating jobs.

In August 2017, the cabinet committee on economic affairs, chaired by Prime Minister Narendra Modi, had approved the renaming of the new central sector scheme—Scheme for Agro-Marine Processing and Development of Agro-Processing Clusters (SAMPADA)—as the PMKSY. The PMKSY is being implemented during 2016–20 coterminous with the 14th finance commission cycle. The key objective of PMKSY is to supplement agriculture, modernize food processing and decrease agri-waste.

The PMKSY is an umbrella scheme incorporating ongoing schemes of the MoFPI such as mega food parks, integrated cold chain and value addition infrastructure, food safety and quality assurance infrastructure. This also includes new schemes like infrastructure for agro-processing clusters, creation of backward and forward linkages, creation and expansion of food processing and preservation capacities.

The PMKSY, with an allocation of ₹6,000 crore, is expected to leverage investment of ₹31,400 crore. It would entail handling of 334 lakh tonne of agro-produce valuing ₹1,04,125 crore, which would benefit 20 lakh farmers and generate around 5.3 lakh direct or indirect employment in the country by the year 2019–20.

The PMKSY is a comprehensive package designed to result in creation of modern infrastructure with efficient supply chain management from farm gate to retail outlet in addition to setting up of food processing units. For mega food parks and agro-processing clusters, all common infrastructure facilities such as storage, including cold storage, ripening and drying chambers, primary processing and raw material collection centers, food testing laboratories, etc., are created which can be used by the food processing units set up inside the parks and agro-processing clusters.

The standard design factory inside the parks can cater to the needs of the entrepreneurs or farmers who can process their raw material on plug-and-play basis without setting up of separate food processing units. The scheme's components such as integrated cold chain and value addition infrastructure and creation of backward and forward linkages provide seamless linkage between the farmers and the food processing industries on one hand and the consumers on the other.

The PMKSY is a big step towards doubling of farmers' income, providing better prices to farmers and creating huge employment opportunities, especially in the rural areas. It is a comprehensive package for creation of modern infrastructure with efficient supply chain management from farm gate to retail outlet. Besides providing a big boost to the growth of food processing sector in the country, it also helps in reducing the wastage of agricultural produce, increasing the processing level, enhancing the export of the processed foods and enabling availability of hygienic and nutritious food to consumers at an affordable price.

**Table 3: Estimated Number of Jobs Created under PMKSY since 2016**

| | *Direct* | *Indirect* | *Contractual* | *Total* |
|---|---|---|---|---|
| 2016–17 | 286 | | | 286 |
| 2017–18 | 157 | | | 157 |
| 2018–19 | 6,741 | 44,940 | 1,16,598 | 1,68,279 |

*Source: Lok Sabha questions/answers 18 December 2018*

As of 31 December 2018, the government has approved 304 proposals for establishing cold chain projects across the country with the financial assistance of the MoFPI under the scheme for Integrated Cold Chain and Value Addition Infrastructure. Dr Saumitra Chaudhuri Committee in 2012, constituted by the then planning commission, had indicated cold storage requirement of 61 million tonne. The current capacity of cold storage in India is estimated at 36.61 million tonne. Through the MoFPI schemes, 4.87 lakh tonne of cold storage capacity has been created in the last four years. One hundred and thirty-five cold chain projects have been completed.

According to government officials, a capacity of 11.58 lakh tonne would be created when all the projects approved by the MoFPI will be completed.

There are several other incentives provided by the government to promote creation of cold chain infrastructure:

1. Services of pre-conditioning, pre-cooling, ripening, waxing, retail packing, labelling of fruits and vegetables have been exempted from service tax in Budget 2015–16.
2. Loans to food and agro-based processing units and cold chains have been classified under 'agriculture activities' for Priority Sector Lending (PSL) as per the revised RBI guidelines issued in 2015.
3. Under Section 35 AD of the Income Tax Act 1961, deduction to the extent of 150 per cent is allowed for expenditure incurred on investment for (i) setting up and operating a cold chain facility; and (ii) setting up and operating warehousing facility for storage of agricultural produce.
4. The government has extended project imports benefits to cold storage, cold room (including for farm level pre-cooling) or industrial projects for preservation, storage or processing of agricultural, apiary, horticultural, dairy, poultry, aquatic and marine produce and meat. Consequently, all goods related to food processing, imported as part of the project, irrespective of their tariff classification, would be entitled to uniform assessment at concessional basic customs duty of 5 per cent.
5. Refrigeration machineries and parts used for installation of cold storage, cold room or refrigerated vehicle, for the preservation, storage, transport or processing of agricultural, apiary, horticultural, dairy, poultry, aquatic and marine produce and

meat are exempted from excise duty.

6. Construction, erection, commissioning or installation of original works pertaining to post-harvest storage infrastructure for agricultural produce including cold storages for such purposes are exempted from service tax.
7. Capital investment in the creation of modern storage capacity has been made eligible for the Viability Gap Funding scheme of the finance ministry. Cold chain and post-harvest storage has been recognized as an infrastructure sub-sector.
8. The government has allowed 100 per cent Foreign Direct Investment (FDI) in trading, including through e-commerce, in respect of food products manufactured and/or produced in India. This will benefit farmers immensely and will create back-end infrastructure and significant employment opportunities.
9. A special fund of ₹2,000 crore in National Bank for Agriculture and Rural Development (NABARD) has been set-up to make available affordable credit at concessional rate of interest to designated food parks and agro processing units.

## WAREHOUSING AND NEGOTIABLE WAREHOUSING RECEIPT

The Reserve Bank of India (RBI) conducted a comprehensive all-India rural credit survey in 1951 under the direction of a committee headed by Mr A.D. Gorwala. The recommendations of the survey committee, which submitted its report in 1954, set the pace and directions for the subsequent years not only for the bank's agricultural credit policy but also for the related polices of the central and the state governments.

The committee had made the following important recommendations to the government:

1. Create scientific storage facilities for the farmers near their doorstep to avoid storage losses in agricultural produce which were estimated to be around 9.6 per cent at that time.
2. Create a negotiable warehouse receipt system in the country to facilitate credit to the farmers.

Decades later, the Ministry of Agriculture had appointed an expert committee on 19 December 2000 to review the present system of agricultural marketing in the country and to recommend measures to make the system more efficient and competitive under the chairmanship of Mr Shankar Lal Guru, a noted economist. The committee, in its report dated 29 June 2001, had suggested various legislative reforms as well as the reorientation of the policies and programmes for the development and strengthening of agricultural marketing in the country. One of the key recommendations of the committee chaired by Guru was the introduction of a system of negotiable warehouse receipts for agricultural commodities in the country to improve credit delivery, better loan recovery and convenience in commodity management.

Warehouse Receipts (WR) are negotiable instruments backed by the underlying commodities and are an integral part of the marketing and financial systems globally as they can be traded, sold, swapped and used as collateral to support borrowing or accepting delivery against a derivative instrument such as a futures contract. In developing countries, the high real interest rates for agricultural loans are often linked to perceived risks. Collateralizing agricultural inventories will lead to an increase in the availability of credit, reduce its cost, and mobilize external financial resources for the sector. It contributes to the creation of cash and forward markets, and thus enhances competition and reduces transaction costs.

WR can be combined with price-hedging instruments such as

a put option which could induce banks to reduce the margin on their lending. A functioning WR system also obviates the need for governments to take physical inventories to support prices as they could simply purchase WR when the prices fall below a certain minimum. The governments also need not hold physical stocks for ensuring food security; they could simply hold WRs.

In 2011, Minister of Consumer Affairs, Food and Public Distribution, Professor K.V. Thomas launched the Negotiable Warehouse Receipt System (NWRS). Under the NWRS, farmers could seek loans from banks against the WRs issued to them against their storage. These receipts issued by the warehouses registered with the Warehousing Development and Regulatory Authority (WDRA) became a fully negotiable instrument backed by central legislation. The WDRA was set up by the government in October 2010 to regulate and develop warehouses in the country.

The committee for Strengthening Negotiable Warehouse Receipts by the WDRA had recommended Electronic Warehouse Receipts (EWRs) in 2015. It stated that the EWRs provide faster movement of information and automatic creation of audit trail. The EWRs can break barriers and promote national market in agricultural goods to benefit farmers. They would promote proper grading, inspection and weighment.

The EWRs will help farmers/depositors to: have access to a large number of buyers nationwide; have better bargaining powers; realize higher prices by selling graded produce; have their prices quoted and immediate payment received and avoid distress sales by getting loans from banks against EWRs.

In 2017, Minister of Consumer Affairs, Food and Public Distribution Ram Vilas Paswan, launched negotiable WRs in electronic format that farmers could use to avail bank credit easily and without fear of losing or misusing it. 'Till now, the receipts were issued manually. Now, it will be given in an electronic format, which will not only benefit the farmers, but also the banks and other stakeholders,' Paswan had said. He had also stated that farmers would not have to worry about losing the receipt—which has details of the quantity, quality and the warehouse where the commodity is stored—as it will be uploaded online and will be accessible to banks while sanctioning a loan.

In the last few years, several measures have been taken by the WDRA in simplifying the warehouse registration rules, digitizing the entire process of registration, monitoring and surveillance as well as creation and management of Negotiable Warehouse Receipts (NWRs) in electronic form through two repositories. The e-NWRs reduce the chances of any tempering, mutilation, fudging, loss or damage and with no possibility of any multiple financing. Hence, these e-NWRs will not only facilitate easy pledge financing by the banks and other financial institutions but also smooth trading on various trading centres like commodity exchanges, electronic National Agriculture Markets (e-NAM) and other electronic platforms.

There are about 55,000 warehouses in the country, out of which only 735 have the capacity of 6.6 million tonnes and a valid registration with the WDRA. Most of them are located in Gujarat, Maharashtra, Madhya Pradesh and Rajasthan. The government officials say that the process of registration of warehouses with WDRA has been simplified. The new rules would result in an increase in the number of warehouses registered with WDRA which would help large number of farmers in the next few years.

## CONSTRUCTION OF WAREHOUSES AND SILOS

The government is deploying latest scientific technology in foodgrain preservation and distribution of foodgrain through

Public Distribution System (PDS). To prevent the post-harvest losses of foodgrains, a number of warehouses have been established by the Food Corporation of India (FCI), Central Warehouse Corporation (CWC) and State Warehouse Corporations across various states. Depending on the requirement in specific areas and for modernization of storage facilities, the government has been implementing following schemes for construction of godowns and silos in the country.

## PRIVATE ENTREPRENEURS GUARANTEE SCHEME

Under this Scheme, which was formulated in 2008, storage capacity is created by private parties, CWC and the state government agencies for guaranteed hiring by FCI. A capacity of 14.18 million tonne has been created so far. Under this scheme, no funds are allocated by the government for construction of godowns and full investment is done by the private parties, CWC, and the state agencies by arranging their own funds and land. After a godown is constructed and taken over by FCI, the storage charges are paid to the investor for a guaranteed period of 9 or 10 years irrespective of the quantum of foodgrains stored.

## CENTRAL SECTOR SCHEME

This scheme is implemented in the north-eastern states along with Himachal Pradesh, Jharkhand and Kerala. The funds are released by the government to FCI and also directly to the state governments for construction of godowns. A total capacity of 1,91,180 tonne has been created by FCI and the state governments during the last five years (2013–2018).

## CONSTRUCTION OF SILOS

In addition to conventional godowns, the construction of steel silos has been undertaken in Public Private Partnership (PPP) mode for modernizing storage infrastructure and improving the shelf life of the stored foodgrains. As on 31 October 2018, a capacity of 11.75 lakh tonne silos has been created. Foodgrains stored in silos are transported in bulk, to reduce the losses due to theft and pilferage. The construction of silos is being carried out using three models—viability gap funding (VGF), without the VGF cover and through CWC, central railside warehousing corporation/state government-owned agencies.

Under the VGF plan, silos would be constructed on the FCI land while the corporation would provide guarantee of rentals for 30 years for silo operation for the private sector to recover capital investment and maintenance charges. Besides, there is a provision for 20 per cent VGF from the government as per infrastructure projects norms. All the silos would have the facility of 'railway siding' for easier transportation of grain.

In case of the non-VGF norm, the private sector would create silos on its own land while FCI would provide guarantee of rentals for grain storage for 30 years while silos owned by the state government-owned agencies like CWC would be used by FCI for grain storage.

Because of the creation of storage facilities, the foodgrains procured from the farmers by paying Minimum Support Price (MSP) by FCI and the state government corporations are scientifically stored with various preservation measures such as fumigation and treatment with pesticides. Only small quantities of foodgrains may become non-issuable due to various reasons such as natural calamities, damages in transit, negligence of officials, etc.

**Table 4: Accrual of Damaged Foodgrains in FCI during the Last Three Years**

| | *Off-take quantity (excluding DCP states) in lakh tonne* | *Damage accrual in FCI (in lakh tonne)* | *% Damaged foodgrain against off-take quantity* |
|---|---|---|---|
| 2016–17 | 473.31 | 0.09 | 0.02 |
| 2017–18 | 452.16 | 0.027 | 0.006 |
| 2018–19 (1 December 2018) | 296.40 | 0.04 | 0.01 |

*Source: Lok Sabha questions 8 January 2019*

In 2015, the Punjab government had disposed of 1.93 lakh tonne of 'rotten' wheat which could have fed a large number of people. Because of the lack of a scientific storage capacity, the wheat stocks got spoiled. However, due to the government's thrust on creating modern silos, for last two years, those at Kotkapura, Faridkot district (25,000-tonne capacity) and Sahnewal, Ludhiana district (50,000-tonne capacity) are being used for storing wheat by the state government agencies. Storage in steel silos, which involves automated merchandised handling of grains, results in virtually 'zero' loss and the grain can be stored for at least a couple of years. The thrust of the government has been to eliminate all the temporary storage facilities such as covered and plinth (CAP), where the grain can be stored for only a few months. This has resulted in a virtual elimination of grain losses, thus, preventing financial losses.

## PREVENTION OF CROP AND POST-HARVEST LOSSES

Crop losses can happen due to biotic and abiotic factors. Biotic factors include pest and disease and other vertebrate pests. Abiotic factors include droughts, floods, extreme weather conditions such as hailstorms, extreme temperature, etc. To prevent crop losses due to pest and diseases, the Department of Agriculture, Cooperation and Farmers' Welfare regulates the manufacture, storage and use of pesticides through the Insecticide Act 1968 and promotes Integrated Pest Management (IPM).

To promote IPM activities, the central government established Central Integrated Pest Management Centres (CIPMCs) in the state of Rajasthan (one each at Jaipur and Sriganganagar). In addition, 34 CIPMCs have also been established in all the states, including one union territory. The purpose of CIPMCs is to conduct regular pest surveillance and monitoring to assess pest/disease situation and issue advisories for timely pest management along with measures to prevent crop losses. The CIPMCs also promote IPM approaches with emphasis on biological control and also produce various biocontrol agents and provide to farmers free of cost.

Annually, about 760 Farmer's Field Schools (FFSs) have been conducted and about 30 farmers have been trained in each FFS. In addition, CIPMCs conduct Human Resource Development programmes of two and five days and Season Long Training (SLT) programmes on major agricultural/horticultural crops throughout the country. The Central Insecticides Board and Registration Committee (CIBRC), under the Directorate of Plant Protection, Quarantine and Storage (DPPQS) has been established to ensure the availability of safer and effective pesticides by implanting regulatory provisions under the Insecticide Act 1968. The IPM package of practices has been developed for 89 crops.

## OPERATION GREENS

In the budget of 2018–19, a new scheme called 'Operation Greens' was announced by Finance Minister Arun Jaitley on the line of 'Operation Flood', with an outlay of ₹500 crore to promote Farmer Producers Organizations (FPO), agri-logistics, processing facilities and professional management. The scheme is being implemented in the 'Tomato, Onion and Potato (TOP)' producing nine states on pilot basis. Recently, the guideline of Operation Greens was released by the MoFPI.

The major objectives of Operation Greens include:

1. Enhancing value realization of TOP farmers by targeted interventions to strengthen TOP production clusters and their FPOs, and linking/connecting them with the market.
2. Price stabilization for producers and consumers by proper production planning in the TOP clusters and introduction of dual use varieties.
3. Reduction in post-harvest losses by creation of farm gate infrastructure, development of suitable agro-logistics, creation of appropriate storage capacity linking consumption centres.
4. Increase in food processing capacities and value addition in TOP value chain with firm linkages with production clusters. Setting up of a market intelligence network to collect and collate real-time data on demand and supply and price of TOP crops.

The key strategy for Operation Greens includes a series of measures:

1. Short-term price stabilization measures:
   The National Agricultural Cooperative Marketing Federation of India (NAFED) will be the nodal agency to implement price

stabilization measures. The MoFPI will provide 50 per cent of the subsidy on two components: transportation of TOP crops from production to storage; and, hiring of appropriate storage facilities for TOP crops.

2. Long-term integrated value chain development projects:
   i. Capacity building of FPOs and their consortium
   ii. Ensuring quality production
   iii. Creation of post-harvest processing facilities
   iv. Agri-logistics
   v. Marketing at the consumption points and creation
   vi. Management of e-platform for demand and supply management of TOP crops.

The pattern of assistance will comprise of grants-in-aid at the rate of 50 per cent of the eligible project cost in all areas, subject to maximum ₹50 crore per project. However, in case where Project Implementation Agency (PIA) is/are Farmer Producer Organisations, the grant-in-aid will be at the rate of 70 per cent of the eligible project cost in all the areas, subject to a maximum of ₹50 crore per project.

The eligible organizations would include state agriculture and other marketing federations, FPOs, cooperatives, companies, self-help groups, food processors, logistic operators, service providers, supply chain operators, retail and wholesale chains and central and state governments, and their entities/organizations. These will be eligible to participate in the programme and avail financial assistance.

## PRODUCTION CLUSTERS OF TOP CROPS UNDER OPERATION GREENS

Tomato:
Andhra Pradesh (Chittoor and Anantpur districts), Karnataka (Kolar and Chikkaballapur districts), Odisha (Mayurbhanj and Keonjhar districts) and Gujarat (Sabarkantha district)

Onion:
Maharashtra (Nashik), Karnataka (Gadag and Dharwad), Gujarat (Bhavnagar and Amreli) and Bihar (Nalanda)

Potato:
Uttar Pradesh (Firozabad, Hathras, Aligarh, Farrukhabad and Kannauj), West Bengal (Hooghly and Purba Bardhaman), Bihar (Nalanda) and Gujarat (Banaskantha and Sabarkantha)

Ensuring the availability of food to the Indian population will be a major challenge in future with decreasing agriculture land and ever-increasing population. One way of achieving this target is to efficiently use the food materials produced; also, saving them as much as possible is another key factor. Thus, it becomes necessary to know about the route/channels through which crop and livestock produce reaches the consumers. The Modi government has embarked upon the right path of saving the leakages and providing longer life to the produce. This will prove to be a milestone in ensuring a better income to the farmers.

***Sandip Das** is a senior journalist who writes on agriculture and food security. He is an alumnus of Jawaharlal Nehru University.*

# MARKETING REVOLUTION: eNAM AND MARKETING PLATFORMS

*Rajesh Singh*

About 90 km from Delhi is the town of Charkhi Dadri in Haryana. It has a history—the nawab of the place, who had expressed token allegiance to the Delhi ruler Bahadur Shah Zafar surrendered to the British in the 1857 revolt and was packed off to Lahore thereafter. The British awarded the small princely state to Raja Swarup Singh, the king of Jind, for his services to the East India Company. Seven years later, his descendant faced revolt from many villages in the region; the rebellion was brutally crushed and the villages that participated in the audacity were razed to the ground. Once a part of Bhiwani district, Charkhi Dadri is today a full-fledged district in itself, with the town bearing the same name serving as its headquarters.

The place came into national limelight in 1996 when two foreign airlines collided in mid-air, above the village, and crashed into the fields below. All 349 people on board the two aircrafts perished in the terrible accident. It remains one of the world's biggest aviation disasters and the worst that has happened in Indian skies. But, there is also a happier reason to remember Charkhi Dadri—the famous Phogat sisters, who have blazed a trail in the world of wrestling, hail from a village in this district.

More recently, in May 2018, Charkhi Dadri shot into the news for a very different reason—its foodgrain and vegetable market (mandi) witnessed an unprecedented scene as the price of tomato crashed to less than one rupee a kilogram. A truck of tomatoes sold for as low as ₹6 for a crate of 25 kg in the wholesale market during bidding, which worked out to be 24 paise per kilogram. The mandi was flush with tomatoes strewn all over, with no takers. The tomatoes then made their way to cow-shelters, but even the cows reportedly developed digestive complications after consuming the abundant vegetable!

It was a severe crisis for the farmers who had invested heavily (approx. ₹4 to grow a kilogram of tomato) in the produce's cultivation. Those who had standing crops were compelled to let them wither. The government had to intervene by fixing support prices and ensuring cash transfers to make up for any loss that the farmers suffered in case they sold the crop for less than ₹4 a kilogram. The main cause of the crisis had been a bumper harvest of tomato in Haryana. Ordinarily, this should have been good news for the farmers and the traders, since it promised them a huge return nationwide. Unfortunately for them, other states, which were markets for tomato from Haryana, had recorded a huge growth of the vegetable too and had no desire to absorb the import from Haryana. Across the country, some 270 million tonne of tomato had been harvested.

But, that was then; today, the Charkhi Dadri mandi wears a new look. There is the usual hustle-bustle, which is associated with a market that trades in foodgrain and other products—loaded tractors and small trucks make a beeline for the market, unload their produce and leave; the market is stacked with massive jute bags of foodgrain and cotton; and farmers, traders and commission agents move around, doing brisk business. But, even in the midst of the hectic activity, there is a kind of order, a level of silence not associated with markets brimming with raucous farmers seeking the best price and traders bidding for the most reasonable rates they can get the produce for. This is because the Charkhi Dadri mandi has been integrated into the e-National Agriculture Market (eNAM) system, where biddings are done online, thus cutting out the chaos and noise that are a result of voice biddings, not to mention heralding other benefits to every stakeholder. The most common crops traded here are wheat, mustard, cotton, gwar (used as fodder) and pearl millet (bajra). Besides the usual vegetables, turnips and cucumbers are also cultivated. A special mention must be made of matira, a kind of watermelon, which is a speciality and is largely grown in the Loharu tehsil.

*eNAM e-Auction hall at Charkhi Dadri, Haryana*

The Charkhi Dadri mandi is considered a 'model' market because it meets a set of criteria. Some of these are: handheld electronic devices at the entry gate; quality check machines inside to determine the moisture level in the produce; e-weighing machines inside the market (these are in addition to the weighbridge installed at the entry gate); a complete range of facilities such as high-speed Wi-Fi services (with a minimum of 5 to 8 kbps speed) and other infrastructure within the market complex such as toilet facilities, restrooms, etc.

Farmers registered at the Charkhi Dadri mandi do not generally have high debts (money taken as loans from various sources, primarily from the traders who recover the amount in the process of purchasing the produce from the farmers). An official of the Ministry of Agriculture, who was posted at the mandi, explained that the region had traditionally been a dry belt with poor irrigation facilities, and the farmers were never certain how their next crop would turn out to be. This uncertainty made them refrain from borrowing because they were not confident if they would be able to repay it on time. The situation has improved over the years. Irrigation facilities have got better and Charkhi Dadri is no longer a dry belt. But, the farmers have retained their reluctance for heavy borrowings and this has placed them on a stronger footing than their counterparts in the rest of the country.

Until the beginning of 2016, the Charkhi Dadri mandi was like any other market across the country that functioned as a part of the larger Agricultural Produce Market Committee (APMC) regime. Farmers arrived with their produce (kharif or rabi), wholesale buyers conducted voice bids (which were often rigged beforehand) and deals were struck. On rare occasions, money exchanged hands promptly, but conventionally, the payments were done to the farmers several weeks or months later, and that too in instalments. Needless to say, farmers were often left short-changed. Even the various reforms in the APMC set-up had failed to bring much relief to them. Things changed dramatically April 2016 onwards, when the eNAM concept was implemented. Online bidding and fund transfers not only led to transparency in dealings but also to prompt payments to the farmers.

However, Charkhi Dadri was not amongst the first two markets in Haryana, where eNAM was initiated as a pilot project; they were Karnal and Ellenabad. Once it came into the fold, the mandi took to the system like fish takes to water. Thanks to the eNAM portal of Charkhi Dadri APMC, Haryana became the first state to start online payment. As of 20 October 2018, Haryana had registered a national best with 15,486 e-payment invoices valued at ₹27.86 crore, which benefitted nearly 4,900 farmers. The momentum provided by the Charkhi Dadri mandi ensured that all 54 APMCs in Haryana would begin online payments through the eNAM platform. Nowadays, purchasers and commission agents are increasingly adopting e-auction mobile apps; traders and purchasers are also being encouraged to seek licences to operate at multiple mandis; and organizations representing rice, dal and oil millers are being persuaded to participate in the eNAM system with a view to broad-base the market for the producer-farmer and bring about an enhanced level of competitiveness which benefits both the producer (in terms of better monetary returns) and the purchaser (by way of better quality products). Farmers are also being shown the way to register at multiple eNAMs so that they can get the best price for their produce.

The Charkhi Dadri e-payment system has reasons to be proud. In the period from 14 April 2016 to 20 October 2018, it generated the maximum number of invoices for e-payments in all of Haryana—1,237. In terms of total value of transactions, it clocked ₹493.52 lakh, which was second only to Faridabad (₹554.90 lakh). In the quantity of transactions (measured in quintals of the produce handled), the Charkhi Dadri market was third in the state during the period mentioned above, with 12,458.56 quintals; Faridabad and Gurugram were first and second, respectively. It also did well in the number of participants in the eNAM system, both the traders and the farmers. While 56 traders associated themselves with the eNAM payment set-up, 366 farmers signed up for the same. Interestingly, Charkhi Dadri outperformed Bhiwani, of which it was once a part, in all parameters except in the number of traders that were part of the system, during the said period.

The eNAM works in a simple enough manner for the farmer and the trader—which is what the aim had been—functioning in the background to ease the wrinkles of logistical and other complexities; after all, the electronic market regime is less than three years old. At the Charkhi Dadri mandi, the farmer brings his produce in a vehicle. If he is already registered, he will possess a unique identity number, which he provides to the employee manning the gate. That identity number is quickly cross-checked on the computer (or a handheld device) and he is allowed entry. If the farmer has not registered, he can do so by providing the relevant documents, including his bank account number to which his sale income can be transferred; he will then get the unique identity number, which he needs to mention when he comes to transact business at later dates.

Once in, the farmer with his produce has to choose a commission agent of his choice. The commission agent's task at this first stage is to organize the unloading of the product and cleaning it (if needed) to enhance its value. That done, the trader steps in to evaluate the quality of the produce and mentally work out the price he would like to pay for the product. Of course, multiple traders assess the produce. Then comes e-bidding, which is done online with the help of specialized software. The highest bidder gets to buy the produce but not always, since the farmer has the option to reject the bid if he is unhappy with the price he is getting. The farmer can then wait for another day and another bid in the same market or a different one. In case he accepts a bid, the successful trader gets into the act. He acquires the services of the commission agent. In the first instance we had seen above, the commission agent is paid by the farmer for unloading and cleaning of the produce. But now, with the agent tasked with unloading and weighing the product, it becomes the trader's responsibility to effect the payment for the services. All of these transactions are done online.

It's the responsibility of the eNAM officials to ensure that the entire exercise, from the time the farmer arrives at the mandi to the time he leaves after the deal is done, is adhered to without glitches. There are established processes to facilitate that such as the Market Setup Report, which has details of the commission agent (also called the agent master), bag type, commodity, farmer's registration number, fee category, trader (also known as the trade master), etc. The Sale Bill reflects the deal done and has the following details: agreement number, agreement date, details of the seller, buyer, commission agent, the commodity, the price bid by the trader and accepted by the farmer, quantity of the produce sold and the break-up of the various charges paid, such as to the commission agent.

But, there are a few challenges too, which are being addressed. Trade is conducted in selective commodities, which restricts the scope of eNAM to bring about large-scale changes. Officials have been working with various stakeholders to broad-base the commodities profile and convince them to bring more products on the eNAM platform. Then, there is the issue of convincing farmers to use the eNAM platform more frequently for direct transfer of sale proceeds to their bank accounts. While the level of transactions pertaining to direct transfer of sale funds through eNAM has been good at Charkhi Dadri, a great number of such proceeds are done through challans, by which the farmer collects money from the buyer either in cash or requests direct deposit to an account that is not registered with the mandi on the eNAM system.

There could be various reasons why the farmers decide to skip the system. It could be because the farmer needs cash in hand on an immediate basis. It could also be that the farmer has loan instalments to settle and does not want the money transferred to his bank account registered with eNAM because part of it could be deducted by the bank against the pending loan amount. Mandi officials are working relentlessly to persuade the farmers to switch over to the eNAM direct payment system on a more extensive basis, and to this end various incentives are being offered. But, mindset changes take time to happen.

The potential for the expansion of fund transfers through eNAM at the Charkha Dadri mandi (and elsewhere) is enormous, which is evident from the figures that represent the overall APMC trade. The volume in APMC transactions at Charkha Dadri for the period 14 April 2016 to 20 October 2018 is as follows—in quantity, it's close to 17 lakh quintals, in rupee terms, it is a little over ₹448 crore. While these include the transactions that have resulted in direct fund transfer to the accounts of farmers through various apps such as Bharat Interface for Money (BHIM), even a cursory comparison of the exclusively eNAM figures to that of the overall APMC, one would be able to see that far more transactions have been done outside of the direct fund transfers through the eNAM platform. The number of buyers registered in the APMC trade during the above period was 210 (as against 56 who participated in the e-payment process), while the number of farmers registered in the APMC trade was 33,625 (as compared to 366 farmers who were part of the e-payment system).

The Charkhi Dadri mandi may not be among the biggest e-markets in the country in terms of sheer volume traded, but it has certainly shown the way in Haryana, and is reflective of the success of the eNAM project. It stands out also because, after having parted with Bhiwani and acquiring its own district identity, Charkhi Dadri had to combat issues of limited size and resources. Besides, the market is a good example of the enormous potential that the eNAM project has in bringing about positive changes in rural India. This was indeed the key aim which led to the conceptualization of eNAM under the Narendra Modi-led National Democratic Alliance (NDA) government and the scheme's rollout.

The Union Budgets of 2014–15 and 2015–16 provided the first clear hints of a major change in the functioning of APMC markets across the country. The budget announcements related to the establishment of an Agri-Tech Infrastructure Fund (ATIF) and the creation of an e-portal for the National Agriculture Market that would link farmers and traders within states as well as inter-state. The ATIF received a budget allocation of ₹200 crore to begin operations and the scheme envisaged the deployment of a common e-market platform—to be called eNAM—in 585 select regulated wholesale agricultural produce markets by March 2018. The overarching aim was to enhance farmer income through the following objectives:

1. To integrate markets—beginning at the state level and then taking the process forward across the country—through a common online market platform that would facilitate a pan-India trade in agricultural commodities
2. To streamline marketing and transaction procedures and

establish uniformity across all markets with a view to promote efficient functioning of these markets

3. To enhance better marketing avenues for both the seller (farmers) and the buyer (traders) through online access, removal of informal asymmetry between farmer and trader, better and real-time price discovery based on actual demand and supply, transparency in the auction process, ensuring price that is commensurate with quality and online payments to plug leakages and delays
4. To put in place quality-testing facilities that would help in better and well-informed biddings by the buyers
5. To promote stability in pricing and ensure availability of quality produce to the end consumer

Clearly, what was envisaged was nothing less than a revolutionary overhaul of the agricultural commodities' marketing mechanism—that too nationwide—and it needed an equally dramatic new ecosystem. The Small Farmers Agri-Business Consortium (SFAC) was mandated with the key task of implementation. It had to manage and seamlessly integrate both the virtual market (eNAM) and the backend 'physical' markets. The online process involved a one-time registration of farmers/sellers, creation and processing of details at the entry gate, weighing, quality checking, auctions/trade transactions, payments by buyers to sellers and other agencies involved in the train of transaction. The physical aspect dealt with the entire market flow of agricultural commodities. But, the implementation could proceed only after an online platform was created.

Experts were roped in to develop a special software for eNAM, which was provided free of cost to any market that opted to join the national network. Besides, any customization that was needed by a particular market was also assured. These were specialized jobs and the Union Ministry of Agriculture Department and Farmers' Welfare (which helmed the scheme) decided to rope in a private player—Hyderabad-based Nagarjuna Group—as its strategic partner after following the due process of selection. The private entity was asked to design, develop, test, implement, maintain, manage, enhance and modify the set of applications and modules of the eNAM platform across various markets in the country; in short, everything from administration to Management Information System (MIS).

The strategic partner was also made responsible for ensuring that software faults were resolved in a time-bound manner, data requests that were received from the SFAC were processed in a time-bound period, etc. Additionally, the private partner had the important task of marketing and publicizing the e-portal system among the various stakeholders, both present and potential, and of training personnel to adapt to the new regime.

The National Informatics Centre (NIC) was taken in as the technical partner for the project. It was made responsible for the following:

1. Hosting of the eNAM software and ensuring that it functioned uninterrupted on the MeghRaj cloud—an initiative for cloud computing
2. Providing and maintaining the necessary infrastructure, including virtual machines (servers), base operating systems, firewall, load balancers, SMS and e-mail services, etc.
3. Offering technical services to the SFAC on functional requirement specifications, software requirement specifications, process design document, etc.

The NIC was also opted as a member of the project monitoring committee with relation to all technical aspects of the scheme.

It should be evident from the above detailing that an enormous amount of back grounding happened before the eNAM's rollout. Given the unprecedented nature, glitches were bound to occur, and they did. But, they were also tackled promptly, with everyone learning more than they knew, in the process. And yet, what we have encountered so far has been largely technical in nature; the real challenge in selling the concept to stakeholders—including the various states—and preparing the administrative groundwork that would take care of the nitty-gritty of assistance under the scheme; the eligibility criteria which needed to be met to get such assistance; the process for the approval of proposals and release of assistance; budget provisions and management; and the precise role of the various agencies involved with the project. We have already detailed the task of the NIC and the strategic partner, but there are other members too.

The Ministry of Agriculture published the operational guidelines for the promotion of eNAM in September 2016. Among other things, the guidelines included the eligibility criteria for getting assistance under the scheme. It emphasized the need for states and union territories to initiate APMC reforms (agriculture is a state subject) in three primary areas to qualify for assistance in operating the e-portal trading system. The first was to have a single trading licence that would be valid throughout the state. The second was to ensure that there was a single point levy of market fee across the state. And, the third was to have the state agriculture marketing department or similar body, which would directly facilitate the provision for e-auction/e-trading. The operational guidelines also observed that appropriate state legislation or an executive order would be needed to establish a single trading licence across the state. Not just that, states would have to take care that prohibitive practices such as charging high-security deposit fees or stipulating a minimum quantity eligible for trading are avoided.

With the guidelines for assistance made clear, the other important step was to clear the assistance. For this purpose, a Project Appraisal Committee (PAC) was formed, and it was to this PAC that states/union territories could apply for approval of detailed project reports and grants under the scheme. A prescribed format was prepared to facilitate the approval with complete transparency. Senior officials of the Ministry of Agriculture were made members of the approval panel. The SFAC became the lead agency to helm the eNAM project with support from the strategic partner. Nagarjuna Fertilizers and Chemicals Limited was appointed as the strategic partner for an initial period of five years from the date of signing the contract.

It would be evident from this brief overview that a great deal of back office work had gone into the implementation of the eNAM scheme. A new work culture, a fresh approach to marketing of agricultural produce, a novel attempt at enhancing the income of farmers—all of this and more drove officials at various levels to make eNAM a success. So far, more than one crore farmers have been registered on the eNAM portal nationwide. The registration of farmers increased drastically from 37.96 lakh during 2016–17 to over 50 lakh during 2017–18. As on 23 March 2018, eNAM had completed the integration of 585 regulated markets on the e-market platform in 16 states and two union territories—this was ahead of the targeted date of 31 March the same year.

Now, the plan is to integrate 415 more markets by March 2020. In totality, more than a lakh traders and over 66,000 commission agents have been registered. Initially started with just 25 commodities, the e-trade facility now covers 114 commodities. As on 30 September 2018, trade recorded on the eNAM portal stood at a value of ₹50,575 crore, and in terms of volume it was more than two crore tonne. The average number of bids per lot across the country too has gone up from 2.4 bids per lot in 2016–17 to 3.4 bids in 2017–18, thus demonstrating the enthusiasm of traders for the e-market portal. It also shows that the portal is fetching better returns to the seller (farmer). It is a growing phenomenon—in September 2018,* the nationwide average bid stood at 4.3 per lot.

The opting of more states into the e-integrated system to facilitate inter-mandi trade is also a work in progress. So far, the states of Andhra Pradesh, Chhattisgarh, Telangana, Haryana, Madhya Pradesh, Uttarakhand and Uttar Pradesh have conducted inter-market dealings. A pilot project was launched in Khammam district of Andhra Pradesh to have inter-state trade as well. Various states have undertaken measures to promote and popularize the eNAM platform, with Uttar Pradesh celebrating eNAM Day on the 14th of every month.

With the benefits of a unified market for agricultural commodities managed through an e-portal being so obvious, why was the system not put in place years ago? The equally obvious answer is—lack of political will. The government of PM Narendra Modi, since its inception, had resolved to put the farming sector on the priority that it deserved, realizing that the aim of a new India could not be achieved if the agricultural economy was allowed to languish. Over the last four years, the budget for the agriculture sector has been nearly doubled to ₹2.12 lakh crore. Various steps have been taken to enhance farm productivity and income, such as higher MSPs increase in irrigation reach, larger use of technology, boost to animal husbandry, etc. The government also resolved to double the farmer income by 2022 through these measures. In line with the new determination, the Modi regime launched the eNAM scheme on 14 April 2016.

The aim of the eNAM system was reflected in the enactment of the state/union territory Agricultural Produce and Livestock Marketing (Promotion and Facilitation) Act 2017, also known as the APLM Act. The legislation was 'to provide for geographically restriction-free trade transaction of agricultural produce, including livestock, across the state/union territory and country; to give freedom to the agriculturists to sell their produce across time and space; to enhance transparency in trade operations and price settlement mechanism through adoption of electronic and other innovative forms of technology; to promote emergence of multiple channels for competitive marketing...'

Among the salient features of the act were the following:

1. Giving freedom to the agriculturists to sell their produce to the buyers at the place and time of their choice; they could sell to whosoever and wherever they got better prices
2. Promotion of direct interface between farmers and processors/exporters/bulk-buyers/end users so as to reduce the price spread, bringing advantage to both the producers and the consumers
3. Provisions for single point levy of market fee across the state and unified single trading licence to realize cost-effective transactions
4. Rationalization of market fee and commission charges
5. Abolition of fragmentation of market within the state/union territory by removing the concept of notified market area
6. Creation of a conducive environment for setting up and operating private wholesale market yards and farmer-consumer market yards, so as to enhance competition among different

markets and market players for the farmer's produce, to the advantage of the latter

7. Providing a level-playing field to the licencees of private market yards, private market sub-yard, electronic trading and direct marketing vis-à-vis the Agricultural Produce and Livestock Market Committee (APLMCs) and removing the conflict of interest that the latter are likely to practise, if both development and regulatory functions are entered in the same authority

Observing that the marketing system that had existed prior to the coming of eNAM, especially under the various State Agricultural Produce Marketing (Regulation) acts, had fallen 'well below the intended objectives', the Statement of Objects and Reasons (SOR) of the APLM Act further noted that the environment was 'neither advantageous to the farmers nor serves well the interests of the consumers'. The SOR said that the 'profile of India's farm produce is changing' and that it was 'getting more cosmopolitan with higher levels of outputs in the domain of horticulture, dairying, poultry and fisheries, besides of course increasing quanta of cereals, pulses and oilseeds'. All of this required an intervention that would do away with the 'restrictive and monopoly-centric agricultural market structure'. The SOR emphasized that the system that then existed was not 'capable of permitting the producers to harvest the economic advantages of place, time and form value of their agricultural commodity'.

It is obvious from these observations that while the model APMC Act of 2003 and Rules therein of 2007 had done their bit to reform the marketing of agricultural products, they had gone obsolete with the rapid changes that had taken place and with the rise of new aspirations and demands of the farmers, not to mention the Modi government's determination to double the farmers' income. The Union government engaged with the stakeholders and the Niti Aayog to chart a fresh course of action, and the first of these was the formulation of a new model act, which would reflect the goals of the eNAM project. Various officials and organizations offered their views—the Union Minister for Agriculture Radha Mohan Singh provided the overall guidance, while the Minister of State for Agriculture Parshottam Rupala, Niti Aayog member Prof. Ramesh Chand, Secretary, Department of Agriculture, Cooperation and Farmers Welfare Dr S.K. Pattanayak contributed with their administrative experience and inputs to the cause. Various others were involved too, including officials of states and union territories.

The need for reforms had been felt for long. Back in 2013, a committee of state ministers incharge of agriculture marketing to promote reforms had submitted its report to the then government. It referred to the need to 'overcome the limitations and constraints of present agricultural marketing system such as lack of sufficient number of markets and adequate marketing infrastructure, high incidence of market fee/charges and lack of competition with long chain of intermediation'. It may be noted that these are precisely some of the observations that the model act of 2017 too highlighted, which the eNAM structure has sought to address. The 2013 panel also said that several states and union territories had tried to combat the challenges by amending their respective APMC laws, but there had been 'variation in adoption of the contents and coverage of reforms to the APMC acts/rules across the states/union territories'. Again, these problems are being effectively tackled in the eNAM ecosystem.

Interestingly, while elaborating under the sub-head, 'Challenges to Agricultural Marketing', the 2013 report mentioned nearly every issue that has been spoken about in the 2017 act, with some of them being taken head-on in the eNAM system. They are—limited access to markets, licensing barriers, lack of market infrastructure, high incidence of market charges, lack of national integrated market, low farmer price realization, large number of marketing channels with long supply chains (resulting in several intermediaries) and high marketing costs that adversely impact small and marginal farmers.

The 2013 committee recommended the following, among others:

1. States and union territories must amend their respective APMC acts
2. The existing system of licencing of traders and commission agents should be replaced with a modern and progressive system of registration that ensures transparency
3. A single unified registration system must be put in place
4. Private markets should be treated at par with the existing APMCs

The panel also, very importantly, recommended measures to maintain quality with a view to ensuring greatest acceptability of produce and highest price realization for that product. It said, 'To promote the grading and testing of agricultural produce, states are required to take initiative for establishing grading units with trained manpower in the market to attend to work of grading and to promote private laboratories for testing of agricultural produce on user-charge basis.' Quality assaying has been an important component in the eNAM scheme. The ministry has been engaged with a number of technological organizations and personnel to develop cost-effective, less cumbersome as well as accurate machines to conduct quality tests on various produce that is traded on the eNAM platform. Nearly all eNAM mandis already have machines that test the moisture level in agricultural products, including crops and oilseeds. But, more are needed to test other parameters, and the e-markets are hopeful of getting them sooner than later. Certain Indian Institutes of Technology (IITs) have been contacted to develop these testing equipment. Once the testing laboratories are adequately equipped and functional at the e-mandis, they will ensure that farmers get the right (higher) price for better quality produce. This will also incentivize the farmers to enhance the quality of their produce.

If we were to travel for more than a couple of days (and nights) from Hyderabad and head north on National Highway 44, we would end up in Jammu & Kashmir. The NH-44 is said to be the longest-running national highway in the country, connecting Srinagar to Kanyakumari, cutting through vast swathes of north and south India, besides passing through the western state of Maharashtra. But, if the goal is to touch on a major foodgrain market that has robustly adopted the eNAM system, there is no reason to venture that far. Less than four hours from Hyderabad is the mandi of Nizamabad. In terms of business, it is the third largest—after Warangal and Khammam—in Telangana. These two markets ride the top spots in cotton and chillies harvest. But, in trade conducted in turmeric produce, the Nizamabad market is the biggest in the state, and third in all of India (after Sangli in Maharashtra and Erode in Tamil Nadu). Spread over 68 acres, the mandi is a proud recipient of the Prime Minister's Award for Excellence in Public Administration for Best Performance in Implementing eNAM in 2017.

As one drives into the market in November, one is confronted with several mounds (called 'lots') of turmeric placed all over the designated market yards, having being brought in by the farmers (sellers). They are cursorily checked by traders for quality and then weighed after being bought by them. It being an e-market, Nizamabad conducts the marketing process through the electronic mode—from bidding to weighing. Mechanical weighing machines are out and the produce in the yards is weighed by electronic weighing scales for accuracy. The scale's software is linked to a handheld device, which simultaneously exhibits the weight as shown on the machine's screen. The handheld device is also connected with the main eNAM platform. Simply put, even as the scale measures the weight, the figure is loaded on to the main system against the name of the concerned seller/buyer, thus cutting down on time and ensuring transparency. Market officials are now working to take the process one step ahead—they are exploring ways, in collaboration with eNAM's technical partner, the Nagarjuna Group, to have the sale bill and sale agreement generated along with the weight bill.

In the old days, before eNAM, processes in the Nizamabad market took an entire day to conclude, often spilling over to the following working day. Mechanical methods guided the process, from the time the farmer came with his produce to the time he sold it and got his amount. The bidding process itself took time, and then there was the task of collating the bids, writing the bids down, declaring it in the market and ensuring that the sale closed in time for the market gates to shut. The complicated system also led to allegations of 'fixing' of prices by traders and inaccuracy in weighing. Now, things have begun to work with speed and accuracy. The Nizamabad market officials had generated a 'bid submission report' within minutes of the closure of secret bidding through the electronic medium. The report listed the names of the traders, commission agents and farmers involved, along with the bid rates. On 19 November 2018, for instance, a farmer named

Goli Narsaiah received as many as 18 bids for his produce, turmeric bulbs, and the list was out well before 4 p.m.

*Nizamabad turmeric market (Photo by Rajesh Singh)*

Statistically speaking, the Nizamabad market has been doing well enough since it adopted the eNAM system, which was the day when the Modi government introduced the scheme with multiple goals, the overarching benefit being the empowerment of the country's farmers. The number of farmers registered under the project in 2016–17 was 39,975; it went up to over 58,000 in 2017–18. The volume traded (in quintals) in 2016–17 was 13,52,439; in 2017–18, it shot up to 1,657,711. In monetary terms, the trade turnover in 2016–17 was a little over ₹542 crore; in 2017–18, that went up to ₹672.31 crore.

Mandi officials have been trying out an experiment—a

dealing directly between the seller and the buyer by cutting out the commission agent. Commission agents, since the eNAM implementation, have been involved in facilitations of a different kind—organizing manpower for unloading of the produce after it enters the market, cleaning (if needed) of the product and loading it after a buyer purchases it. Unofficially, though, they continue to exert some influence on the potential buyer as well as the seller. The elimination of the commission agent in the present circumstance would mean that the market officials have to organize the task that the agent did. But, the Nizamabad market staff has done a commendable job in this direction. In the period 2017–18, pursuant to the officials' efforts, more than 2,600 farmers registered for the Direct Sales Platform, and more than 16,000 quintals of produce was traded as a consequence. Interestingly, the direct farmer-trader linkage is the predominant theme of the eNAM system that seeks to eliminate all intermediary parties and thereby offer the best deal for both the seller and the buyer.

Apart from the Direct Sales Platform, the other innovative initiative taken at the Nizamabad mandi by the agricultural market committee is to help small and marginal farmers with short-term financing called the Rythu Bandhu Pathakam. Although it is an old scheme (introduced in 1983 and working uninterruptedly since then), under which farmers get short-term loans from the committee against their produce, farmers have begun to show added interest in the facility after being empowered through the eNAM system. With the assurance that their product will fetch the best market prices and that they will no longer be short-circuited by wily traders and commission agents, the farmers have summoned the courage and confidence to avail the loans. Figures tell the story—the number of farmers who benefitted from the scheme in 2015–16 (before the scheme was implemented) was 130. It more than doubled in 2017–18. The total loan amount disbursed was a little over ₹2.5 crore; it jumped to more than ₹3.34 crore.

The Nizamabad market's quality-testing processes have been sound, although officials admit that more can and needs to be done. Incidentally, this is something that even the officials in the Union Agriculture Ministry agree with and are working to meet the challenge. Let's take the instance of turmeric. A typical 'Sample Assaying Result' sheet would present the following:

1. Assaying number
2. Assaying date
3. Lot code number
4. Commodity (turmeric finger)
5. Name of the farmer
6. Name of the commission agent

There are seven assaying parameters to establish quality, and the results fall in three 'ranges'. In the case of turmeric finger, the range is decided on the parameters of foreign matter, defective rhizomes, insect damaged matter, curcuminoid content, uniformity and moisture. As an example, if a turmeric lot sample is found to have 0–10 per cent (by weight) of moisture, it would fall in the range one category, which is good. Anything with over 11 per cent of moisture would be considered in range three and would fetch comparatively lower rates. Similarly, the more lustrous turmeric finger would come under range one, while those of poor lustre would fall in range three. The biggest advantage of quality testing laboratories is that it encourages farmers to cultivate better quality crops for bigger returns on the eNAM platform. These laboratories, across the country, are presently operated by the National Collateral Management Services Limited (NCML), which has expertise in testing and certification services since 2005.

These achievements apart, the most outstanding feature one noticed of the Nizamabad regulated market was the perfect coordination between various agencies in the successful implementation of the eNAM project. The enthusiasm of the state officials, their rapport with representatives of the technical partner, the Nagarjuna Group, and their wholehearted acceptance of a central scheme helmed by a party that is a political opponent is commendable. For all of them, the farmer comes first.

Nearly halfway between Hyderabad and Vijayawada on the National Highway lies the town of Suryapet, which is also the headquarters of Suryapet district in Telangana. The agricultural market there came into the eNAM fold on 1 July 2016, and since then, both farmers and traders have tapped into the enormous opportunities the system has provided them. The principal kharif crop in the region is paddy, and if one were to visit the market yards, one would find enormous lots of paddy neatly placed all over. Tucked in each heap is a sheet of paper that bears the lot-IDs, which the farmer/seller obtains from the eNAM cabins located in the market premise. Licenced traders (purchasers) are seen hovering over such lots, feeling the grains in the palm of their hands to ascertain prima facie quality. By evening, the process—which begins with the arrival of the produce in the market and ends with the acceptance of the highest bid and money exchanging hands—comes to a close. Farmers begin to arrive as early as late night, and from 6.30 a.m. to 10.30 a.m., they are issued their lot-IDs. Soon after their details are fed into the eNAM system, they receive a confirmation message on their mobile phones, kicking off the rest of the process.

The Suryapet market complex may not be as sprawling as the Nizamabad one, but it's no less efficient in the performance of the eNAM system. It was only a little after 12.30 p.m. and the final printed list of the successful bidders was on the table of the mandi secretary. There is an interesting Lot Tracker Report, which keeps tabs on the bidding underway, though not even the officials know at that time what the highest bid would be. A typical Lot Tracker Report at a certain time would have the following details—commodity (various varieties of paddy), quantity arrived (in number of bags and in quintals), lots approved, lots pending approval, lots with bids, lots without bids and the number of sale agreements. Two Lot Tracker Reports at two different times would obviously be different; the later one would normally have a lower number of lots pending bids, for instance, thus demonstrating the process between the earlier and later hours. For example, a Lot Tracker Report generated at 10.43 a.m. on 16 November 2018 said that 353 lots had received no bids; the report generated at 12.45 p.m. the same day showed that only 12 lots were without bids. This would be the story other days too, for other crops.

Fifty-eight-years-old Venkannah hails from Warayanguta village, 18 km from Suryapet town. He grows paddy on 5 acres of land he owns. Besides, he has taken another 5 acres on lease for cultivation. Last year, 2018, was his first year at the eNAM platform; he had gone with 160 bags (roughly 60 kg of produce per bag) of paddy to be sold in the market to the highest bidder. He is fortunate to have access to irrigation—his fields are close to the Nagarjuna water canal, also known as the Krishna river canal. Until now, every year, he would approach rice millers with his produce. But, when he was told by fellow farmers that he should try out the eNAM platform for better rates, he loaded his produce and came to the Suryapet mandi. 'I am happy with the price here. Also, there is transparency and I can be assured of not being short-changed,' he said.

*Chinna Laxmaiah s/o Ramulu Village: Gudlanarwa, Mahabubnagar District (Photo by Rajesh Singh)*

Some 30 km from Suryapet is the village of Gadala Malkapuram, which comes under the administrative jurisdiction of Penpahad mandal. A farmer, Narasaiah, has brought 70 bags of IR-64 paddy for disposal at the best price he can get in the e-market. 'Previously, I used to sell the crop locally to a buyer out of convenience. But, I never received a satisfactory price for the hard effort I put in. Fellow farmers advised me to change my mindset and try out the e-market. I was initially apprehensive because of the new system, but summoned the courage to experiment.' He beams in confirmation when asked whether he had found the eNAM to his benefit.

Saida could not be more than 40 years of age. He hails from the village of Khambad, 15 km from Suryapet. He is in the market accompanied by his mother D. Bulli. Both mother and son are more than happy with the eNAM regime. He noted, 'We have gained in many ways. Time is saved, rates are better (we get around 20 per cent more than what was paid outside) and there is transparency.'

Many of the farmers one interacted with in November of 2018, were barely educated. But the 24-year-old Rajashekhar proudly told us he was an M.Sc. in Chemistry. Although with a regular job, he helps his father in farming, and it was his idea to try out the eNAM set-up. He came from Husseinabad village, some 25 km from Suryapet, with 120 bags of paddy to be sold at the best price he could get through secret bidding by traders. He counted his gains—'apart from the time-saving the eNAM system has led to'—winning bid is known soon after the bid closes, weighing of the produce is accurate, bids are no longer rigged and the hold of 'syndicates' has all but collapsed. eNAM applications also help in understanding price trends in various markets and prepares one to plan for the best day and market to maximize returns.

*Kashanna, s/o Veeraiah, Village: Vattem (Photo by Rajesh Singh)*

Devareddy Janakiram Reddy, a farmer-cum-commission agent who said he ought to be close to 60 years of age, is a satisfied person, though he naturally wishes to be more better-off. He has cultivated red grams and paddy in his three acres of land. He wholeheartedly endorses the eNAM system and says, 'Earlier, the entire process used to take two to three days, and we farmers would still not be happy with the rates our produce fetched. But, we had no option and continued to be exploited. Today, with eNAM, work gets done in a day and we get paid promptly. Besides, we have even the right to reject the highest bidder's rates if we feel that we can get a better price later on.' He also endorsed the opinion of other farmers on the greater accuracy of electronic weighing machines. 'In the old days, we lost out also because our products were not weighed properly—they were almost always under-weighed and couldn't do anything.'

*Mekala Bangaraiah, s/o Chinna Ramulu, District: Nagarkurnool (Photo by Rajesh Singh)*

It's not just the farmers that are a happy lot; market officials too have heaved a sigh of relief. A senior officer at the Suryapet said, 'the eNAM system had greatly reduced the workload while at the same time ensured that accuracy at all stage was maintained. In those mechanical days, we were a harried lot, running helter-skelter in a desperate attempt to keep up with the pace of work. And yet, there were deficiencies and we had to bear the brunt of the anger of farmers, traders and the commission agents. Besides, our staff had to work continuously for two to three days at a stretch, and we had to give them a day off as a result. Now, we have smooth functioning, and the level of satisfaction among the staff has led to greater efficiency in functioning.'

If states such as Telangana and Haryana are doing a commendable job in eNAM's implementation, there are those such as Uttar Pradesh that face a challenge of convincing the farmers about the gains to be had by connecting with the system. Officials of the agriculture department are working ceaselessly in that direction, but clearly mindsets take time to change. A good example is that of the mandi in Pratapgarh, which is some 55 km from Prayagraj (formerly Allahabad). It adopted eNAM in September 2016, becoming one among the first six regulated markets in the state to come on board. Since then, 100 more have implemented the electronic trading system. More than 40,000 farmers and over 300 traders have so far been registered. Mandi officials are working overtime to persuade more farmers to join and the registered farmers to trade more. This is no small achievement in a situation where the farmers and traders are still not fully tuned to the new system.

The Pratapgarh experience is critical to further ensuring the success of eNAM in Uttar Pradesh—or at least in the eastern part, given that western Uttar Pradesh has done better in the matter. One lesson to be learnt is that the eNAM must take into account local factors such as productivity of a particular product. Pratapgarh is the centre of amla or aonla (Indian gooseberry) cultivation, with the product finding a ready market in the country and abroad, for a variety of uses including medicinal. The trade in Pratapgarh mandi heavily depends on this produce. In 2015–16, it traded in 2,19,565 quintals; in 2016–17, it was 4,25,660. As of October 2018, 45,531 quintals had arrived in the Pratapgarh regulated market. However, amla is not one among the 114 listed products that can be traded on the eNAM platform. Hectic consultations have been going on between the market and the state-and central-level officials over the issue. It's mainly vegetables that are traded electronically there. One senior mandi official remarked, 'It would be good for the farmers and for the NAM here if amla was included in the eNAM system.'

That apart, local market officials admit that they have to make even more strenuous efforts in reaching out to the farmers to induce them into eNAM. 'We need to go to the villages, talk to the farmers and explain to them the benefits of electronic trading. They need to understand that they will benefit hugely from the initiative.' That there is much that can be done is evident from the following figures: the e-payment report for the period 1 February 2017 to 20 November 2018, shows that a little over 113 quintals had been traded, and the value of transaction was roughly ₹1.83 lakh. In terms of overall trade in the mandi, between 14 April 2016 and 20 November 2018, more than 19,000 quintals were dealt with, and the total trade value in rupee terms was ₹1,702.93 lakh.

Despite the relatively low figures on the eNAM platform, Pratapgarh market officials are confident that they can turn things around. By and by, farmers are getting round to understanding that they stand to gain through secret competitive bidding that eNAM ensures. But most of them deal in Indian gooseberry, cultivating traditional crops such as paddy only to the bare minimum—enough for their family consumption. As a consequence, such traditional crops are rarely traded in the market.

In other respects, the Pratapgarh market is no different than others that are there in the rest of India. Like elsewhere, the stranglehold, which traders have over farmers by virtue of the former often serving as a money lender to the latter in times of need, is there in Pratapgarh too. Everyone agrees that eNAM is a way out of this crisis.

There is no doubt that the eNAM platform has the potential, in the coming months and years, to completely change the pattern of farmers' income in a positive manner. As more agricultural products get added to the e-trade list, as more regulated markets adopt the system, and as the existing eNAM markets expand and fine-tune the setup, we can expect an explosion of sorts in the way farmers trade their produce. There still are glitches, and obstacles to a more complete rollout of the process in many parts of the country. More awareness among farmers coupled with better coordination between the centre and the states to ensure that farmers are not short-changed and they get to drive the benefits of the eNAM project, will propel the scheme to greater heights. As the examples of Charkhi Dadri, Nizamabad and Suryapet have shown, the right intent and committed implementation can work wonders. The Pratapgarh market, on the other hand, highlights the potential that remains untapped. The eNAM project is an important vehicle for the Modi government to realize its ambitious goal of doubling farmers' income by 2022. It's not the only means, but it's certainly among the most critical ones.

***Rajesh Singh*** *is a former opinion editor of the Pioneer and regularly contributes to Vivekananda International Foundation, WION, etc.*

# BALANCING ACT: ANCILLARY ACTIVITIES

*Chandra Shekhar*

To think that farmers' income will double by 2022, as envisioned by PM Narendra Modi, on its own without any extra effort by the government or the farming community would be living in a fool's paradise. It will not happen on its own. However, if the right policies are pursued with firm determination in a mission mode with the cooperation of all the stakeholders—may it be government functionaries, small farmers or those engaged in allied activities such as fishing, beekeeping, dairying, etc.—this vision can be realized.

Doubling the income of the farmers by a specified date is by no means a small task, it requires a lot of planning, a concrete action plan and a spirited government machinery to push through the difficult agenda. With this end in view and also to understand how the whole scheme has worked to the benefit of the farmers, it may be worthwhile to take stock of probably the most ambitious programme undertaken by any government since Independence.

In order to achieve the target of doubling the income of farmers by 2022, the government came out with a seven-point all encompassing strategy. The focus of this strategy has been to improve all components connected with the rural life in a balanced manner with a view to promote sustained development and collective prosperity of large number of people depending on farm and allied activities for their livelihood. The areas identified for special attention also include allied activities which can play a major role in increasing as well as supplementing the income of the farmers. These are activities that a farmer can undertake in addition to core agriculture activity, which is producing cereals and vegetables.

Although promotion of ancillary activities like poultry, beekeeping and fisheries has been mentioned as the seventh and the last point, in no way does it diminish the importance of these economic activities and the role they have been playing and can play in substantially increasing the income of farmers and those associated with them. These ancillary activities are significant as they provide stable income to farmers. The main reason being that while the prices of cereals and vegetables fluctuate widely depending upon demand and supply, edible items such as eggs, chicken, honey, fish, etc., remain in demand throughout the year. These products are less prone to ups and downs of seasonal demand, and hence, anchor the income of the farmers, besides giving them useful and rewarding work throughout the year. Also, they add to the nation's wealth, the gross domestic product (GDP) and the national income.

Keeping in view the interest of individual farmers, the Ministry of Agriculture and Farmers' Welfare, during the last four years, has strengthened several ongoing schemes, has launched new programmes and initiated concrete action on many fronts to transform rural landscape of the country. Major initiatives have been taken by the ministry with regards to the development of fisheries, poultry, dairying, beekeeping, etc., as part of the development of allied activities with the overall objective of improving the income of farmers. In fact, small and marginal farmers and poor households living in villages have been the main focus of the development programmes of the present BJP-led NDA government.

## FISHERIES

For a country with a vast coastline of over 8,000 km, an exclusive economic zone of 2.02 million sq km and an extensive network of rivers, fishing ought to play an important role in the economic life of people, and it has done so for ages. However, what is significant at this juncture is to promote scientific methods of fishing with a view to not only tap the existing natural resource but also to expand it for the benefit of those who will follow this vocation in the years to come. This will also play a crucial role in meeting the nutritious needs of the vast populace of the country.

Moreover, with constant innovation and support being extended by the government through various programmes and schemes, fisheries has increasingly become an important allied activity for those who are living away from the coastline. And, for those living near the coastline, it has always been an important full-time economic activity and will continue to be so.

The government, it may be recalled, had set a target of increasing the country's fish production by 50 lakh tonne by the end of 2020. This increase in the output of fish from the brackish and marine waters as well as fresh water is aimed to be achieved through extensive use of modern technology. Efforts are being constantly made to utilize technological inventions which have been languishing in laboratories for want of proper government-supported schemes and programmes.

One such technology is 'cage culture', which is being touted as the future of fisheries. The extensive use of this technology, which is possible given the landscape of our country, has the potential to revolutionize the fishery sector, making it an engine for self-employment in villages, semi-urban areas and in coastal areas. As many as 1,095 cages have been installed all along the coast with the technical support of Indian Council of Agricultural Research-Central Marine Fisheries Research Institute (ICAR-CMFRI), Kochi.

As a result of the initiatives taken by the NDA government, the production of fish has increased substantially. According to the latest available statistics, fish production has increased from 355.16 lakh tonne during 2010–14 to 447.55 lakh tonne during 2014–18. The increase works out to be 26.01 per cent, which is the result of the steps initiated by the Modi government since it took office in May 2014.

On account of increasing the focus on diversification, the annual carp seed production has gone up to 25 billion and that of shrimp to about 12 billion. Along with fish-food culture, ornamental fish culture and high value fish farming have also gained importance in the recent past. According to an official report, over 2.4 lakh fishing crafts operating in the coast, six major fishing harbours, 62 minor fishing harbours and 1,511 landing centres are functioning to cater to the needs of over 3.9 million fisher folk.

More significantly, fish and fish products have emerged as the largest group in agricultural exports of India, with 10.51 lakh tonne in terms of quantity and ₹33,442 crore in value. This accounts for around 10 per cent of the total exports of the country and nearly 20 per cent of the agricultural exports. More than 50 different types of fish and shellfish products are being exported to as many as 75 countries around the world.

Has this happened on its own without the efforts of the government machinery combined with the hard work of all those engaged in the business of fishing? The simple answer is a definite

'No'. The pragmatic policies of the government and its strong leadership team along with the efforts of all those involved in the implementation machinery and the hard work of individual fishermen have contributed to this significant increase in the output of fish and its export. All this has added to the income of fishermen and also of those engaged in the business of fishing, both in the informal as well as the formal sector.

The strategy for promoting fishery, in fact, forms a part of the Blue Revolution launched by PM Narendra Modi. Encompassing multidimensional activities, the Blue Revolution focusses on increasing fisheries production and productivity from aquaculture and fisheries resources, both inland and marine.

As elaborated by the Ministry of Agriculture and Farmers' Welfare, the five clear objectives of the Blue Revolution are: to increase the overall fish production in a responsible and sustainable manner for economic prosperity; to modernize the fisheries with special focus on new technologies; to ensure food and nutritional security; to generate employment and export earnings; and to ensure inclusive development and empower fishermen and aquaculture farmers.

Integrated Development and Management of Fisheries, the centrally-sponsored scheme, was a result of restructuring of several existing schemes by the NDA government with a total central outlay of ₹3,000 crore. Several ongoing schemes were merged with a broad aim to provide an integrated and focused approach to this important economic sector. The Blue Revolution dealt with development and management of fisheries, including inland fisheries, aquaculture, marine fisheries, deep-sea fishing and all activities undertaken by the National Fisheries Development Board (NFDB).

The focus was also on post-harvest operations, strengthening of database and Geographical Information System (GIS), institutional arrangement for the sector, Monitoring, Control and Surveillance (MCS) and other need-based interventions, besides a national scheme of welfare of fishermen.

Demonstrating its priority for the fishing sector, the central government earmarked ₹732.45 crore for funding various schemes in this sector in their 2018–19 budget. Of this, as much as ₹632.61 crore was for schemes under the Blue Revolution. The central government has also been increasing allocation for development of fishing infrastructure. As per an official report, the government intends to spend as much as ₹7,522 crore during the five-year period, including 2018–19 on schemes under the Fisheries Infrastructure Development Fund.

On 9 March 2018, the government had introduced a scheme for assisting deep-sea fishing under the existing component 'development of marine fisheries, infrastructure and post-harvest operations' of the Blue Revolution scheme. The scheme was aimed at promoting capacity building in traditional fishermen to venture into deep-sea fishing and to support their livelihood with comparatively higher income generation.

The sub-component also sought to introduce intermediate size of modern deep-sea fishing vessels (DSFVs) to the traditional fishermen for operating in the Indian Exclusive Economic Zone (EEZ), beyond the territorial waters, to enable them to harness fishery resources in the deep sea. During the financial year 2017–18, the central government had released ₹300 crore to the governments of Tamil Nadu, Andhra Pradesh and Gujarat.

The union government in its 2018–19 budget has set aside a large sum for setting up a dedicated Fisheries and Aquaculture Infrastructure Development Fund (FIDF). The fund, according to an official report, has the potential to benefit over 40 lakh marine and inland fishers especially women, Self Help Groups (SHGs) and weaker sections, due to the availability of modern infrastructure and added value of produce. The FIDF has also been providing concessional finance to the state governments/union territories, state entities, cooperatives, individual entrepreneurs, etc., for the development of fisheries infrastructure and facilities both in marine and inland fisheries sector.

The fund, the report added, is aimed at: filling the large infrastructural gaps in the fisheries sector, create employment opportunity for the rural population in fishing and allied activities, contribute towards the enhancement of fish production and productivity, offer manifold benefits and fulfill the requirements of tapping the full fisheries potential and achieving the vision of doubling the farmers' income.

It may also be mentioned that during the two financial years (2016–17 and 2017–18), creation of four new fishing harbour projects and the modernization of one existing fishing harbour at Sassoon Dock, Mumbai, (at a total cost of ₹642.75 crore with central liability of ₹337.67 crore) have been jointly taken up by the centrally-sponsored scheme of Blue Revolution of Ministry of Agriculture and Farmers' Welfare and Sagarmala of Ministry of Shipping.

More importantly, the government has continued to provide insurance cover to fisherfolk on easier and attractive terms. The annual insurance premium for fishermen was brought down from ₹29.00 to ₹20.34. Further, the insurance premium has been fixed to ₹12 after integration with the Pradhan Mantri Suraksha Bima Yojana (PMSBY), while insurance coverage has been increased to ₹2 lakh from ₹1 lakh for accidental death and permanent disability.

The importance of fishing should also be viewed from the point of food, its nutritional value as well as the pressing need to preserve biodiversity. In India, fisheries and aquaculture are important sectors of food production, providing nutritional security to the food basket and contributing to the agricultural export with the engagement of about 14 million people in different activities.

Constituting about 6.3 per cent of the global fish production, the sector contributes to 1.1 per cent of the GDP and 5.15 per cent of the agricultural GDP, says an official document, adding 'paradigm shifts in terms of increasing contributions from inland sector and further from aquaculture' are needed over the years.

'There is a huge untapped potential in fisheries and aquaculture, which can contribute considerably to improve the livelihood of fishermen and also help in women empowerment,' said a report prepared by the NFDB. The future development of aquaculture, it added, would depend on adoption of new and innovative production technologies, management of less utilized water resources and proper market tie-ups. It would be a 'win-win' situation for both the fish producer and the consumer.

## ANIMAL HUSBANDRY

In case of the animal husbandry sector, not only new schemes were launched but also earlier ones were modified, strengthened and fine-tuned to yield better results. The unsaid mantra of the Modi government was that no government scheme should continue just for the sake of it. In this light, the government re-evaluated the ongoing schemes and only those that were found relevant were retained and re-launched with added vigour. In fact, this process was followed by the government in several other sectors and animal husbandry was no exception.

With a view to accelerate the development of livestock, the NDA government launched the National Livestock Mission

(NLM) in 2014–15, in the very first year after assuming office at the centre. The objective of the NLM was to ensure quantitative and qualitative improvement in livestock production systems and capacity building of all stakeholders. It also aimed at promoting sustainable development of the livestock sector with a focus on improving the availability of quality feed and fodder. Being implemented by all the states, NLM is covering everything germane to the improvement of livestock productivity. It has been supporting projects and initiatives dealing with almost all aspects of livestock from fodder to medicine.

The NLM has four sub-missions to cater to separate aspects of livestock development. These are: Fodder and Feed Development, Livestock Development, Pig Development in Northeastern Region and Skill Development, Technology Transfer and Extension. As the name suggests, the sub-mission on Fodder and Feed Development has been addressing the problem of scarcity of animal feed resources. Under the sub-mission on Livestock Development, efforts were being made towards productivity enhancement, entrepreneurship development and employment generation. It also deals with projects related to strengthening of infrastructure of state farms, modernization, automation and biosecurity, conservation of threatened breeds, minor livestock development, creation of rural slaughterhouses and fallen animals and livestock insurance.

The other sub-mission dealt with the development of piggery in the north-eastern region of the country. This sub-mission was adopted in deference to the long-standing demand of the north-eastern states for central assistance for all-round development of piggery in the region. The central government for the first time agreed to support the state piggery farms. The whole scheme was aimed at benefiting the people of the region by enhancing the livelihood opportunities for them. Besides, the aim was also to make protein-rich diet available to the people of as many as eight states of the northeastern region. It has also helped in effectively disseminating the larger message—the people of north-eastern region are on the radar of the central government and their development too is a priority for New Delhi.

The most important sub-mission and the linchpin of the NLM was skill development and technology transfer. Nothing is actually possible without proper training and the intensive use of appropriate technology. The foremost objective of this sub-mission was to strengthen the weak and dilapidated extension machinery for livestock activities at the field level. That was in fact the weakest link in the whole structure and prevented the latest technologies developed by research institutions from reaching the farmers. This sub-mission focussed on training and capacity building to help and enable the farmers to adopt the newer technologies and benefit from research being done in laboratories across the country.

What has been the result of the NLM? Has it helped in increasing productivity, raising the income of farmers or has it just remained another government scheme on paper? To quote a few statistics, the production of eggs has increased to 342.98 billion in 2014–18 as compared to 273.96 billion during 2010–14. The increase works out to be 25.19 per cent. Also, the per capita availability has increased to 69 eggs per annum. As a result of research, nine new varieties of pigs were developed and released. These improved crossbred varieties attain more than 75 kg of body weight as compared to local variety weighing around 35–40 kg, thus providing double the income through sale on live weight basis at 8 months of age.

Besides NLM, one of the major initiatives of the Modi government was launching the Rashtriya Gokul Mission (RGM) in December 2014. This is significant as the country has 299.6

million bovine population of which 190.9 million are cattle and 108.7 million are buffaloes. Of the total, 80 per cent of cattle are indigenous and of nondescript breeds. The programme for the development of indigenous breed was initiated with an initial outlay of ₹2,025 crore. The main objectives of the programme were to conserve indigenous breeds through selective breeding in the breeding tract and genetic upgradation of nondescript bovine population. The two components of the scheme were called National Programme for Bovine Breeding (NPBB) and National Mission on Bovine Productivity (NMBP).

Besides conserving indigenous breeds, the objectives of the Gokul Mission also included increasing bovine stock, enhancing milk production and productivity of bovine population by increasing disease-free high genetic merit female population and keeping a check on spreading of diseases, upgrading nondescript cattle using elite indigenous breeds such as Gir, Sahiwal, Rathi, Deoni, Tharparkar, Red Sindhi, distributing disease-free high genetic merit bulls for natural service, bringing all breedable females under organized breeding through Artificial Insemination (AI) or natural service using germ plasm of high genetic merits, organizing quality AI services at farmers' doorstep, creating e-market portal for bovine germ plasm for connecting breeders and farmers, enhancing trade of livestock and livestock products by meting out sanitary and phytosanitary (SPS) issues and promoting select breeding bulls of high genetic merit at a young age through application of genomics.

As part of the mission, the government has also established Gokul Grams which function as integrated cattle development centres with a specific focus on promoting indigenous bovine breeds. These centres attempt to promote indigenous cattle rearing and conservation in a scientific manner besides propagating high genetic merit bulls of indigenous breeds. These grams also seek to optimize modern farm management practices and promote common resource management. Another focus of the scheme is to utilize animal waste in economical way, i.e., cow dung and cow urine. The government has already approved the establishment of 20 Gokul Grams in 13 states with an outlay of ₹197.67 crore.

As per a latest report, two new National Kamdhenu breeding centres (one in north India in Madhya Pradesh and one in south India in Andhra Pradesh) have been established with the central government releasing ₹50 crore for the projects. A new frozen semen centre with a capacity of 50 lakh doses per annum is being established at Maranga, Purnia District, Bihar. Along with this, 28 semen centres were strengthened all over the country under National Dairy Plan I.

In order to encourage the farmers to rear indigenous breeds and improve production, the government instituted various annual awards—Gopal Ratna award (for farmers maintaining the best herd of indigenous breeds and practising the best management practices) and Kamdhenu awards (for the best managed indigenous herd by institutions/trusts/NGOs/gaushalas or best managed breeders' societies). There are three Gopal Ratna awards and three Kamdhenu awards, respectively, for five regions—hill and north eastern, north, south, east and west. Each award consists of a citation and an incentive of ₹5 lakh, ₹3 lakh and ₹1 lakh each for first, second and third position, respectively, in every region. As per the latest data, as many as 22 Gopal Ratna and 21 Kamdhenu awards have been given to the winners.

Among other initiatives, the central government in its 2018–19 budget proposed to set up an Animal Husbandry Infrastructure Development Fund (AHIDF). It earmarked ₹2,450 crore for development of basic infrastructure in the animal husbandry sector. This unique initiative of the government is aimed at enabling the small and poor farmers, entrepreneurs, self-help groups among weaker sections and all other stakeholders to get access to latest infrastructure facilities, benefit from technological advancements and, most importantly, obtain better remuneration for their produce.

The government has also set up a similar fund for the development of infrastructure for the dairying sector. The Dairy Processing and Infrastructure Development Fund was established with the specific objective of doubling the income of dairy farmers. Besides, it also aimed at accelerating the efforts made under the White Revolution, a highly successful initiative launched in the 1970s. The fund has a corpus of over ₹10,000 crore. Under the scheme, financial assistance is provided to milk cooperative societies through the National Bank for Agriculture and Rural Development (NABARD) at a subsidized rate of 6.5 per cent. As per the official estimates, as many as 95 lakh dairy farmers will benefit as a result of the scheme.

This ambitious target set by the Modi government in the dairying sector includes establishment of 28,000 Bulk Milk Coolers (BMCs) in 50,000 villages; additional milk chilling capacity of 140 lakh litres per day; and additional milk processing capacity of 126 lakh litres per day. It was also envisaged to set up 59.78 lakh litres per day capacity for the production of value-added milk products, with a view to ensure better remuneration to farmers.

As a result of these initiatives, India has continued to remain the largest producer of milk in the world, contributing about 19 per cent of total production. What is more noteworthy is that the production of milk increased by 23.69 per cent during 2014–18 as compared to the output in 2010–14. The per capita availability of milk also increased by 21.49 per cent in 2017–18 as compared to 2013–14. Also, the purchase of milk by dairy cooperatives increased by 39.54 per cent in 2014–18 as compared to 2010–14. Most importantly, the income of dairy farmers went up by 30.45 per cent during the last four years.

The other significant initiative of the present government was to set up e-pashuhaat, a portal to help farmers obtain information regarding indigenous bovine breeds. The portal also allows farmers to sell and purchase animals or other products. The use of the portal by the farmers is fast trending and, as per the latest available information, as many as 6.6 crore frozen semen doses, 372 embryos and 7,95,334 live animals have been made available on the portal. Through the portal, effort has been made to remove the involvement of middlemen in the sale and purchase of the germ plasm. This kind of portal with information on all types of breeds of animals is not available even in advanced countries, pointed out an official paper.

Another important step initiated by the Modi government was with regard to insurance cover. As a part of the extensive drive to save farmers from any unforeseen events, the government made efforts and also succeeded in increasing the scope and coverage of livestock insurance from 300 to all 716 districts. In addition, the coverage of livestock insurance expanded from 2 milch animals to 5 milch animals/other animals or 50 small animals. Livestock insurance coverage was increased by as much as 135 per cent. At the same time, the Foot and Mouth Disease (FMD) control programme and the free vaccination drive were increased substantially. As a result of the initiative, FMD outbreaks came down from 2,379 during 2010–13 to 632 during 2014–17, reflecting a reduction of 73.43 per cent.

The impressive advancement in the animal husbandry cannot be sustained in absence of qualified veterinary manpower. In this regard, it is imperative to increase the number of veterinary colleges as well as the number of seats wherever possible. The results are for everyone to see. The number of veterinary colleges have increased from 36 to 46 between 2014 and 2017. The total number of veterinary graduates from first schedule colleges increased from 2,311 during 2013–14 to 3,340 during 2017–18.

The approach of the NDA government in revitalizing the animal husbandry sector has already started showing results and helping the farmers to supplement their income from allied activities. The results are clearly visible in terms of increased production of milk, eggs and other products and in reduction of the incidences of FMD. Moreover, better infrastructure and increasing number of qualified veterinary experts coming from good colleges will go a long way in sustaining the growth of the animal husbandry sector in the years to come.

## HORTICULTURE

One of the key components of the government's drive in the allied sector was horticulture. With a view to promote the horticulture sector, the Modi government, soon after assuming power in May 2014, came out with the well-thought-out Mission for Integrated Development of Horticulture (MIDH).

The centrally sponsored MIDH scheme covered fruits, vegetables, roots and tuber crops, mushrooms, spices, flowers, aromatic plants, coconut, cashews, cocoa and bamboo, besides focussing on the overall development of the horticulture sector across the country. The broad objective was to accelerate the growth of horticulture and ensure sustained income for the farmers.

As per the MIDH scheme, 60 per cent of the total outlay is borne by the central government, while the 40 per cent is contributed by the respective state governments. Under the Horticulture

Mission for Northeast and Himalayan states (HMNEH), 90 per cent fund is provided by the central government and remaining by the respective state governments. The contribution of the central government is 100 per cent in case of National Horticulture Board (NHB), Coconut Development Board (CDB), Central Institute of Horticulture (CIH), Nagaland and the national-level agencies.

The NHB has been playing a key role in implementing various schemes of the government. The key schemes include development of commercial horticulture through production and post-harvest management, capital investment subsidy scheme for construction/extension/modernization of cold storage for horticulture products, technology development and transfer for promotion of horticulture, promotion of mechanization in horticulture and making quality planting material available in horticulture.

The broad aim of the scheme is to provide essential support to farmers, including quality seeds, storage facility, processing infrastructure and marketing assistance, with a view to prevent distress sale as well as wastage of the farm produce.

Among other initiatives in the horticulture sector, the Modi government also launched Operation Greens to ensure that the farmers do not suffer losses for producing staple vegetable items such as tomato, onion and potato, which are consumed by the people round the year. It was for the first time that the central government came up with a specific scheme to ensure that the farmers get the right price of these essential kitchen items. A budgetary provision of ₹500 crore was made for Operation Greens. To achieve the objective of preventing wastage and also ensuring reasonable prices for the consumers, the NHB provided financial assistance for 3,120 cold storage projects across the country with a total storage capacity of 137.22 lakh tonnes.

As per the latest statistics, the achievements under the

various components of the MIDH scheme have been quite significant during 2014–18. There has been a substantial increase in the productivity through sustainable horticulture, value-chain development, connecting farmers to the market and promoting the ownership of farmers over entire value chain from the fields to the market. The horticulture production of the nation has reached 306.8 million tonne during 2017–18, outpacing the foodgrain production and helping India retain its position as the second largest producer of fruits and vegetables globally.

The increased horticulture output, according to NHB, is a result of the MIDH scheme, which has played a vital role in accelerating the planned development of this sector, mainly through extensive use of technology developed by the country's premier institutes and agriculture universities.

As per the NHB report, some of the highlights of the development during 2017–18 'include the establishment of 2,012 commercial horticulture projects in an area of 4,483.54 ha (open field condition and protected condition), creation of 1,25,289 million tonne capacity of cold storage with 21 units, 96 pack house/grading packing line/pre-cooling units/cold rooms/ripening chamber units/reefer vans projects, 37 mushrooms units and plant and machinery projects and 115 primary processing units. Approximately 203 fruit and vegetable nurseries were also accredited during the year.'

Thanks to various initiatives by the Modi government and the hard work done by officials and other stakeholders, the advances made in horticulture is playing a pivotal role in supplementing the income of the farmers, not in a small way but in a sustained manner. If things continue at this pace, a time will soon come when the rural youth would prefer to stay in the villages and not migrate to cities for better career prospects.

## BEEKEEPING

'If you take care of bees, the bees will take care of your needs and also of the other farmers and the society,' so believes the veteran, well-known and respected beekeeper of Jind town in Haryana, Anil Singh Sandhu. Through his grit, hard work and determination, he has earned a name for himself as a successful beekeeper. He presently owns and manages 2,000 boxes with his team of dedicated and equally committed co-workers. A self-confident Sandhu is an inspiration for both the youth and fellow farmers as he shows how to earn a decent and respectable livelihood, how to increase farm productivity as well as family income with little but smart efforts. Sandhu takes satisfaction from the fact that his state of Haryana as well as the central government have recognized beekeeping as an important allied agricultural activity with huge potential.

Sandhu has a word of advice for potential beekeepers. The first and the foremost is to remain fully committed to the bees by taking good care of them. The more the dedication and commitment, the better would be the results, asserts Sandhu. Besides commitment, one also ought to follow scientific methods of beekeeping as unguided and misguided hard work might not yield the desired results. According to Sandhu, the capital is not a big problem but the training is. Beekeeping is a craft which anyone with a sense of purpose and commitment can learn.

The importance of beekeeping lies in increasing the income of people living in rural areas, raising farm productivity and achieving the ambitious target of doubling the farmers' income. But, as many people may doubt, where can one obtain good initial training to pursue the vocation of beekeeping? It is no more a problem as good training is being offered by various government agencies, owing to a major policy shift by the Modi government in allied agriculture activities. In order to promote scientific beekeeping, the central government under the Mission for Integrated Development of Horticulture (MIDH) is running several training programmes. These training programmes are being organized by the Horticulture Departments of States and National Bee Board (NBB), which was earmarked as a national-level agency for coordinating and promoting various activities.

Beekeeping was initially promoted by the All India Khadi and Village Industries Board (KVIB), which was set up in 1954 to encourage traditional village industries. Later in 1981, the ICAR launched an All India Coordinated Research Project on Honeybee Research and Training with the involvement of various agricultural universities. In 1994–95, the agricultural ministry launched a central sector scheme for Development of Beekeeping for Improving Crop Productivity.

The National Bee Board (NBB) was later set up to achieve the objective of promoting scientific beekeeping by 'popularizing the state-of-the-art technologies relating to nucleus stock production, capacity building and training bee breeders and beekeepers, processing, etc.' Its present focus is on promoting Integrated Beekeeping Development Centres (IBDCs)/Centres of Excellence (CoEs) on beekeeping in each state. Most of the IBCDs have been equipped with infrastructural facilities for developing and promoting scientific beekeeping. These centres are helping beekeepers and farmers adopt scientific beekeeping methods in an integrated manner with a view to get better results and improved productivity of the crops in adjoining areas.

Besides, the elaborate list of programmes being promoted by MIDH through liberal financial assistance includes organization of conference, workshops, national- and international-level seminars, training camps at several places and exposure visits of beekeepers within India and abroad. The NBB in the last four years has trained about 12,300 farmers/beekeepers in scientific beekeeping, including production of high-value beehive products like bee pollen, propolis, royal jelly and bee venom.

According to Sandhu, training and education is an ongoing process and it is imperative for a successful beekeeper to keep up with the latest developments in the sector. These could include adoption of better methods of upkeep of bees, their breeding, extraction of honey and other by-products, hygiene and marketing of products, etc. The list can go on and on. There is no end of learning as there is no end to development of newer techniques, newer methods of beekeeping and newer processes.

In order to encourage scientific beekeeping, MIDH provides several grants and assistance for various activities associated with the craft of beekeeping. It extends liberal assistance for development and multiplication of bee stock. Under the scheme, as assistance of ₹20 lakh is provided per project to research institutes for production of nucleus (pedigree) stock. Assistance is also provided to the extent of 40 per cent of the project, subject to a ceiling of ₹4 lakh, for production of bee colonies by bee breeders.

Under the scheme, MIDH provides an assistance of 40 per cent of the project cost subject to a ceiling of ₹800 per set of bee colony and beehive, supers, etc. The scheme also covers the distribution of eight frame bee colonies (50 beehive colony per beneficiary). Also, 40 per cent of the cost, subject to a ceiling of ₹8,000 per set per beneficiary, is provided for the distribution of bee equipment, which includes a set of honey extractor of four frames, ten containers, a net and other tools.

These schemes of the government, according to Sandhu, are there to encourage people to take up beekeeping as a successful enterprise with a view to supplement the family income. The onus is definitely on the young to take advantage of the government schemes, obtain necessary skill set and finances and become an entrepreneur. Instead of job seekers, they can be job providers in addition to contributing their might to the nation building.

Providing a back of the envelope calculation, Sandhu said that one box of beehive, which might cost somewhere between ₹4,500 to ₹5,000, could provide an annual income of ₹2,000. To achieve the economies of scale, one needs to start with a minimum of 50 boxes, he said. The income projections would mainly depend upon the price of honey in the market, Sandhu added.

But, that is not the end, he said, explaining that by scientifically extracting and selling other by-products, including beeswax, royal jelly, pollen and bee venom, a beekeeper can substantially increase his or her income. Giving his own example, Sandhu said that he had been able to increase his income by as much as 40 to 45 per cent through the sale of the by-products other than honey.

According to the economics of beekeeping worked out by the NBB Executive Director Dr B.L. Sarswat, a unit of 100 bee colonies could yield an annual income of ₹2 to ₹2.5 lakh per year. These estimates were based on prices prevailing in 2016 and may not be true to the last dot in all cases as prices of input and output, especially honey, change with time and place.

However, Dr Sarswat's analysis does provide the basic financial structure of beekeeping enterprises and profits that can be earned with small investment and financial assistance from organized sources. No one can deny the fact that beekeeping as a standalone activity or as an allied activity can help in supplementing the income of the farmers, directly as well as indirectly.

The biggest advantage of beekeeping is that it provides ample opportunities for sustainable livelihood to people residing in rural areas, tribal land and around forests. An unemployed youth can start his own business of beekeeping with as little capital as ₹1 lakh to ₹2 lakh.

According to an NBB analysis, 10,000 bee colonies in bee hives can generate 3.75 lakh man days of employment and the income from 100 bee colonies could be in excess of ₹2.5 lakh to ₹3 lakh per annum. Moreover, it can also help in doubling the farmers income by supplementing and complementing agriculture and other horticulture activities.

The other advantage of beekeeping, from the point of view of employment generation, is that it also creates work for people engaged in manufacture and maintenance of appliances and equipment used in the process of beekeeping. According to estimates, 75,000 man days are needed for manufacturing appliances for 10,000 bee colonies.

As regards the potential of beekeeping, consumption and demand for honey and other products, the potential is huge in India. According to NBB figures, the number of honey bee colonies in the last four years has increased from 20 lakh in 2013–14 to 34 lakh in 2017–18, while the honey production rose from 76,150 metric tonnes to 1.05 lakh tonne during the same period. Is it sufficient or much less than the potential? A comparison with the beekeeping activity in China will provide us some clue as to where we are and where we can go.

China produces 2.5 lakh metric tonne of honey per annum, besides 13,000 metric tonnes of beeswax, 1,000 metric tonne of pollen and 800 metric tonne of royal jelly. As a major exporter of bee products, China is implementing an ambitious plan to substantially increase the number of bee colonies in the coming decades, with a view to increase its dominance as the global player.

Indian beekeeping industry too can look forward to the huge potential of the domestic market as well as exports. At first, the domestic consumption of honey in the country is extremely low. According to estimates, the per capita annual consumption of honey is just about 10 gm, as against the global average of 250–300 gm. The per capita annual consumption of honey is highest in Germany at 2 kg. Among the Asian nations, Japan accounts for the highest per capita annual consumption of honey at 600 gm.

The opportunities for exports are immense. Honey exports increased by 81.64 per cent during the last four years to 51,547 metric tonne in 2017–18. The major destinations for Indian exports are Germany, USA, United Kingdom, Japan, France, Italy and Spain. These markets provide better returns, but, at the same time, are highly quality conscious.

## IMPACT ON AGRICULTURE PRODUCTION

Beekeeping ought to be promoted by the government not only to create opportunities for self-employment but also for a host of other factors. The most important reason being that bees help in improving farm productivity through widespread pollination. Bees move constantly to collect nectar and in the process play a very crucial role in pollinating the plants. That is the nature's way of protecting and promoting flora and fauna. The role being played by the bees in pollination cannot be replaced by any other method, artificial or natural.

According to a scientific research, as many as 90 per cent of the pollination is done by animals and only 10 per cent by wind. It has also been established that as much as 85 per cent of the crops grown worldwide need pollinators for pollination for which honey bees are best suited.

The role played by bees in pollinating the plants has a direct impact on the productivity of the agriculture sector. It has been conclusively established that bees have immensely helped in increasing the per acre yield of various agriculture and horticulture crops. In the US, beekeepers provide their bee colonies on rent to farm owners for pollination. According to studies conducted by agricultural scientists in the US, the yields have increased by as much as 15–20 times on account of pollination services rendered by bees.

Significant impact of bee pollination was witnessed in oilseeds (mustard, rapeseed, toira, sarson, safflower, linsed, niger and sunflower) and orchard crops (apples, pears, plums, cherry, strawberry, raspberry, persimmon, litchi, grapes, guava, papaya, mosambi and orange). The positive impact of bee pollination was also seen in the case of pulses (alfalfa, berseem, vetches, broad beans, dwarf beans, kidney beans, runner beans and arahar), vegetables (radish, cabbage, turnip, carrot, onion, brinjal, cucumbers) and other crops like cotton, buckwheat and coffee. As per the study, bees were found to be major pollinators for spice crops such as cardamom, clovers, fennel, coriander, cumin seeds, fenugreek seeds, carom thymol seeds, etc.

The yields of all the crops mentioned above have increased by substantial measure on account of bee pollination. As per the experiment, yields went from 5 per cent to as high as 33,150 per cent, a number which is difficult to visualize even by experts.

Beekeeping helps the farmers on several counts. First, it brings in additional income from sale of honey and other by-products. Secondly, it improves farm productivity and fights pests and diseases. The end result is more disposable income, better living standard and greater prosperity. Not a single activity can be more useful to a farmer than beekeeping.

The onus of taking advantage of the government's schemes rest on the farmers, especially the young people living in the rural areas. In view of the sustained focus of the Modi government on encouraging self-employment, it is now much easier for individuals to obtain loans, often without any collateral, for starting a business. With easier availability of loans, it is not difficult to set up a beekeeping enterprise. But, funds are not all that is needed for the success of a business. It is also about creating job opportunities for others and helping the nation in achieving exponential increase in farm productivity.

***Chandra Shekhar*** *is a senior economic journalist with more than three decades of experience.*

# INDIA A GLOBAL FOOD FACTORY: BOOSTING AGRI-EXPORTS

*Sandeep Singh*

- Indian skipper Virat Kohli and the team management have requested for bananas to be available in abundance when they travel to England for the 2019 World Cup.
- India has leapfrogged 65 places to the 77th rank in the 2018 World Bank Global Ease of Doing Business Index ranking. It was ranked 142 in 2012. In the Ease of Trading Across Border ranking, India is at the 80th rank, up 46 places from 2014. (To put it in context, in Ease of Doing Business ranking for 2018, China is at the 46th place having experienced a fall of 27 places; it was ranked 19th in 2014.)

Mentioned above are the two pieces of news in the newspaper, which I read as I sat down to pen a snapshot of the journey of the Indian agricultural export in the last four and a half years. These two headlines actually, in a way, tell the story of the Indian agricultural export as well.

With a production of over 259 million metric tonne (mn MT), India is the second largest producer of fruits and vegetables in the world. The country is the world's largest producer of bananas (29.7 mn MT), papayas, mangoes and guavas; the second-largest producer of potatoes, green peas, tomatoes, cabbage and cauliflower;

the fourth largest producer of citrus fruits; and the fifth largest producer of apples.

India witnesses nearly 5–18 per cent wastage in fruit and vegetable annually due to inappropriate harvesting practices and inadequate cold chain infrastructure. In the last four-and-a-half years, initiatives have been taken to reduce wastage levels, build adequate infrastructure, including cold chain, processing infrastructure, Research and Development (R&D) for processable grades development, packaging, innovation in farm preservation systems, skill development and much more.

## BANANA BOOST

Let's understand some of the initiatives taken by the government with respect to bananas; after all, it is a question of the Cricket World Cup!

The union cabinet has approved the Agriculture Exports Policy, 2018, which seeks to double the farm exports to $60 billion by 2022. The policy, which also aims to integrate Indian farmers and agricultural products to the global value chain, talks about 'developing sea protocol' in point 6.4.B.

It says:

> Developing sea protocols for perishables must be taken on priority for long distance markets. Export of perishables requires special storage, transportation and handling at desired temperatures. Time is a major constraint and air freight proves costly for exporters while low volumes and poor infrastructure make it unviable for airlines to transport produce. However, India's export of fresh produce can grow exponentially if sea protocols are established across

> exported/exportable varieties of shortlisted commodities. A sea protocol will indicate at what maturity level harvesting can be done for transportation by sea. This exercise has to be carried out in partnership with shipping lines, reefer service providers, Indian Council of Agricultural Research (ICAR) and Agricultural and Processed Food Products Export Development Authority (APEDA). Philippines and Ecuador are a classic case in point—both the countries were successful in developing sea protocols for exporting bananas for 40 and 24 days of sea journey respectively. Philippines has been shipping bananas to the Middle East which takes around 18 days while India has only been able to ship produce around 2–4 days transit period. Trials of sea protocol held at strategically important ports across India are therefore an immediate requirement that must be taken up on war-footing. This will go a long way in promoting trade.

Report on the 'Development of Sea Protocol for the Trial Sea Shipment of Traditional Nendran Banana to Dubai' says:

> India is the largest producer of bananas with an annual production of 30 million tons in an area of 0.8 million hectares. Though Cavendish bananas are ruling the banana export in the world trade, traditional bananas like Nendran, Ney Poovan and Red Banana find their place in hyper malls especially in West Asia and South East Asia markets due to the settlement of ethnic population from India. Nendran, the commercial plantain variety available in Kerala, Tamil Nadu and parts of Karnataka, occupies 50 per cent of the total area in these states and maximum quantity of the fruit is sold locally. Presently, the fruits are being exported through air cargo which incurs much higher expenses and the scope

> for sustainability and profitability of the business is getting diminished. Therefore, to set a new voyage by sea to Dubai with its 'Made in India' farm fresh Nendran bananas, in a first-of-its kind attempt, ICAR-NRCB (National Research Centre for Banana), Trichy and APEDA, New Delhi entered into a Memorandum of Understanding (MoU) for a consultancy project 'Development of Sea Protocol for the Trial Sea Shipment of Traditional Nendran Banana to Dubai' in partnership with M/s. Fair Exports India Pvt Ltd, Kochi, on 20 April 2017.

The project was started with the target that it will be completed within five months from the date of approval/issue. Accordingly, the project was initiated by the last week of April and culminated with the supervision and survey in the Dubai market by the end of the first week of August 2017. The project ended one month ahead of its planned schedule.

The process of exporting quality Nendran banana to Dubai began with the identification of suitable orchards for the selection of export quality bunches. An expert team from ICAR-NRCB, Trichy visited the four Nendran banana-growing fields in Valliyur (Nagarcoil), Cumbum (Theni), Mettupalayam (Coimbatore) and Sathymangalam of Tamil Nadu and one field in Chamaraja Nagara of Karnataka. Finally, Chamraj Nagara, Karnataka was selected for the trial study and farms were identified and suitable pre-harvest recommendations were given to the farmers before the harvesting of bananas. It is important to note that both are non-BJP-ruled states.

For any market, the maturity index (fruits harvested before optimum maturity may not ripe adequately and may not develop adequate flavour, while fruits harvested late, have a shorter post-harvest life and deteriorate rapidly) must consistently meet two requirements—minimum acceptable eating quality and a long storage life. Therefore, for the export market, the hands of 80–85 per cent maturity were harvested. Harvesting of bananas was done manually by a team of two persons, where one person used to cut the bunch and the other carried it away.

Dehanding was done with a sharp chisel type dehanding tool and care was taken to leave maximum crown attached to the hand. Crown was cut evenly, so that its outer finger does not get detached. A very sharp knife was used to give a clean, smooth cut in a single movement. For 10 minutes, the separated hands were spread on a clean surface to drain the latex. After the removal of latex, the fruits were packed in 20 kg perforated boxes, which were foamed at the bottom and on the sides to avoid abrasions and compression injury during transport. Foams were also placed in between hands to avoid bruises during the handling and transportation.

Well-experienced and trained personnel were deputed to check for minimum finger length and caliper grade as well as different types of damages and marks the hands or whole bunches might have received. On this basis, the bananas were rejected or selected. The selection procedure of the bananas continued at the water tanks of the packing plant.

The boxes were unloaded carefully and were not exposed to sun or rain after unloading to avoid physiological loss in weight and possible infection by micro-organisms. The crown was removed after careful inspection, if necessary, before placing the fruits in a wash tank. As soon as the hands were drained from latex, they were placed in the wash tank to remove dirt and latex, which exudes from the cut of the crown. All the damaged fruits and the ones with undesirable size and shape were removed using a knife.

The second tank was filled with water containing alum (@10

gm/litre to remove the latex and destroy the microorganisms). The dehanded fruit was washed for four minutes.

The most effective postharvest control of the crown rot is provided by the treatment with benzimidazole group of fungicides. Bavistin @ 1.5 g/litre for 10 minutes was used for arresting the fungal growth.

Once the hands were removed from the third tank, which has fungicides, they were air dried by placing them on cushioned drying tables. High-capacity fans were mounted on the wall or on the ceiling to provide air for faster removal of water from the skin.

The air-dried hands were weighed and packed in 100 gauge polypropylene bags which were lined in the 5-ply-corrugated-fibre board boxes holding an average fruit weighing 10.5 kg–12 kg to avoid moisture loss. Two pouches of KMnO4, an ethylene absorbent/oxidizer were used to control the ethylene release and to enhance the shelf life. The air was removed from the polyethylene bag using vacuum.

The packed boxes were stacked and loaded in the pre-cooling room to bring down the temperature of the fruit. The RH of 85–90 with the temperature of 13.5°C was maintained in the room.

For the trial shipment, 40-inch insulated reefer container was used. These reefers were then transported to the ship by road. The containers were transported by sea to Dubai port and then by road directly to the ripening chamber and cold storage room. Fruits were shipped under refrigeration to prevent the initiation of ripening before they arrive at their destination. Storage temperature of 13°C and humidity level of 90–95 per cent were maintained during the voyage.

At the destination, depending upon the demand, the fruits were ripened by keeping the boxes in the ripening chamber, where the temperature was maintained at 20–24 °C and relative humidity at

90–95 per cent. Ethylene gas was applied at 100–150 ppm for 24 hours. After 24 hours, ventilation was done to remove the ethylene from the ripening chamber. The ripened fruits were displayed in the hypermalls for sales.

The consignment received through the trial shipment was not only popular among the consumer but was sold at a premium price.

APEDA-sponsored, ICAR-NRCB technology-supported trial shipment was a success.

After the successful sailing of two consignments, Fair Export Pvt Ltd, Kochi started sailing 20 tonne of Nendran bananas through sea every week to Dubai with the volume of 1,000 tonne per year. With the saving of roughly ₹40,000 to ₹50,000 per tonne compared to airlifted bananas, the company started realizing savings of ₹4 crore to ₹5 crore per year.

Sea protocol for Nendran banana is just one example of many steps taken by the government for different products. This example also demonstrates how different institutions coordinated to make the project a success.

Looking at the concerns of exporters, APEDA had mandated Yes Bank Ltd to conduct a study on the difficulties faced by the exporters in the supply chain of agricultural products. Some of the recommendations of the report are:

1. From the export perspective, the importing nations are becoming more and more stringent with respect to the production norms/traceability at the farm level.
2. Unregulated input (chemicals) usage at the farm level.
3. Inadequate harvest and post-harvest management affects quality and shelf life of the produce.
4. Besides the other common challenges, one specific challenge is with respect to the right harvesting time. There is a scarcity

of skilled labour for harvesting and handling of commodities specially mangoes and pomegranate.

5. Documentation and procedures to be followed for exports.
6. The availability of quality packing material to suit the export requirement is a challenge. The packaging is important as it adds value to the product.
7. Reduce wastage at the farm level. Currently, the wastage account for fruits and vegetables is 4.6 per cent to 15.9 per cent.

The above points and many more have been taken care in the Nendran banana sea protocol project.

To further strengthen the export, as part of the draft Agricultural Export Policy 2018, point 6.1 talks of clusters. It says:

> While presenting the budget for 2018–19, the finance minister emphasized the need for focussing on a cluster development approach to boost the agricultural and horticultural production in India. A similar approach in export-centric clusters is likely to result in a more focused pre- and postharvest management of the production as well as in upgrading the supply chain to attain much higher levels of export from those clusters.
>
> Exporting horticultural products requires significant volumes of high-quality produce of the same variety with standard parameters matching import demands. Small landholding pattern and low farmer awareness in India has often meant limited volumes of different varieties of multiple crops with little or no standardization. Export-oriented cluster development across states will be key to ensuring surplus produce with standard physical and quality parameters which meet export demands. The success of such a scheme will depend on the state government's infrastructure.

It has been recommended that this scheme should be implemented in partnership with private exporters who will have a natural incentive to promote such clusters. Subject to successful implementation of these clusters, transition Agri Export Zones (AEZs) could be thought of to facilitate value addition, common facility creation and higher exports from such zones. Special Economic Zones (SEZs) facilitate production of goods at a comparatively lower price for exporters aiming to be globally competitive. India has many successful SEZs established in public and private sectors like IT, textiles, pharmaceutical, some even being multisectoral. There are opportunities for developing Agriculture Export SEZ mainly aimed at producing agriculture commodities for certain countries which are largely dependent on import of agriculture products. The interest of some countries (having substantial gap in domestic availability of grains, vegetables and fruits) can be explored for bringing in Foreign Direct Investment (FDI) into Agriculture Export SEZ in order to ensure food security of that country. There can be complete buyback arrangements by the countries, which are bringing in FDI, thus providing a stable market for Indian exports.

Stakeholders have recommended for creation of a corpus for export-oriented horticultural production through development of clusters. This will be the key to boosting volumes of standardized, good quality exports.

Fifty unique product-district clusters (provisional) have been identified for export promotion. This list is tentative and will be fine-tuned in consultation with the respective state governments. Below are the identified district-wise clusters for bananas:

| *Product* | *Region* | *State* | *District* |
|---|---|---|---|
| Banana | South | Andhra Pradesh | Kadapa, Anantapur |
| | | Tamil Nadu | Trichy, Theni, Pollachi |
| | West | Maharashtra | Jalgaon, Kolhapur, Solapur |
| | | Gujarat | Bharuch, Narmada, Surat |

APEDA, Marine Products Exports Development Authority (MPEDA), Export Inspection Council (EIC) and other commodity boards will provide the framework for ownership of the supply chain starting from farmer registrations, Farmer Producer Organizations (FPO) formation, provision of quality inputs, price discovery, farmer training through technical organization and third party certification. The implementation would require full involvement of the state agriculture and horticulture department, the state agricultural universities, ICAR institutions and the food processing department. This programme can be clubbed with the Public-Private Partnership for Integrated Agriculture Development (PPP-IAD) scheme under RKVY as involvement of private industry is critical to market success. The effort will be to focus on developing export-oriented infrastructure in the identified cluster areas, where integrated post-harvest, processing facilities, laboratories, etc., would be set up with the support from Ministry of Food Processing Industries (MOFPI)/ Ministry of Commerce and Industries (MoC), Trade Infrastructure for Export Scheme (TIES)/Mission for Integrated Development of Horticulture (MIDH), etc.

The draft of the Agricultural Export Policy also talks about marketing and promotion of the 'Produce of India' in the point 6.3. It says:

> Marketing campaigns should be created for individual fruits or products such as 'Wonderful Pom' and 'Bananas of

> India'. This fund would primarily be utilized for a sustained communication campaign in the form of a branding blitz across key targeted markets. This must utilize both digital and traditional media platforms.

It is great to see that the government is not only thinking of exports but also of marketing. In fact, the government is talking of branding. It is natural that when a product moves from commodity to brand, its value goes up significantly. It will also help the farmers, the last man in the product chain, increase their incomes.

When one reads the above, one can see the vision of PM Narendra Modi of doubling the farmer income taking shape.

With so much effort, there are chances that by 2019, Indian cricket team will have access to swadesi banana in England during the World Cup.

However, one is not sure how banana-producing countries and private corporations dealing in it will react as and when India grows into a substantial exporter of banana. After all, because of banana, Honduras and Guatemala, did suffer at the hands of United Fruit Company, Cuyamel Fruit Company and the US. India is not Honduras or Guatemala, but the international market of agriculture product is not as simple as one might think. There are a lot of players in the international market who react differently not only to India's growing export in agricultural products but also to India's self-sufficiency in few product categories. The worry is that if India is self-sufficient today, tomorrow it might become an exporter, that is, a potential competitor. To understand the same, let's look at the example of pulses.

## PULSES WAR

'Much as India seems to have won the battle, a war might be a worst thing to experience'—this threatening line is from the article 'India Import Ban on Tanzania Pigeon Peas: When a Winner Loses All' by Zirack Andrew, National Coordinator of Tanzania, Pulses Network, Dar Es Salaam.

Andrew also says, 'And this won't be the first time. It happened in the year 1254, when young Marco Polo travelled to China where he found spaghetti. In no place on earth, other than China, spaghetti was produced. But, young Marco changed the game after coming back to Italy. He introduced the produce and many people joined the bandwagon. Now, Italy is the leading producer of pasta followed by the US, Brazil, Russia and Turkey. Complacency didn't leave China on the safe side; today it is not even in the top five leading countries in producing the product. Can it happen to India also?'

It is not important to discuss the relevance of the example or the threat by Zirack Andrew. What is important is to understand why the national coordinator of Tanzania, Pulses Network, is writing these lines. Let us understand from his article where he writes:

> What happened in that last season is that we mobilized our farmers [to increase pigeon peas production] and India produced a lot; so that was the problem. They [Indians] convinced us [to produce pigeon peas]. Now, after being self-reliant, they imposed a ban on countries which had no bilateral agreement with, but [surprisingly]they did the same to Tanzania while we have a bilateral agreement which we entered into with them in 2000, and so we told them,' said

> Charles Mwijage, Minister for Industry, Trade and Investment while addressing the press on 4 September 2017, soon after coming back from New Delhi on Tanzania-India Joint meeting where he met his counterpart and discussed the possibility of lifting the ban.

He also quotes a threat of 'a case must be lodged to the International Court of Arbitration for breach of contract'.

The above are excerpts from different articles of January 2018 issue of *The Pulse Pod*, an e-magazine of Global Pulse Federation. The e-magazine has nine articles, out of which five are on India's pulse production.

In the same issue, an article 'A Path Forward for Pulses', Gordon Bacon, of *Canada Pulse* says:

> India and Canada are the two global superpowers of the pulse world. India is the world's largest producer and the largest consumer of pulses. Canada is the world's largest exporter of pulses. India's growing population, strong economic growth and inevitable variability in production and harvest quality (weather dependent) all point towards the need for a more comprehensive policy approach that recognizes that food security relies on trade.
>
> The current challenges with pulse trade in India signal that the time has come for the pulse superpowers to come to one view on how to address both the short-term and long-term commercial and political realities of pulse trade.
>
> Both the countries have a lot at stake. No government will benefit if actions end up creating unintended consequences like reduced pulse plantings in 2018. The wrong signals from pulse superpower India could drive farmers in countries like Canada to sharply reduce pulse

plantings, setting the stage for a potential shortage of pulses for the 2018–2019 crop year.

Each country's response is directly proportional to the financial and social hit it will take due to the growth in pulse production in India. Tanzanian economy may go back by few years, hence the strong reaction.

The reason for quoting the above is to make Indians realize how self-sufficiency in pulse production by India can impact international equations. (Imagine what will happen if India becomes self-sufficient in other products, like defence, petrol, etc.? Also, do think why a set of opposition parties and NGOs are so against development in India?)

Before proceeding further, here is another interesting fact on Tanzania:

International Trade Centre, a joint agency of the United Nations and the World Trade Organization, is implementing a five-year project called 'Supporting Indian Trade and Invest for Africa' (SITA). With the intention of encouraging farmers and providing stable price for the farmers, Mahindra & Mahindra came out with the innovative idea of Minimum Assured Price (MAP) in pulses segment to be piloted in Arusha, Tanzania. This is a first-of-its-kind concept in pulses segment, which guarantees farmers a minimum price based on the cost of production plus a fair profit margin. Under SITA, Kingori SACCOS, a Tanzanian farmers' organization, is shortlisted for this pilot project. Under this unique model, Mahindra and Kingori SACCOS have agreed on a minimum price based on the cost of production plus a fair profit margin.

So, it is not that India left the farmers of Tanzania in a lurch. The pulse exporting countries have completely forgotten that they used to monitor the Indian market conditions closely, and the moment they found a low production of pulses in India, they would happily jack up the export prices to India.

Coming back to pulse production, it is important to understand what happened in 2018 that the pulse producers are up in arms against India?

Following table, listing the pulse production and pulse import over the years, has the answer:

| *Pulses Production Vs Imports (million tonne)* | | |
|---|---|---|
| *Financial Year* | *Production* | *Imports* |
| 2000–01 | 11.06 | 0.35 |
| 2005–06 | 13.38 | 1.70 |
| 2010–11 | 18.24 | 2.70 |
| 2013–14 | 19.25 | 3.66 |
| 2014–15 | 17.15 | 4.58 |
| 2015–16 | 16.35 | 5.80 |
| 2016–17 | 23.13 | 6.61 |
| 2017–18 | 24.51 | 5.65 |

Pulse production in India has grown by 50 per cent in the last two years, which is leading to cut in imports. In the year 2018–19, the reduction in imports will be visible more starkly, and one will be able to understand why pulse exporters to India are up in arms.

Research paper titled 'Changing Consumption Patterns and Roles of Pulses in Nutrition, and Future Demand Projections' for the International Food Policy Research Institute in Washington by Praduman Kumar, P.K. Joshi and Shinoj Parappurathu has estimated the likely demand for pulses in India till 2030, which will further upset the pulse exporting nations. As per the paper, the total domestic pulses demand under three different income growth scenarios are as follows:

1. At current GDP growth rate, the demand is expected to go up to 21.87 million tonne in 2020 and 26.58 million tonne by 2030.
2. If the GDP growth is 'low' (25 per cent below existing rates), the demand would rise to only 21.40 million tonne in 2020 and 25.22 million tonne in 2030.
3. The corresponding numbers in a 'high' growth scenario (25 per cent above current rates) are 22.36 million tonne and 28.07 million tonne, respectively.

Harish Damodaran commenting on the report says, 'There are two important things to note here. The first is that the 23–24 million tonne pulses production achieved by India in the last two years already exceeds the 22.36 million tonne demand projected in the Washington-based institute's study. Secondly, even if output were not to rise further over the next decade, the country will not have to import more than four million tonne annually in 2030. If production increases the way it has in the last two years, India, far from being an importer, may even end up being a net exporter of pulses.'

So, the government has not only solved the pulses problem in a short term but also for the future. Before understanding what PM Narendra Modi-led government did, let us look into what was wrong with pulse production in India.

As per Professor Ashok Vishandass, 'Since 1966, pulse crops have been neglected with the agricultural policy environment favouring the spread of green revolution technology to a few crops such as paddy and wheat for food security reasons, crowding out pulse production. Phosphorus deficiency is one of the most widespread soil fertility problems in pulses. Pulses fix nitrogen nutrient by themselves and thus do not require urea. Given that urea is the only fertilizer which is controlled and sold at subsidized notified sale price, pulse cultivators are implicitly excluded from fertilizer subsidy regime.'

The above is just an example of what was majorly wrong with pulse production. In 2016, when the price of pulses was skyrocketing, the government took a lot of steps, apart from importing pulses without any import duty in a holistic way. Following is a glimpse of some of the steps taken by the government in 2016:

1. The government concentrated towards the procurement of pulse crops and offered a steep hike in MSP.
2. Under the National Food Security Mission (NFSM), ₹1,630 crore were allocated out of which central government has allocated ₹1,100 crore and 430 crore were allocated by the state governments. Of this amount allocated for NFSM, 15 per cent goes for production of new varieties of pulses.
3. During UPA tenure, grant being given through state governments for distribution of new seeds varieties was ₹12 per kg till 2013–14, which was increased to ₹25 per kg from 2014–15.
4. For the expansion of cultivation of new kind of seeds, ₹7.85 lakh mini-kits were distributed to farmers free of cost in the year 2016–17 through state governments.
5. In the year 2016–17, demonstration of new techniques for pulse production was carried out in 31,000 ha by 534 Krishi Vigyan Kendras through ICAR and state agriculture universities and ₹25.29 crore were allocated for this purpose.
6. Seed hubs were created through different organizations such as ICAR, state agriculture universities and KVKs for ensuring the availability of new kind of seeds.
7. In three years, the establishment of 150 seed centres and

availability of 1.50 lakh quintal improved seeds were to be ensured by the central government. For this purpose, ₹139.50 crore was approved for the establishment of 93 seed centres during 2016–17 to 2017–18, out of which ₹80.44 crore was for 2016–17.

8. The government worked for a new variety of pulses crops. To increase the availability of new types of breeder seeds of pulses, ICAR Institute and state agriculture universities have been provided ₹20.39 crore during 2016–17.
9. Inter-cropping of pulses with oil seeds, cotton and other crops as well as summer moong and cultivation of tur dal on paddy fields is being encouraged.
10. The government is encouraging farmer-producer organizations (FPO) to grow seeds, to buy and use efficient technology and to ensure adequate prices to small and marginal farmers for their produce.
11. A new variety of pulse (pigeon pea) called pusa arhar 16 developed by ICAR-IARI, New Delhi, was released. The variety is extra-early maturing, semi-dwarf (95 cm to 120 cm tall), determinate, high-yielding and will be available to farmers from next kharif season. While the traditional varieties take 170 days to mature, this new variety takes lesser time, that is 120 days only. This plant type allows dense plant population of 3,30,000 plants per ha when planted with row X row spacing of 30 cm and plant X plant spacing of 10 cm. High-density planting is important to realize higher yield and mechanization. Traditional varieties do not allow high-density planting as their plant type is indeterminate and spreading type. All the items of farm machinery used for wheat from sowing to harvesting are fully utilizable for cultivation of NPT Arhar.

The government waged a war on all fronts against pulses just like it did for sea protocol of banana and it has succeeded.

In the 2015–16 crop year (July–June), a mere 1.19 lakh tonne (lt) of pulses were procured under the Price Stabilization Fund set up by the Narendra Modi government: 50,422.53 tonne during kharif and 69,049.08 tonne in the rabi marketing season.

In 2016–17, procurement by the National Agricultural Cooperative Marketing Federation (NAFED), Food Corporation of India (FCI) and Small Farmers Agro Consortium (SFAC) rose over 13 times to 15.62 lakh tonne. This included 14.74 lakh tonne of kharif pulses (11.66 lakh tonne tur, 2.20 lt moong and 0.89 lakh tonne urad) and 0.87 lakh tonne of rabi pulses (0.60 lakh tonne chana and 0.27 lakh tonne masoor).

In the current year, procurement, which is ongoing, is set to double further. NAFED, the only government agency now procuring under the Price Support Scheme (PSS), has till now bought 14.59 lakh tonne of chana, 8.58 lakh tonne of tur, 2.95 lakh tonne of moong, 2.03 lakh tonne of urad and 1.36 lakh tonne of masoor. That adds up to around 29.50 lakh tonne. The final figure could well cross 30 lt which is unprecedented, as far as pulses go.

Recently, when the prime minister of Canada, Justin Trudeau visited India, the issue of pulse trade was high on his agenda. Now, India is in a position to dictate the terms to a few nations on foreign policy.

So in the end, India is not only winning the pulse war but a lot of other wars along with it.

## NATIONAL PROGRAMME FOR ORGANIC PRODUCTION (NPOP)

Organic products are grown under a system of agriculture without the use of chemical fertilizers and pesticides with an environmentally and socially responsible approach. This is a method of farming that works at grass roots level preserving the reproductive and regenerative capacity of the soil, good plant nutrition and sound soil management, and produces nutritious food rich in vitality that has resistance to diseases.

India is bestowed with a lot of potential to produce all the varieties of organic products due to its various agro-climatic regions. In several parts of the country, the inherited tradition of organic farming is an added advantage. This holds promise for the organic producers to tap the market that is growing steadily in the domestic as well as export sector.

As per the available statistics for 2018, India's rank in terms of World's Organic Agricultural Land was 9th and in terms of total number of producers was 1st (Source: FIBL & IFOAM Year Book 2018).

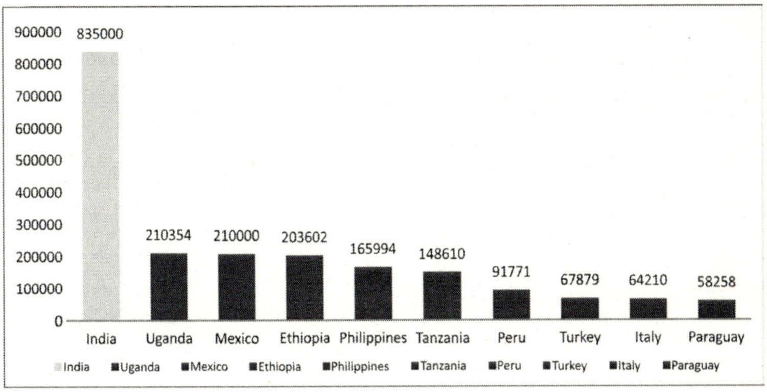


*Source: The World of Organic Agriculture. Statistics and Emerging Trends 2018, FIBL & IFOAM*

The government of India has implemented the National Programme for Organic Production (NPOP), which involves the accreditation programme for certification bodies, standards for organic production, promotion of organic farming, etc. The NPOP standards for production and accreditation system for unprocessed plant products have been recognized by European Commission and Switzerland as equivalent to their country's standards. Similarly, United States Department of Agriculture has recognized the NPOP conformity assessment procedures of accreditation as equivalent to that of the US. With these recognitions, Indian organic products duly certified by the accredited certification bodies of India are accepted by the importing countries.

As on 31 March 2018, the total area under organic certification process (registered under National Programme for Organic Production) is 3.56 million ha (2017–18). This includes 1.78 million ha (50 per cent) cultivable area and another 1.78 million ha (50 per cent) for wild harvest collection.

Among all the states, Madhya Pradesh has covered largest area under organic certification followed by Rajasthan, Maharashtra and Uttar Pradesh.

During 2016, Sikkim had achieved a remarkable distinction of converting its entire cultivable land (more than 76,000 ha) under organic certification. This provided impetus to other states to pursue similar objectives. Meghalaya, for instance, aims to make the switch by 2020.

India produced around 1.70 mn MT (2017–18) of certified organic products, which includes all varieties of food products namely oil seeds, sugarcane, cereals and millets, cotton, pulses, medicinal plants, tea, fruits, spices, dry fruits, vegetables, coffee, etc. The production is not limited to the edible sector but also to fibre and other functional food products, etc.

Madhya Pradesh is the largest producer of organic products

followed by Maharashtra, Karnataka, Uttar Pradesh and Rajasthan. In terms of commodities, oil seeds are the single largest category followed by sugar crops, cereals and millets, fibre crops, pulses, medicinal plants, herbal and aromatic plants and spices and condiments.

The total volume of export during 2017–18 was 4.58 mn MT. The organic food export realization was around ₹3m 453.48 crore ($515.44 million). Organic products are exported to the US, European Union, Canada, Switzerland, Australia, Israel, South Korea, Vietnam, New Zealand, Japan, etc.

In terms of export value realization, oilseeds (47.6 per cent) lead among the products followed by cereals and millets (10.4 per cent), plantation crop products such as tea and coffee (8.96 per cent), dry fruits (8.88 per cent), spices and condiments (7.76 per cent) and the rest.

The top consumer of organic products for 2016 was the US (€38.9 billion sales), followed by Germany (€9.7 billion sales) and France (€6.7 billion sales). According to an Ecovia Intelligence and Forschungsinstitut für biologischen Landbau (FiBL) survey, the data on the organic retail sale of food and beverages showed a compound annual growth rate (CAGR) of 10.4 per cent from 2000 to 2016 with the global sale having increased to $90 billion in 2016 from $17.9 billion in 2000. It is further projected to record a growth of over CAGR 16 per cent during 2017–20.

India currently holds the 9th position among 178 countries that actively practise organic agriculture. Organic farming has been in prevalence in India for centuries, which is based on organic manures and domestic techniques. It may be new technique for the world, but it has been exercised in our country since long. Almost 2 lakh farmers across the world practise organic farming; 80 per cent of these farmers live in India.

India's export of organic products increased by 17 per cent between 2015–16 and 2016–17.

India is the second-largest exporter of organic products in Asia after China. The increasing export market coupled with the government's support is making organic cultivation in India highly successful. Indian organic food exports were estimated at $299 million during 2015–16 with total volume of 2,63,688 million tonne. The major export destinations were the US, European Union, Canada and New Zealand. Oilseeds comprised half of India's overall organic food export, followed by processed food products at 25 per cent. The growth in the export of organic products is shown in the graph below:

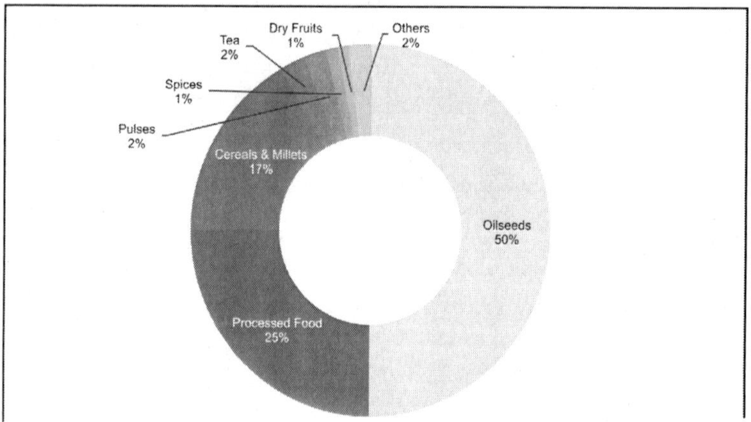


*Source: APEDA*

The global organic food industry was valued at $88.1 billion in 2015 and is expected to grow at a CAGR of 12.1 per cent to reach $156.3 billion by 2020.

On the production front, the government has rolled out several schemes to incentivize organic cultivation such as National Program for Organic Production (NPOP), National Project on Organic Farming (NPOF), National Mission on Sustainable Agriculture (NMSA)/PKVY, RKVY, Mission for Integrated Development of Horticulture (MIDH), National Mission on Oilseeds and Oil Palm (NMOOP) and Network Project on Organic Farming of ICAR.

The most exciting scheme of the ones mentioned above is the Mission Organic Value Chain Development for North Eastern Region—a sub-mission under National Mission for Sustainable Agriculture, started in January 2016.

Northeast India is organic by default. This means most small farms have never used pesticides or fertilizers. Farmers are still using traditional methods of farming. Old-fashioned farming has become their strength. In other words, because the Northeast has been so far behind the times, farmers still use old-fashioned farming methods. They now have a big advantage because this naturally ascribes the land as the best organic farming region.

The advantages of Northeast India for organic agriculture are listed in a report titled 'Opportunities for Organic Agriculture in North Eastern Hill Region' by Aditya Kumar Singh and Lala I.P. Ray:

1. North Eastern Region (NER) is home to some niche crops such as Assam lemon, Joha rice, medicinal rice and passion fruit which has high market demands.
2. NER accounts for 45 per cent of total pineapple production in India and an Agri-Export Zone (AEZ) is already set up in Tripura.
3. Sikkim is the largest producer of large cardamom (54 per cent share) in the world.
4. NER is the fourth largest producer of oranges in India.
5. The best quality ginger (low fibre content) is produced in

this region, and an Agri-Export Zone for ginger has been established in Sikkim.

6. Extent of chemical consumption in farming is far less than the national average.
7. Approximately 18 lakh ha of land in NER can be classified as 'Organic by Default'.
8. Thin population density per square kilometre (13–340 compared to 324 at national level).
9. Dependence of mid- and high-altitude farmers on farm renewable resources.
10. Time-tested indigenous farming systems and use of indigenous technical knowledge in agriculture.

Realizing the potential of organic farming in the NER of the country, the Ministry of Agriculture and Farmer Welfare has launched a central sector scheme entitled 'Mission Organic Value Chain Development for North Eastern Region' (MOVCDNER) for implementation in the states of Arunachal Pradesh, Assam, Manipur, Meghalaya, Mizoram, Nagaland, Sikkim and Tripura, during the 12th plan period. The scheme aims at the development of certified organic production in a value chain mode to link growers with consumers and to support the development of entire value chain, starting from inputs, seeds, certification, to the creation of facilities for collection, aggregation, processing marketing and brand-building initiative.

The scheme 'Organic Value Chain Development for North Eastern Region' is being implemented in a mission mode. The mission structure at the central government's level will consist of the National Advisory Committee (NAC), the Executive Committee (EC), the Mission Monitoring Committee (MMC) and a mission headquarter at Department of Agriculture Cooperation & Farmers

Welfare. At the state level, the mission will be implemented by the State Level Executive Committee (SLEC) and executed through a designated State Lead Agency (SLA) in the form of a state 'Organic Commodity Board' or 'Organic Mission'. The SLA shall function under the overall supervision of the Department of Agriculture and shall be manned by professional experts on contract.

The central sector scheme was launched on 11 January 2016 with an outlay of ₹400 crore for three years from 2015–16 to 2017–18. The scheme is being implemented in NER states through SLAs to cover an area of 50,000 ha in three years. So far, 2,406 farmer cluster and 79 FPOs have been formed.

The government has also established a National Organic Farming Research Institute in Tadong (Sikkim). The organic research institute will promote research and education on organic farming and provide research and technological backstopping to organic production systems, especially in the North East Hills Region of India.

**Amount Released during 2014-17 under MOVCDNER**

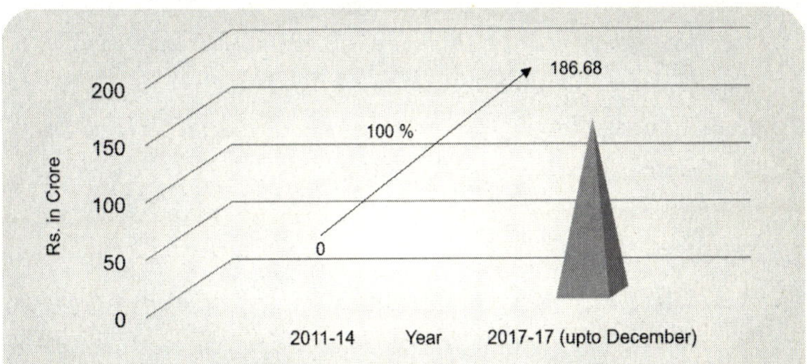


Substantial increase in the budget under MOVCDNER during the year 2014-17

During the 'Swachhta Hi Sewa Abhiyan', the National Centre of Organic Farming had participated in the Pandit Deen Dayal Upadhyaya Krishi Unnati Mela and demonstrated the waste decomposer technique and organic farming to farmers

Under the Pandit Deen Dayal Upadhyaya Unnat Krishi Shiksha Yojana, 130 training programmes on organic farming/natural farming and cow-based economy in 32 SAUs has been organized.

In order to recognize outstanding contribution of organic farmers, the ICAR had instituted an award titled Haldhar Organic Farmer Award in 2015. A citation and award money of ₹ 1,00,000 each shall be presented on 16 July every year, i.e., the Foundation Day of ICAR.

Under PKVY, assistance to farmers for cluster formation, mobilization of farmers, PGS certification, conversion of land to organic farming, establishment of vermi-compost unit, labelling or branding of organic products, etc., is provided. Financial assistance is provided for collection and transportation of organic produce to market at ₹1,20,000 maximum assistance for one cluster. Every farmer of a cluster will be provided financial assistance of ₹50,000 per ha. During the three year period, 10,000 organic clusters of 20 ha will be developed to cover certified area of 2 lakh ha. So far, 10,000 clusters have been formed.

'Opportunities for Food Imports from India' is a report published in January 2018 by Yes Bank and Trade Promotion Council of India (TPCI). It classifies the key export products under different categories based on the current export values, India's potential for the produce and growth trends across the globe in the following three groups:

| *Export Drivers* | *Untapped Stars* | *Future champions* |
|---|---|---|
| Rice | Fruits and vegetables fresh and processed | Organic |
| Tea | Nuts | Indian ethnic food |
| Spices | | Minor millets |
| Other cereals | | |

So far, we have seen the efforts made by the government for one product from the 'Untapped Stars', that is bananas and one from the future champions, that is organic food. The way growth has been seen in 'pulse' production, soon it might form the part of 'untapped champion'.

Before we proceed further, we must take note of an important development in the category of 'export drivers'.

In an agreement signed on 9 June 2018, China agreed to import non-basmati rice from India as well. China till now allowed import of only basmati rice from India, but with this agreement, now even non-basmati rice can be exported. Non-basmati rice exports from India during April 2017–February 2018 stood at $3.26 billion as against $2.53 billion in 2016–17.

One can see that the government has not left any stone unturned in the process of improving agricultural export from India, across different categories.

Before we proceed further, we must take a look at the agricultural product that is being exported from India from time immemorial, and which got whole lot of Europeans and Mughals to India. Yes, I am talking about spices. India is still a global leader in the trade of spices. India produces about 75 of the 109 varieties listed by the International Organization for Standardization (ISO). The current production of spices stands at over 7 mn MT. India accounts for over 18 per cent of the global trade, and within the Indian agri-export basket, spices rank 7th in terms of value contribution.

During 2016–17, a total of 9,47,790 million tonne of spices and spice products valued ₹17,665 crore ($2633 million) have been exported from the country as against 8,43,255 million tonne valued ₹16,238 crore ($2,483 million) in 2015–16 registering an increase of 12 per cent in volume, 9 per cent in rupee terms and 6 per cent in dollar terms. The US, China, Vietnam and Indonesia are the key importers of Indian spices. These countries contribute close to around 40 per cent to India's exports. Spices exports have registered substantial growth during the last five years, registering a CAGR of 10 per cent in rupee terms and 5 per cent in dollar terms.

It is clear that India is holding on to its strengths while adding new products in its export kitty as far as agricultural products are concerned. It is the very factor looking at the global food trade. The current global agricultural exports are valued at around $1.58 trillion, which account for around 10 per cent of the total exports taking place globally. Of the total agricultural trade worth $1.58 trillion, approximately $1.35 trillion is accounted for food products. The other non-food products such as timber, wool, cotton, rubber, etc., account for the remaining $0.23 trillion exports. India exported food products worth $30 billion (in 2016), and its share in global export currently stands at about 2.2 per cent taking it to the 9th position in the world food exports. For India, export of agricultural products contributes about 13 per cent to the agriculture GDP, and therefore, has a large impact on the nation's economy, and that's why it merits attention.

After the increase in agricultural products, the natural and logical next step is to move up the value chain through processing and value addition and bring in more stringent quality parameters and implementing checks and balances to adhere to the global standards. This will increase India's share in the global trade in value terms exponentially. The government has taken a lot of concrete measures for the same.

## FOOD PROCESSING

India presents abundant sources of raw material to meet the demands of food processing industry. The agro-climatic advantage and diversity of climatic zones makes India a home to a variety of fruits and vegetables, spices, cereals, marine produce, plantation crops and ingredients, which are relished all over the world. The production advantages are huge, however, the level of processing for perishables continues to be very miniscule at round 10 per cent and even lower for fruits and vegetables (~2 per cent). On the other hand, the level of wastage of agri-produce is very high and is estimated at over $ 15 billion annually. These two factors pose both challenges and opportunities. Challenge to the government in terms of creating an ecosystem and enabling environment for investors to invest in food processing sector; and, on the other hand, creating an opportunity for investors to benefit from what the sector has to offer.

To facilitate investment in the food processing sector, the Government of India has undertaken several major reforms and initiatives. One of the key economic reforms is permitting 100 per cent FDI under the automatic route in food processing industries and 100 per cent FDI in trading, including e-commerce, for food products manufactured or produced in India through government approval route. A number of fiscal incentives are provided to food processing and related activities to promote food processing sector. 100 per cent Income Tax exemption is permitted on profit for new food processing, preservation and packaging units for first five years and 25 per cent (30 per cent in the case of companies) thereafter for next five years. Approximately 150 per cent investment linked deductions is permitted on capital expenditure for setting up and operating cold chain. The government has also implemented Goods and Services Tax (GST) by merging a number of central and state taxes.

Implementation of GST has made India truly one country, one tax and one market. This major reform is aimed at reducing tax cascading, adding to logistics efficiency, and making it easier to do business. Under GST regime, nearly 80 per cent of raw and processed food products are covered in lower tax slab of 0 per cent, 5 per cent and 12 per cent conveying pro-investment commitment of the government in food processing sector with an overreaching objective of doubling farmers' income by 2022.

Another important initiative has been the introduction of one umbrella scheme—the Pradhan Mantri Kisan Sampada Yojana (PMKSY), which is being implemented with an allocation of around$1 billion. The PMKSY is a comprehensive package of support which will result in creation of modern infrastructure with efficient supply chain management from farm gate to retail outlet. It will not only provide a big boost to the growth of food processing sector in the country but also help in providing better returns to farmers and is a big step towards increasing farmers, income, creating huge employment opportunities, especially in the rural areas, reducing wastage of agricultural produce, increasing the processing level and enhancing the export of the processed foods.

India's geographical location gives it a unique advantage, having convenient connectivity to Europe, the Middle East and Africa (amongst others) from the western coast and Japan, Singapore, Thailand, Malaysia, Korea, Australia and New Zealand (amongst others) from the eastern coast. Given the huge production base of agri-produces, incentives offered by the government to promote food processing sector and its unique locational advantage, India has all the potential to become the food factory of the world.

With a view to showcase the strengths of India in the food processing and allied sectors, to connect domestic and international businesses for possible partnerships and facilitate collaboration, investment flow and encourage sourcing from India, the Ministry of Food Processing Industries (MoFPI) organized World Food India in November 2017. The mega event attracted participation from 61 countries. Sixty Global CEOs and more than 200 global companies participated.

The event provided an opportunity for the Indian and global stakeholders to come together and explore mutually collaborative areas of interventions.

During the event, the MoFPI also unveiled its investors' portal—Nivesh Bhandhu—which brings together all relevant information related to food processing, thus enabling investors to take informed decisions. The portal provides information on central and state government policies, incentives offered for promotion of food processing sector, state profiles and geo-tagged information on district level resources in terms of agri-production clusters, processing infrastructure, Industrial Estates/SEZ/Food Park, cold chain, testing laboratory, communication network, etc. The unique feature of the portal is the platform for business networking by the farmers, processors, traders and logistics operators.

Today, starting a new business in India has become much easier than ever before with simplification of procedures for obtaining clearances from various governments and government agencies.

A large number of archaic laws have been repealed, unnecessary compliances have been removed and services have been integrated with provision for online applications on a 24*7 basis.

With all these positive developments, India is emerging as an attractive investment destination. India is also rapidly progressing on the Global Innovation Index, Global Logistics Index and Global Competitiveness Index. With all these positive developments, it was only expected that the World Food India event witnessed investment undertakings worth $14 billion. Today, India's food sector has emerged as a high-growth and high-profit sector, which any investor can hardly ignore.

In order to take the growth story forward, a major announcement have been made in the Budget 2018–19—the allocation for food processing sector has been doubled (over the preceding year) to ₹1,400 crore, which also marks the culmination of a series of initiatives the government has been taking over the last few years for promoting food processing sector. Apart from increasing the size of the allocation, the announcement highlighted a series of steps to be taken for holistic development of the sector and increasing farmers' income. These included support for cluster approach for increasing agri-produce for processing and expansion of processing facilities, connecting farmers with consumers, strengthening agri-logistics and supply chain infrastructure, promoting professional management, increasing the flow of credit through establishment of agro-processing financial institutions, etc. An 'Operation Green' programme, with an allocation of ₹500 crore, has been envisaged for three basic vegetables—tomatoes, onions and potatoes, covering all these elements to connect farmers directly to consumers.

Last but not the least, a friendly process is also needed for export and government has worked on the same effectively. The government's steps are effective and reflects the World Bank's Global Ease of Doing Business Index as mentioned in the beginning of the article.

## MERCHANDISE EXPORTS FROM INDIA SCHEME (MEIS)

As per highlights of the Foreign Trade Policy (FTP) 2015–2020, the Department of Commerce, Ministry of Commerce and Industry, Government of India have introduced 'Merchandise Exports from India Scheme' (MEIS).

The MEIS has replaced five different schemes of earlier FTPs (Focus Product Scheme, Market Linked Focus Product Scheme, Focus Market Scheme, Agriculture Infrastructure Incentive Scrip, Vishesh Krishi Gram Udyog Yojana) for rewarding merchandise exports that had varying conditions (sector specific or actual user only) attached to their use.

There would be no conditionality attached to the scrips issued under the scheme. Notified goods exported to notified markets would be rewarded on realized Free on Board (FOB) value of exports.

Under the MEIS, higher rewards have been granted for the following category of products:

1. Agricultural and village industry products presently covered under VKGUY
2. Value added and packaged products
3. Eco-friendly and green products that create wealth out of waste from agricultural and other waste products that generate additional income for the farmers, while improving the environment
4. Labour intensive products with large employment potential and products with large number of producers and/or exporters

Markets that are supported:

1. Most agricultural products supported across the globe

Global support has been granted to the following categories:

1. Fruits, flowers, vegetables

2. Tea, coffee, spices
3. Cereals preparation, shellac, essential oils
4. Processed foods
5. Eco-friendly products that add value to waste
6. Marine products
7. Handloom, coir, jute products and technical textiles, handmade carpets. Other textile and readymade garments have been supported for European Union, the US, Canada and Japan.

It goes without saying that the MEIS will come as a huge boost to export of agricultural products from India.

The government has not only intervened in the export policy but also in the agriculture at farm level itself in the form of crop insurance, availability of fertilizers, soil health card, etc. All these will help the farmer take more risks and increase the productivity in the farm.

But, the farming is not dependent on farm alone. Better farming also needs better road, better electricity, and the government has connected the remotest village through electricity and road in the last four years.

Indian farming is dependent on rain and from the last 1,000 years not much has been done for irrigation at a national level till the current government started river-linking projects. It will increase the farm productivity tremendously.

Most importantly, good farming needs a happy and a healthy farmer. With Ayuhshman Bharat and Jan Dhan Yojana, the government has achieved both these objectives. With the disappearance of middleman, the benefits—financial and otherwise—of the central government are reaching the farmers directly.

The government has used technology to help farmers and prevent pilferage of urea by unscrupulous elements. In January

2015, the government allowed urea producers to produce up to 100 per cent of production as neem-coated urea. Further, the government made it mandatory to produce at least 75 per cent of domestic urea as neem-coated. The current policy is that the government has mandated all indigenous producers of urea to produce neem-coated urea only. This small but unique step has far-reaching consequence in the agricultural productivity of India. Earlier, the farmers used to wait for months to get urea; it was also sold in black market. But, Prime Minister Narendra Modi, with his one decision, has changed the face of farming in India.

No other government has looked at the small and big issues, simple and complicated issues in such detail and has worked with a missionary zeal to solve them. Indian agriculture export will have his golden days in the near future, and India definitely has all the potential to become the food factory of the world.

***Sandeep Singh** is the author of 'Third Curve: Women and Child Development in Gujarat' and eight other books.*

# SAFEGUARDING INCOME: MINIMUM SUPPORT PRICE

*Chandra Shekhar*

To speak about that importance of agriculture is like showing light to the sun. Agriculture, undoubtedly, is the mainstay of a large country like India, which has to feed over 125 crore people every day. For that, our farmers have to grow cereals, pulses, fruits and vegetables to suit the taste and nutritional requirement of people spread across the length and breadth of this great country. It is by no means an easy job given the fact that the agriculture sector has to year after year brave the vagaries of nature like floods, droughts, hailstorms, etc. Also, Indian agriculture, to a large extent, depends upon the monsoon that plays a pivotal role in increasing or decreasing farm productivity.

Giving due importance to the farming sector, the Modi government decided to put in place policies with the specific objective of doubling the income of the farmers by 2022. The components of the seven-point strategy being pursued by the government are: special focus on irrigation with sufficient budget with the aim of 'Per Drop More Crop'; provision of quality seeds and nutrients based on soil health of each field; large investments in warehousing and cold chains to prevent post-harvest crop losses; promotion of value addition through food processing; creation of a national farm market; removing distortions and e-platform across 585 stations; introduction of a new crop insurance scheme to mitigate risks at affordable cost; and promotion of ancillary activities such as poultry, beekeeping and fisheries.

This strategy had helped in raising the income of the farmers to a great extent. But, this is only half the story. The other part is to save the farmers from the volatility in the movement of the price of their produce—protect him from the trap of falling prices on account of excessive production.

These crop-insurance schemes can protect the farmers from floods, droughts and other natural calamities. In the same manner, a farmer's interest is ought to be safeguarded in the event of overproduction, falling demand and depressed prices. The farmer ought not to be penalized for working hard and producing more, which often may not be completely in his own hands. At the time of sowing the seeds, there is no way a farmer can look forward in time and guess with any amount of certainty about the demand-supply situation and the resultant prices. Ironically, his returns depend less on his own labour and investment, and more on the market conditions at the time of harvesting.

In order to save the farmer from declining prices on account of overproduction and also to incentivize him to produce more, the government had long ago devised the system of minimum support price (MSP). The primary objective of the MSP is to ensure guaranteed prices and assured market to the farmers and also to insulate them from unwarranted price fluctuation caused by a host of unforeseeable domestic and international factors. The prices of agriculture produce are often influenced by intensity of monsoon, international demand-supply position and other market imperfections. The other objective is to encourage the farmers to adopt newer technology and innovations with a view to increase production and also to grow multiple crops.

The MSP also plays a vital role in operating the public distribution system (PDS), which is essential in providing foodgrains to people at a reasonable price. The mechanism helps in creating a buffer stock of foodgrains to effectively deal with shortages resulting from drought, floods, spurt in international prices or any other reason. Although the emergence of the MSP as an essential tool to deal with the issues facing the agriculture sector can be traced to food scarcity faced by the country after independence, it has today become an integral part of the nation's farm policy, ensuring balanced growth of the sector.

Based on the recommendations of the Commission for Agricultural Costs and Prices (CACP), the government announces the MSP for agricultural commodities, which are widely grown, have large area under cultivation, consumed by masses and have fairly long shelf life. These commodities are also essential from the point of maintaining nation's food security.

Presently the government fixes the MSPs for 22 major agricultural crops—paddy, jowar, bajra, maize, ragi, arhar, moong, urad, groundnut-in-shell, soybean, sunflower, sesamum, nigerseed, cotton, wheat, barley, gram, masoor (lentil), rapeseed/mustard, safflower, jute and copra. The government also announces the Fair and Remunerative Price (FRP) for sugarcane after obtaining the views of state governments. In addition, the MSP for toria and dehusked coconut is also fixed on the basis of the MSPs of rapeseed/mustard and copra, respectively. These agricultural crops, as per official estimates, account for around 99 per cent of the agricultural output of the country.

In addition to the MSP, the government also operates the Market Intervention Scheme (MIS) for horticultural crops, which are perishable in nature, and also some other agricultural crops, which are not covered under the MSP on the request of state/union territories (UT) governments' concerned. The MIS also aims at protecting the growers from making distress sale in the event of bumper crop when the prices tend to fall below the economic level/cost of production. Losses incurred by the procuring agencies are shared by the central government and the concerned state government on 50:50 basis (75:25 in case of northeastern states). Profits, though earned rarely by the procuring agencies, are allowed to be retained by them.

The real issue before the government has been the quantum of MSP. The second issue is to make the whole scheme of MSP more effective so that large number of farmers can benefit from it. The quantum of MSP has several dimensions. First, higher MSP would encourage farmers to grow more to get better returns on their labour and investment. It has a downside also; higher MSP also tends to fuel inflation, which might dampen the demand of that particular agriculture commodity, leading to other complications.

The third dimension of the MSP is the implementation machinery. The mere announcement of the MSP will not serve any purpose in the absence of a strong network of procurement agencies to buy the produce at a given price at those locations, which farmers can approach easily. Fourthly, the implementation of the scheme involves a lot of funding, which has to come from the budget. This has implications of fiscal deficit and other government expenditure, which may be equally pressing. The availability of public resources too is critical for operationalization of the MSP scheme. Also, what is significant is that the whole scheme should be designed and operated in such a manner that it does not violate the norms established by the World Trade Organization (WTO). India, an ardent votary of rule-based global trade, cannot afford to be WTO non-compliant.

The government has assigned CACP the task of deciding the quantum of MSP of different agricultural produce. The CACP takes into account the cost of production of a commodity, in addition to various other expenses. In fact, it considers all costs in a comprehensive manner. These include all paid-out costs such as those incurred on account of hired human labour, bullock labour/machine labour, rent paid for leased land, expenses incurred in cash and kind on the use of material inputs such as seeds, fertilizers, manures, irrigation charges, depreciation on implements and farm buildings, interest on working capital, diesel/electricity for operation of pump sets, etc., miscellaneous expenses and the imputed value of family labour.

After undertaking the elaborate exercise based on all data from across the country, the CACP suggests the MSP with a view to ensure that the farmers do not suffer any loss in case the prices dip below a certain point. By declaring the MSP, the government guarantees to buy the produce at a floor price. The objective is to ensure that the price will not fall below that point, come what may.

The Modi government gave a new dimension to the time-tested practice of announcing the MSP. The government raised the bar by accepting and implementing the recommendations of the National Commission on Farmers (NCF), which had been hanging fire for long. Headed by India's most respected agriculture expert, Dr M. S. Swaminathan, the NCF recommended that the MSP should be at least 50 per cent more than the weighted average cost of production. Unfortunately, when the National Policy for Farmers 2007 was finalized by the then Congress-led UPA government, this recommendation of providing 50 per cent returns over cost of production was ignored.

With a view to achieve the target of doubling the income of the farmers by 2022, the NDA government decided to increase the

MSPs for all mandated crops guaranteeing a return of at least 50 per cent of the cost of production for the season 2018–19. This decision of the Modi government is historic in the sense that it fulfills the government's commitment to the farmers to provide 50 per cent return over the cost of production for specified crops. In fact, this has happened for the first time in the history of independent India and is something for which every stakeholder should be proud of.

To give a few examples, the Modi government has announced the MSP of ₹1,750 per quintal for paddy (common) during fiscal 2018–19. On face of it, the number may not reveal much. In fact, it is an increase from ₹1,550 over the last year's MSP. That too will not reveal much. However, what one needs to do is to see whether it fits into the formula suggested by the NCF. The NCF Head Dr. Swaminathan had suggested that the MSP should be 50 per cent over the cost of production to make the farming profitable and lucrative. The cost of production, as worked out by the CACP, was ₹1,116 per quintal. After taking into account the cost of production, the MSP announced by the government works out to be 50.1 per cent. This is in line with the suggestions made by the NCF.

Similar increases were noticed in other kharif crops for which the government announces the MSP. For instance, in case of jowar (hybrid), the MSP was 50.1 per cent over the cost of production. For bajra, it was as high as 97 per cent; for arhar (tur), it was 65.4 per cent; and for urad, it was 62.9 per cent. Over 50 per cent increase was witnessed in all 14 kharif crops for which MSPs were announced by the government.

In case of rabi crops, the story is even better. For wheat, the government fixed the MSP at ₹1,840 per quintal during 2018–19. It was ₹1,735 per quintal during the previous fiscal. The cost of production worked out by the CACP for wheat was ₹866 per quintal. Over this cost, the MSP fixed by the Modi government was ₹1,840. Now, one can look at the increase in percentage over the cost of production. It works out to be 112.5 per cent, more than double of what was suggested by the NCF. The MSP for rapeseed/mustard was 89.9 per cent over the cost of production for 2018–19. For masoor (lentil), the increase works out to be 76.7 per cent; for gram, it was 75.2 per cent; and for barley, it was 67.4 per cent. For the six rabi crops, the MSP was more than 50 per cent of the cost of production, a definite improvement over the formula suggested by the NCF.

The other important crops on which the government announces MSP are copra (milling) and jute. In case of both these crops, the MSP was 50 per cent or more over the cost of production—for copra (milling), it was 50 per cent and for jute, it was 63.2 per cent. In addition to the MSP, the government announces the Fair and Remunerative Price (FRP) for important and politically-sensitive sugarcane. The FRP for sugarcane was fixed at ₹275 per quintal by the central government, much more than the production cost of ₹155 per quintal. In percentage terms, the MSP works out to be 77.4 per cent over the cost of production. In case of other crops too, the government has not only adhered but also exceeded the recommendations of the NCF.

The MSP, it may be emphasized, is only a guaranteed minimum price and does not restrict the farmers from selling their produce in the open market at a better price. This, in fact, would mean that farmers will always get more than 50 per cent of the cost of production.

In addition, the central government has also launched an umbrella scheme called Pradhan Mantri Annadata Aay Sanrakshan Abhiyan (PM-AASHA). Under PM-AASHA, the Department of

Agriculture, Cooperation and Framers' Welfare (DAC&FW) under the Ministry of Agriculture and Farmers' Welfare implements a Price Support Scheme (PSS) for procurement of pulses, oilseeds and copra.

**Cost*, Minimum Support Price (MSP) & percent return over cost**

(Rs. per quintal)

| *Sl. No.* | *Commodity* | *2017–18* | | | *2018–19* | | |
|---|---|---|---|---|---|---|---|
| | *Kharif Crops* | *Cost* | *MSP* | *% Return over cost* | *Cost* | *MSP* | *% Return over cost* |
| 1 | Paddy (Common) | 1117 | 1550 | 38.8 | 1166 | 1750 | 50.1 |
| 2. | Jowar (Hybrid) | 1556 | 1700 | 9.3 | 1619 | 2430 | 50.1 |
| 3. | Bajra | 949 | 1425 | 50.2 | 990 | 1950 | 97.0 |
| 4. | Maize | 1044 | 1425 | 36.5 | 1131 | 1700 | 50.3 |
| 5. | Ragi | 1861 | 1900 | 2.1 | 1931 | 2897 | 50.0 |
| 6. | Arhar (Tur) | 3318 | 5450 | 64.3 | 3432 | 5675 | 65.4 |
| 7. | Moong | 4286 | 5575 | 30.1 | 4650 | 6975 | 50.0 |
| 8. | Urad | 3265 | 5400 | 65.4 | 3438 | 5600 | 62.9 |
| 9. | Cotton (Medium Staple) | 3276 | 4020 | 22.7 | 3433 | 5150 | 50.0 |
| 10. | Groundnut in Shell | 3159 | 4450 | 40.9 | 3260 | 4890 | 50.0 |
| 11. | Sunflower Seed | 3481 | 4100 | 17.8 | 3592 | 5388 | 50.0 |
| 12. | Soyabean | 2121 | 3050 | 43.8 | 2266 | 3399 | 50.0 |
| 13. | Sesamum | 4067 | 5300 | 30.3 | 4166 | 6249 | 50.0 |
| 14. | Nigerseed | 3912 | 4050 | 3.5 | 3918 | 5877 | 50.0 |
| | Rabi Crops | | | | | | |

| | | | | | | | |
|---|---|---|---|---|---|---|---|
| 1. | Wheat | 817 | 1735 | 112.4 | 866 | 1840 | 112.5 |
| 2. | Barley | 845 | 1410 | 66.9 | 860 | 1440 | 67.4 |
| 3. | Gram | 2461 | 4400 | 78.8 | 2637 | 4620 | 75.2 |
| 4. | Masur (Lentil) | 2366 | 4250 | 79.6 | 2532 | 4475 | 76.7 |
| 5. | Rapeseed/ Mustard | 2123 | 4000 | 88.4 | 2212 | 4200 | 89.9 |
| 6. | Safflower | 3125 | 4100 | 31.2 | 3294 | 4945 | 50.1 |
| | Other Crops | | | | | | |
| 1. | Copra (Milling) | 4758 | 6500 | 36.6 | 5007 | 7511 | 50.0 |
| 2. | Jute | 2160 | 3500 | 62.0 | 2267 | 3700 | 63.2 |
| 3. | Sugarcane# | 152 | 255 | 67.8 | 155 | 275 | 77.4 |

**Includes all paid out costs such as those incurred on account of hired human labour, bullock labour/machine labour, rent paid for leased in land, expenses incurred on use of material inputs like seeds, fertilizers, manuers, irrigation charges, depreciation on implements and farm buildings, interest on working capital, diesel/electricity for operation of pump sets etc, miscellaneous expenses*

*# Fair and Remunerative Price (FRP)*

*Source: Lok Sabha Question No. 1353, 18 December 2018*

For oilseeds, DAC&FW has implemented the Price Deficiency Payment Scheme (PDPS). The states/UTs have the option to choose either the PSS or the PDPS in a given procurement season with respect to a particular oilseed crop for the entire state. Besides, DAC&FW has also launched Private Procurement and Stockist Scheme (PPSS) for oilseeds on pilot basis giving option to states to implement PPSS in district/selected Agricultural Produce Market Committees (APMCs) of district involving the participation of private stockist.

In addition, the government also operates the MSP scheme for Minor Forest Produce (MFP). Under the scheme, the government provides funds to the state governments for the procurement of

MFP and creates facilities for the proper storage of the procured MFP items. The state governments procure the notified MFP only in the event of its market price falling below the notified MSP. The government is also working on new market architecture to ensure that the farmers get remunerative prices on their produce. These include setting up of Gramin Agricultural Markets (GrAMs) with a view to promote 22,000 retail markets in close proximity of a farm gate; develop a competitive and transparent wholesale trade at APMC through e-NAM; and create a robust and pro-farmer export policy.

Under PM-AASHA, the procurement for paddy, wheat and coarse grains is done by the Department of Food and Public Distribution (DFPD) through Food Corporation of India (FCI). Cotton and jute are procured by the Ministry of Textiles through Cotton Corporation of India (CCI) and Jute Corporation of India (JCI), respectively.

As a result of the host of initiatives taken by the Modi government, the procurement of wheat under a central pool has increased substantially. As per the official data, the procurement of wheat went up from 229.62 lakh metric ton (LMT) in 2016–17 to 308.24 LMT in 2017–18 and further increased to 357.95 LMT during 2018–19. Similarly, the procurement of paddy under a central pool in terms of rice has been 357.95 LMT in 2016–17, 381.85 LMT in 2017–18 and is expected to further go up in 2018–19. It was also pointed out that under the Price Support Scheme (PSS), during the Kharif Marketing Season (KMS) 2017–18, sanctions were accorded for procurement of 33,94,290 MT of pulses and oilseeds in nine states through 866 centres and for KMS 2018–19, sanctions were accorded for pulses and oilseeds for 50,20,499 MT (including PDPS) in 11 states through 2,066 centres.

The real test of the government, however, lies in dealing with the crisis situation which cropped up in the sugar sector. The sugar industry faced crisis on account of excess production and depressed prices. As a result, the cane price arrears of farmers peaked to ₹14,538 crore based on the Fair and Remunerative Price (FRP) and ₹23,232 crore based on the State Advised Price (SAP) in May 2018.

In order to resolve the crisis, the central government stepped in with a host of measures. These included fixing of MSP, extension of financial assistance to sugar mills, creation of buffer stock and extension of soft loans for setting up new distilleries and installation of incineration boilers to augment ethanol production. In addition, the government also notified the new National Policy on Bio-Fuels 2018 under which sugarcane juice has been allowed for production of ethanol. Further, the government has fixed remunerative price of ethanol produced from C-Heavy molasses and B-Heavy molasses/ sugarcane juice separately for supply under the Ethanol Blended Petrol (EBP) Programme during ethanol season 2018–19.

Have these initiatives yielded results—a fair question to ask. According to the information provided by the government in the parliament in December 2018—'as a result of various measures taken by the government, the cane price arrears for the sugar season 2017–18 have come down to ₹1,924 crore and ₹5,465 crore on FRP and SAP basis respectively on all India basis.' This substantial reduction in cane arrears would have definitely helped the cane growers. Also, the initiatives taken by the central government in dealing with the problems of the sugar industry will go a long way in providing stability to the sector which will also benefit the mill owners as well as the farmers.

Here it may be worthwhile to ask about the efficacy of the MSP mechanism in mitigating the woes of the farming sector and that whether it can be improved further. After all, huge amount of public resources are being spend every year directly and indirectly to operate this system to save the farmers from hardship being caused by excess production and falling prices.

The important limbs of this mechanism are: the announcement of the MSP by the government, presence of procurement machinery to buy agriculture produce at the decided MSP, the storage of the procured produce and finally disposal of procured goods. In addition, the farmers must know the MSP before sowing so that they can take informed decisions. There are several other aspects of the MSP mechanism that are needed to be examined and improved to make the scheme more effective.

The NITI Aayog, a body that was created by the Modi government to act as the country's premier think tank, came out with an 'Evaluation Study on Efficacy of Minimum Support Prices (MSPs) on Farmers' in January 2016. Based on the data collected from large number of respondents across the country, the study found that 'the MSP has succeeded in providing floor rate for major foodgrains like paddy and wheat and other produces such as gram (black and green), spices and oilseeds (groundnut, mustard, til), sugarcane, jute and cotton, and it did not allow market prices to fall below the MSP fixed for them.'

The data collected from the respondents also revealed that the MSP has continued to play a critical role in stabilizing the market prices in addition to helping the beneficiaries in adopting modern technologies in farming. Many farmers also revealed that they sold their produce in the open market to get better returns.

The evaluation study, after extensive analysis of the responses, concluded that 'almost all the beneficiaries were unanimous with the view that the MSP should continue as it insulated them from an unfavorable market condition by assuring them a minimum return for their produces.'

At the same time, it would be wrong to assume that everything is hunky-dory with the MSP scheme. The study also pointed out various shortcomings and suggested ways to improve them to make the MSP scheme more effective to the benefit of farmers.

Some of the issues flagged by the study are: non-availability of procurement centres within close vicinity; delay in opening of procurement centres; lack of covered storage/godowns facility for temporary storage of produces; absence of electronic weighing equipment in some places; and delay in payments to farmers for procured goods. Another problem which was highlighted by the study was the delay in announcement of the MSP; often, the MSP is announced after the crops have already been sown by the farmers. It was observed that this delay in announcement of the MSP deprives the farmers of planning their crops. It was also emphasized that the MSP should be appropriate to cover the rising cost of the farming.

In order to improve the efficacy of the MSP system, the study came up with a host of important suggestions. The first and foremost was that all efforts should be made to increase awareness about the MSP among the farming community. It was pointed out that the timely dissemination of information at the lowest level would definitely increase the bargaining power of the farmers. Armed with the knowledge of the MSP, the farmers would not have to resort to distress sale of their produce and, on the other hand, would be armed with requisite information to negotiate a better deal. The study also recommended that the government should not delay the MSP payments as it makes the farmers vulnerable.

The other suggestions are: the MSP should be announced well in advance of the sowing season so as to enable the farmers to plan their cropping; improved facilities should be provided at the procurement centres such as drying yards and weighing bridges;

more godowns should be set up and maintained properly for better storage and reduction of wastage; there should be meaningful consultations with the state governments, both on the methodology of computation of the MSP as well as on the implementation mechanism; the criteria for fixing the MSP should be current year's data and based on more meaningful criteria rather than the historical costs; the small and marginal farmers should be provided with some exemption in Fair Average Quality (FAQ) norms to provide them with a source of income; procurement centers should be in the village itself to avoid transportation costs; and overhaul of the scheme should be undertaken in states, especially in the northeastern region, where the impact varies from 'nil' to 'at-best marginal'.

It is not that the Modi government is not aware of the shortcomings in the MSP scheme and is not doing anything to make it foolproof to the benefit of the farmers, especially with a view to double their income by 2022. NITI Aayog is on the job. It has already started work on a mechanism for effective implementation of the MSP scheme for different agricultural crops.

The NITI Aayog, in consultation with representatives of states and central ministries, is presently deliberating on three options to make the MSP more effective. The first one is related to Market Assurance Scheme, which proposes procurement by states and compensation of losses up to a certain extent of the MSP after the procurement and price realization out of sale of the procured produce.

Second option relates to the Price Deficiency Payment Scheme. Under this scheme, if the sale price is below a modal price, then the farmers may be compensated to the difference between the MSP and the actual price subject to a ceiling which may not exceed 25 per cent of the MSP. No compensation would be due if modal price in neighboring states is above the MSP. And, the third option concerns the PPSS, which relates to procurement by private entrepreneurs at the MSP. Under this option, the government will provide some policy and tax incentives and a commission to such private entities which may be decided on the basis of transparent criteria and bidding for undertaking procurement operations.

The third option offers great promise as it will reduce the fiscal implications for the government by involving private entities as partners in agriculture marketing and also improve competition in the market. The government's liabilities for storage and post procurement management and disposal will also be reduced.

The NITI Aayog is expected to come out with its report by March 2019 and hopefully its suggestions will add more vigour to the MSP scheme making it a truly farmer-friendly scheme, rendering farming more profitable and transforming India's countryside into an attractive place to live for rich and poor alike.

***Chandra Shekhar** is a senior economic journalist with more than three decades of experience.*

# INDEX